A MAN OF THE THEATER

A MAN OF THE THEATER

Survival as an Artist in Iran

Nasser Rahmaninejad

New Village Press ▪ New York

Published in the United States by New Village Press

bookorders@newvillagepress.net
www.newvillagepress.org

New Village Press is a public-benefit, nonprofit publisher

Distributed by NYU Press

Paperback ISBN: 978-1-61332-110-2

Publication Date: February 2020

First Edition

Library of Congress Control Number:2019957357

Library of Congress Cataloging-in-Publication Data
Available online at http://catalog.loc.gov

Front cover illustration: Faramarz Pilaram (from Mehr Theater Group poster for 1966 production in Tehran of Arthur Miller's *Incident at Vichy*)
Cover design: Lynne Elizabeth
Interior design and composition: Leigh McLellan Design

In memory of my father and mother

CONTENTS

MY STEEL HEART

—Nima Youshij

Let my horse go
And my provisions
And my saddlecloth
And myself, who cannot stop cursing,
For a wild idea drew me
To the door.

I come from a faraway land
There are no joyful hearts there
In that far off land full of turmoil, rioters
Whose work is killing and murder
In every corner of that country,
Instead of seeds, in spring
They plant the wounds of corpses.

As I was riding here,
I was thinking that a traveler
Could pass through this lethal desert
If he had a heart of steel
Which through bad and good
Looked at difficulties with ease
And knew that the world
Is full of enmity murder and ruin
With no one to help.

But now, to the same lethal desert
I must return, must use my wits,
My gift from the previous journey
Was a horrible and shocking nightmare.

Whenever I open my eyes
In that split second
I see my whole life burning
In its fire.

For me, who was ruined by that journey
There is no moment in which to stop.
I am, of everyone in this hour,
The most plundered,
Everything has fallen from my hands,
And my steel heart is no longer with me,
All I had was my heart
And now I see that my steel heart
Has been left on the road.
That tribe made my steel heart doubt
That malicious tribe, who in the arms of spring,
Gathers, instead of flowers, the bleeding of the wounded.

Now my thought goes to my brothers
Unjustly rolling in blood,
Innocently rolling in blood
In whose blood
My steel heart is rusting.

Translated by Kathleen Au and Nasser Rahmaninejad
Edited by Esmail Khoi

I

WATER (*Aab*)

We did not have tap water. Most residents of Tehran, the capital of a major oil-producing country, lacked tap water. Probably somewhere in the wealthy north end of the city, water flowed pure and clean, right into the kitchen sinks, but not where we lived, downstream, in the southern neighborhood of Ferdows Garden.

Most of Tehran's water flows down from the Alborz Mountains, about fifteen kilometers north of the city. At the source, Tehran's water was clean, pure, and cold. Large channels along Pahlavi Avenue and Old Shemiran Road carried water from Tajrish, in the foothills, down to Tehran. These channels were about two meters wide and lined with concrete at the sides and stones on the bottom. After reaching Tehran, the channels narrowed to less than a meter, branched into innumerable streets, and finally reached the poor southern neighborhoods, like ours. By the time they reached us, the channels had dwindled to open gutters that were not even concrete-lined. Little bridges crossed these channels, but sometimes car or bicycle wheels and even children fell into them.

Each house had a clay duct leading its share of water into a courtyard pool or to a subterranean reservoir. People used the water from the gutters for washing dishes, clothes, and baby diapers, and for watering plants and washing sidewalks. In most parts of southern Tehran, the streets and sidewalks were not paved. On summer afternoons every shop owner would send an aide to spray the sidewalks and sweep them with a broom to keep the dust down. Of course some portion of dust from the unpaved streets, along with any runoff from the struggle to subdue it, inevitably landed back in the gutter-supplied water.

In the 1940s, when I was growing up, even rich neighborhoods lacked a modern sewage system. The houses had sewage pits—just holes in the ground—not lined septic tanks. The pits were about ten to fifteen meters deep. At the bottom was a space to contain the sewage—larger or smaller depending on the number of residents in the house. If people washed clothes in the courtyard pool, the water would drain into the sewage pit, but many people washed clothes in a separate tub so they could throw the wash water out into the street. People did not want their sewage pits to fill up. A full pit meant that workers had to be hired to dig out the sewage, load it into wagons, and drive to the south end of town to dump it—or sometimes they would drive the wagons out to farms and dump the sewage into the fields as manure. To avoid this household expense, residents would empty their wash water into the alleys, where it would flow back into the gutters—and back into the city's water supply.

The city arranged to distribute water into the houses each month, on a different night for each neighborhood. At night, when few people used water, there was little visible dirt in it. Night by night, city workers would release the water into the gutters of each neighborhood so that the residents could refill their courtyard pools as well as the little subterranean reservoirs in their cellars or beneath their yards. Sometimes there would be fights. Neighbors would disagree over who would be allowed to fill their reservoir first, each wanting to finish the process earlier and be able to go to bed. There was supposed to be a city worker in the neighborhood to manage the distribution of the water, but often he failed to show up, so people had to take care of it on their own. Sometimes, aggravated citizens bribed the city workers to come to do them a favor.

In addition to household reservoirs, most old neighborhoods had a large public reservoir, which was built not by the government but by neighborhood benefactors who had enough money to underwrite the expenses. Usually these reservoirs were named after the people who funded them—all around old Tehran were reservoirs named for wealthy men. The steps down to the big neighborhood reservoirs were usually dark and scary, and some had no kind of lighting at all. As a child I would test my courage by walking down the steps whistling. People were constantly afraid that their children would drown in these reservoirs, deep underground, where no one could hear them scream.

Besides the gutters, we had one other source of water. Most people bought drinking water from big yellow barrels loaded onto two-wheeled wagons pulled by *yabu*, a kind of draft horse. The source of this water was the Nasseri Qanat, one of Tehran's underground irrigation channels, also called Aab-e Shah, "Water of the King," which conveyed water from the Alborz Mountains. The pumping station where the barrels were filled was also called Aab-e Shah. The wagons would arrive at Aab-e Shah before dawn, and the station would begin pumping at four o'clock in the morning. Large pipes were fixed to two short concrete walls along both sides of the street. Each pipe had a row of faucets. The water would run from the faucets through rubber pipes and into hatches on top of the wagon barrels. Each morning, long lines of yabu-drawn wagons parked on both sides of the street, stretching to Bagh-e Melli, the National Garden, a beautiful place with big, old trees and a historic, beautifully crafted iron gate.

The area where the pumping station was located had been a military training site in the late 19th and early 20th century, but after Reza Khan (the father of the Shah who was toppled in the 1979 revolution) seized power from the Qajar Dynasty in 1925, it was redeveloped by the new government. By mid-century, the Central Police Station, the State Department, the main Post Office of Tehran, the Registration Administration, the Anglo-Iranian Oil Company, and the Museum of Ancient Iran were all clustered there. The northern end housed a military complex, which included the Military Treasury Administration, the Supply Administration, and the Military Police Administration and its prison; warehouses and depots for clothing and food; a bakery and a tailoring factory; plus, a block north of this complex, the Ministry of War and the Joint Chiefs of Command. The Aab-e Shah Pumping Station was built on the south side of the area, against the wall of the Police Provisional Prison, which later became the infamous *Komiteh*.

Despite the separate distribution of drinking water, many people, especially children, died of typhoid and other water-borne diseases. They died because they were impoverished and too poor to live in neighborhoods other than those like Ferdows Garden, where people were crowded together at the bottom of the sloping plain of the city and which thus were among the last neighborhoods to receive the water after it had washed through all the streets and alleys of Tehran.

2

OUR NEIGHBORHOOD

The southern neighborhoods of Tehran are still poor and, in terms of altitude and social status, the lowest in the city. Ferdows Garden, my old neighborhood, vanished long ago; a charity institute and a maternity hospital now occupy the area where the public garden used to be. My family's house, the first house that I clearly remember, had a large courtyard, with families of three, four, or five people living in single rooms in the two-story buildings around it. My family lived in two rooms on the second floor. Our rooms were sunny all day. For a short time, five of us lived there, until my sister Manijeh died at age five, when I was three years old. I have a vivid memory of the morning my parents left home to bury her. My mother carried Manijeh out of the house with outstretched hands, as if offering a precious gift. My father followed silently, sorrowfully. I ran out after them, because I knew something bad had happened. A horse-drawn carriage stood in front of the door. My parents climbed into the carriage and sat there with my sister on my mother's lap covered in a blanket. I stood in the open doorway, watching. My mother told me, "Go inside. We will be back soon."

But when they came back, they came without my sister. After that I was lonely at home, because my brother was older and already away at school all day. My sister had been my closest friend and my playmate. Like so many other children in the southern neighborhoods, she had succumbed to typhoid.

My parents were very simple, ordinary people and I always loved and appreciated them. Although my father was in the army and a lifelong military man, he never forced us to do anything. He was not aggressive or violent. During most of my boyhood—the last ten years of his life—he did office work for his unit. My mother was ready to give everything for her children and for whomever she loved. I learned the meaning of love from her. I got a sense of freedom from both my parents, because they never ordered us to do this or that. My father wanted me to be an engineer, but he always said, "I won't force you; do whatever you like." He was thinking of my future; he just wanted me to be safe financially. Whenever I was in need it was my mother who suffered. She was always willing to help me with money, to look for me when I was arrested, to visit me in prison, trying to get me out, and later suffering from separation when I fled Iran into exile.

My whole family was close: my brother, Mansour, was five years older than me; my second sister was ten years younger than me and called Manijeh after the sister who had died. Her birth name was never used, and Manijeh in a real sense replaced her deceased sister for the rest of the family. My mother always wanted her little girl back.

■ ■ ■

Ferdows Garden, which was the name of the neighborhood's park, sat within the larger neighborhood of Chaleh Meidan. *Chaleh,* means "pit" and *meidan* usually means "square," but in this case it meant "market." Before the local city administration (*barzan*) gathered all wholesalers of fresh vegetables and fruits into a big *caravansarai* called Anbar-e Gandom, a former wheat depot, they were crowded at the southern end of the Tehran Bazaar, or Bazaar-e Hazrati. This area was a jumble, with almost no recognizable method used in categorizing goods for sale. Besides the wholesalers, there were also vegetable retailers, mostly women, who displayed chives, parsley, radishes, cilantro, basil, and the like on pieces of cloth on the ground. Most of them were clustered in the area called Amin Soltan Square along with purveyors of seasonal cooked beets, barbecued liver, beef tripe and *sirab shirdoun* made from lamb or sheep stomach; *ferni*, a kind of rice porridge made of starch or rice powder, sugar, milk and water; and *jaghour baghour* (fried onion with veal's larynx, skin, fat, and every other scrap left over from the butcher's). These popular dishes, served hot on small aluminum plates, were something like the *chitlins* of poor blacks in America or the *menudo* of Mexico. In Tehran's poor areas, vendors used cast-off animal parts to create a cuisine so well spiced, so delicious, that you would forget you were eating the cheapest and unhealthiest ingredients.

Mingling with the market crowd were pickpockets—both teenaged amateurs and adult professionals—stealing an apricot here or an apple there from the vendors and picking the pockets of poor men and women, trying to gather enough for a meal. There were also more sophisticated petty thieves—skillful con artists who worked in teams to swindle the unwary. One of them would start a card game and the other would pretend to be an ordinary passerby who would somehow just be always lucky, winning and taking money from the "mark". These con artists were fast, articulate, and extremely compelling. This is part of the reason that, even today, if you are trying to reproach someone for bad behavior, you might say, "Did you grow up in Chaleh Meidan?"

Like poor urban neighborhoods everywhere, Chaleh Meidan had, in addition to these petty thieves, its share of serious gangsters. Our local criminals organized gambling houses and opium dens (*shireh-kesh khaneh),* and extorted money from businessmen and other better-off people. In addition to these dependable money-making ploys, they launched a number of other schemes on the side.

The most famous gangster in our neighborhood was Tayeb Haj Rezai, who was usually referred to by his first name. One of the main sources of Tayeb's income was the wholesale fruit and vegetable trade, especially once it was moved to Anbar-e Gandom. At each of two gates of the market there was a kind of office where Tayeb's minions (*nowtcheh)* illegally "taxed" everybody who purchased produce wholesale. There were of course no specific regulations on this tax, because the whole business was unlawful. The term for this daily robbery in the produce market was *dar baghi* (literally, "garden door"). It operated in broad daylight under the semisecret protection of the local police, who took their daily cut of the money that Tayeb stole from the poor grocers and other small businessmen.

Other lucrative neighborhood activities were run by Tayeb's relatives or other, less powerful associates. There was an opium den just a few houses from Tayeb's house, run by his cousin Mahmoud Soltanali. The whole neighborhood knew him well. Mahmoud had organized a very skillful group of thieves who would travel to the north of Tehran to rob the wealthy and to the central districts to burglarize the houses of the better-off *haji bazaari* (traditional merchants in the bazaar) and others. This crew was famous for jumping from second-floor windows with bags of loot in their arms. But Mahmoud was no Robin Hood; he robbed the small-time merchants of the southern neighborhoods as well.

The opium dens were particularly horrible. The servant women of the opium houses, called *saghi*, were the most exploited, miserable people in Tehran. Addicts themselves, they were under pressure from all sides: from the owner or manager of the opium den, from the customers, and from their own desperate addictions. Not only was the position of saghi considered a filthy, gruesome job in our culture, but saghis were also assumed to be prostitutes. Because of this perception, some customers expected to have sex with them. These women were virtual slaves, not accepted anywhere outside of the opium houses, and they were brutalized and degraded. The image of the saghi of the opium den was particularly disturbing and sadly surreal; in classical Iranian culture, the saghi appears in countless poems and painted miniatures as a muse and companion—a young, beautiful, and enchanting woman carrying a jug of wine serving men.

The gangsters wielded barely concealed power over the neighborhoods. In our neighborhood, the one who had the most power was Tayeb. He was somehow, directly or indirectly, involved in everything that went on in the area, and profited from everything. He was considered the local boss. Supposedly he could be helpful when needed. A story circulated about Tayeb and Ferdows Garden when I was a child. I never knew whether it was actually true; nonetheless, it gives an accurate picture of the power relations in our neighborhood at the time.

Someone from our neighborhood raped a young boy. This action outraged everyone, especially because a few years earlier there had been a serial killer, Asghar Ghatel—"Asghar the Murderer"—who had raped and killed boys. The story of Asghar Ghatel still haunted people's minds. Tayeb, in his role as protector and power figure, found the perpetrator, grabbed his arm, and dragged him into Ferdows Garden. There, in broad daylight, Tayeb beheaded the rapist while the neighbors waited outside.

After he finished the job, Tayeb walked out and left the area. Everyone knew what had happened, but no one said anything. If the story is to be believed, Tayeb protected the neighborhood by killing a rapist, although he and his associates profited from the daily rape and exploitation of the saghi women.

These gangsters in the poor neighborhoods, who seemingly had no role in the larger society, were instrumental in at least two major events in twentieth-century Iranian history. During the early 1950s, Prime Minister Mohammad Mossadegh, a popular elected official, nationalized the Iranian oil industry in an attempt to let the people keep a larger portion of the profits from the sale of their natural resources. In response, British and American government agents jointly organized and backed a coup that ousted Mossadegh and consolidated all local power in the hands of the Shah, Mohammad Reza Pahlavi. Local gangsters played an important part in the 1953 coup, acting as paid agents, demonstrators, rioters, and assassins.

The second instance of gangster participation on the national scene took place during the 1979 revolution. Local gangsters were used by the clerics who were organizing against the Shah in mosques and poor and lower middle class neighborhoods. Gangsters were used to threaten, intimidate, beat, and murder leftists and other secularists as the mullahs, the Islamic clerics, struggled to consolidate power. Our Tayeb did not survive long enough to participate in the revolution. He had already been executed by the Shah because he had supported the Ayatollah Khomeini in the riots of 1963. Although the mullahs were already a powerful force in the 1960s, they were not yet the dominant force, and Khomeini had been forced into exile. Tayeb was sufficiently ignorant of power relations at the top that his siding with the mullahs was premature, and this miscalculation cost him his life.

■ ■ ■

When I was a little older, we moved to an alley called Doukhteh Foroush-ha, "Ready-Made Clothes Dealers." It was here that my brother, Mansoor, organized a theater group with the children in the neighborhood. We put on plays for the neighbors in the alley. I was in the fifth grade at the time but was already completely entranced with acting and theater. The plays we staged were of a particular genre called *Takht-e howzi* (*takht* meaning "board" and *howzi* meaning "pool"), a traditional style of theater that takes place in homes (mostly the homes of the wealthy), at wedding parties and other ceremonial and family occasions, such as circumcisions. The courtyard pool is covered with boards over which rugs are spread to form a stage. As the last entertainment of the evening, after dinner has been served and after the musicians have finished playing, usually around 11 o'clock, or even midnight, the families of the bride and groom and their guests gather in the courtyard around the stage as the actors climb onto the boards laid across the pool and begin the play. These shows often go on until two or three in the morning.

This style of traditional theater also has another name: *Siah-bazi* (*Siah* meaning "black" and *bazi* meaning "play" or "show"). Siah-bazi is named for the traditional protagonist, a black family servant who always has a direct relationship with the audience, whom he addresses in asides—letting them in on the tricks he plays on the master of the house. Traditional actors playing this role burn cork to blacken their faces, just like white minstrels used to do in the United States. They put on red lipstick and a red costume with a long tunic and belted baggy pants with a red pillbox hat—like a fez without a tassel. There is no script in this traditional Iranian theater; rather, it is based on improvisation. I do not think anyone knows the exact origins of the Siah-bazi, but its roots are obviously in slavery, although the character is not a slave. He is a servant who lives in the master's house. He's funny, he has an accent, and under the guise of not understanding certain words he turns them cleverly against the master. The audience understands that he is clever, that he is purposely mistaking the meaning of the words in order to use them as weapons.

This character has different names—Almas (diamond), Mobarak, or Firouz—and during the show he slyly says or does wrong things in order to aggravate his master so as to get laughs from the audience. When the master calls him—"Fi-i-i-rouz!"—the audience laughs, because they know something funny will likely happen soon. This black character serves as a metaphor for the Iranian masses. The audience always sympathizes with him; he is their hero, always outwitting the master. Also, he acts as a confidante to whoever is relatively powerless or oppressed in the play. If the master's son has difficulties—loves a girl whose father won't let her out of the house, for example—Firouz will act as a go-between. The son and the daughter always trust him. When my brother formed the theater group with the neighborhood kids, I was always the one who played this black hero. Siah-bazi was the style of theater we knew best. All kids would see it at wedding ceremonies and knew the stories and characters, especially the black character and his master, Haji.

But my acting career predated my role as Firouz. My mother told me that when I was two years old I used to make fun of family members, especially my father's friend, the colonel. I would mimic him, walk like him, holding my hands behind my back. I do not really remember, but that is what my mother told me. The other experience I had as a child actor was in school, in the second grade. We had a chanting class, in which we sang patriotic songs—the national anthem, things like that. The teachers, who were usually musicians, taught us the notes. One played flute and clarinet. To us he was a comic character, tall and slow with thick glasses; none of us took him seriously. Sometimes he let us play his clarinet, and we would laugh at the spittle incurred in playing a wind instrument. Once he directed a little play in class. I had a small part: someone is lost in the desert and I show him the way. I remember the gesture I used to show the lost fellow the way: I raised two fingers in a V shape in front of the lost man with a flourish and told him to look between them.

"What do you see?" I asked him?

"A minaret and—"

"Well, that's where you go."

I used the same gesture many years later in a play and the adult audience laughed just as much as the second graders had. At any rate, these were my first theatrical experiences.

My passion was fueled and developed by my father, who began to take me to the theater when I was a little boy. My father's second cousin Abdolvahab Shahidi was a famous actor and singer. Theater was very expensive in Iran at the time and my father was an ill-paid warrant officer, but because of this famous relative we were able to go to plays for free. Without this connection I would never have had the chance to feed my growing passion for the stage.

Abdolvahab Shahidi used to perform at the Jame'eh Barbod Theater, the sole company producing classical Iranian musical theater. I began to attend these plays with my father when I was very young, even before I entered school. Right from the start I was entranced. I remember so clearly, even now, the lobby of the theater, the large carpets on the floor, the lights, the chandeliers, the bar, and—moving through these magical spaces— the people, the members of the audience, dressed in beautiful clothes. The contrast between this magical world and my own life left me anxious to return again and again; to walk with my father through the crowded lobby into the auditorium to find our seats; to share the excitement of the audience in the moments before the curtain rose! The bell rang three times before the opening of the curtain: the first was a three- or five-minute warning, the second was a minute before, the third was less than one minute, and then, the dimming of the lights.... When the curtain finally opened on that other world, I was somewhere else—completely transported. All of this was so wondrous to a boy from Ferdows Garden. Regardless of where I have traveled and which places I have lived, that wonderment has never dwindled in my mind; it has sustained me through the hard times and enriched the pleasure of the better ones.

3

ANAHITA THEATER

I began my life in theater immediately after I finished high school. It was 1959—1338 according to the Iranian calendar. By that time my family had moved to a new neighborhood in the east of Tehran called Shahbaz. I was completely crazy about theater; I could not see myself as anything but an actor. I applied to the Anahita acting school, where for the first time in Iran they were teaching Method acting—the Stanislavsky System, as it is called in Iran and elsewhere. I signed up and paid for three months of classes, to be followed by an audition, hoping that the directors—the husband-and-wife team of Mostafa and Maheen Oskoui—would recognize my talent and my potential for the stage.

Anahita acting classes required, at the time, a monthly tuition of thirty tomans. After three months, each student received an evaluation based on a short piece of theater, either a scene from a play or a novel or something created from one's own writing. Whoever won first place would be granted the rest of his classes tuition free. The course of study was two years. I did not have enough money and I did not want to ask my mother for help. A friend of mine, Parviz, who lived next door to my house, was a typesetter. I explained my situation and asked if he could help me find temporary work in a print shop. He and his coworkers soon found Latin typesetting work for me in the same print shop where he was working.

I was very slow in the beginning. I had to search for each letter in the typesetting box. I prepared small pieces of paper, wrote the letters of the alphabet on them, and glued them to each letter space to see the letters more readily. I was typesetting an English textbook, *Direct Method*, and gradually became familiar with the typesetting box. After two weeks I was able to earn ninety tomans—about thirteen dollars at the time—enough to pay the first three months of tuition. It was a painstaking and time-consuming job, but I was determined to win first place in the evaluation. I did capture first-place honors, but I continued working in the print shop until I finished typesetting the textbook.

As my audition piece, I chose a Chekhov short story, "The Joy," about a young man who gets drunk one night and is involved in an accident. Stumbling heedlessly out of a cafe, he is run down by a horse-drawn carriage. No serious injury is involved and the next morning he experiences only slight aches and pains in his legs. Because he lives in a very small town, however, the accident is news: the morning paper prints an account in which his name appears. The young man is very excited about this—he's famous now! He buys a copy of the newspaper and carries it home. He flings open the door and holds up the paper for his parents to see: "I never expected it; no, I never expected it!" Acting the scene, I pretended that the two directors were my father and mother; I banged the door open and addressed the couple directly, shouting, "My name has been published! Now all Russia knows of me!" That's how I joined Anahita Theater.

When I entered acting school, I was twenty. I had just graduated from my high school, Honarestan-e Sanati-e Tehran, the Industrial School of Tehran. I chose this technical school myself in order to join a friend whose brother-in-law was a teacher there who had told him that this was a good school for building a future. In Iran at that time, students typically attended elementary school for six years, beginning at age seven, before going on to a six-year high school. One would normally graduate at age nineteen, but I was held back because I was a troublemaker. Actually, I was a well-behaved student until the middle of high school; I don't know what happened then, but I became an incorrigible troublemaker—but only at school, never at home.

The first four years at the Honarestan were hands-on. We learned to do everything: ironwork, blacksmithing, fabrication of lamps, and manufacturing of industrial molds, bolts, screws, and many other items using a variety of metals and tools. These courses were taught in Farsi. Then, for the last two years, students had to select a major: mechanical field or electrical field. I chose electrical. The technical and language professors for the senior students were all German.

The school had been established in 1907 and had gone through many ups and downs during the twentieth century. It was located northwest of a military training site near the National Garden—the training site that I mentioned in the first chapter. The school was shut down from 1916 to 1920 due to pressure from the British and Russian governments, and to the discontinuation of financial aid from Germany and the Iranian monarchy. After the war and the coup by Reza Khan in 1920 (1299 on the Iranian calendar), the new government reopened the school with a new budget in February 1921.

In 1941, during World War II, when British forces in the south and Soviet forces in the north occupied Iran, the school was threatened again. The British and Soviet militaries forced the Iranian government to seize all of the German engineers and technicians and deport them. The subsequent lack of technical and scientific specialists crippled the school, and for years after the end of the war the institution barely limped along.

In 1953, the year I entered the school, there was only one elderly German engineer, in the machine and mechanical section. Later, with changes in the Ministry of Education and the establishment of a science and technology treaty with Germany, several German technicians and teachers, including a German language teacher, Herr Weiss, returned to the school. As I mentioned, during my last two years, when I specialized in electricity, we had German teachers in the technical and language courses.

Due to its curriculum and the composition of the student body, ranging from the very poor to the very rich, coupled with the high quality of its teachers, the school possessed a special potency and force. Many prominent figures in the fields of industry, politics, arts, and theater graduated from this school. Some teachers at the school, such as Nima Youshij and Bozorg Alavi, played an influential and important role in Iranian contemporary literature, and Nour Ali Boroumand, one of the most important figures in Iranian music, taught there. Nima Youshij, whose poem "My Steel Heart" I quote at the beginning, is widely acknowledged as the founder of Iranian New Poetry. His revolutionary role in poetry and his writings on literature clearly mark the departure from lingering tradition and the beginnings of literary modernity in Iran.

Bozorg Alavi, a pioneer of the new style of novel writing, helped alter the whole conceptualization of both style and content in fiction. Iranians who have read Alavi's *Fifty-Three Persons* might recognize the main building of the school described in the narrative as the place where Reza Shah's secret police arrested him.

By the time I graduated from Honarestan and entered Anahita Theater, I knew something about nuts and bolts, and a little bit about electricity too. I also had learned about art and literature, about the history of my country, and especially about theater. Despite my father's wish that I become an engineer, I was certain that I would become an actor. All through high school, and beyond, I felt insatiably hungry for any knowledge about this profession. The only literature I knew that addressed theater were two books written in Farsi, both of which had been banned because their authors were from the leftist Saadi Theater. One of these books, *The Art of Theater*, was written by the founder of modern theater in Iran, Abdol Hossein Noushin; the other, *The Technique of Theater*, was written by an actor and director who was a colleague of Noushin's, Hossein Kheirkhah. These books were apolitical technical treatises; nonetheless, they were banned by the Shah. We could buy used copies of them if we could afford three or four times the original price; the cost was high because of their scarcity. To purchase them, I had to save the pocket money my mother provided me. There was always a little money in our house for books and movies, because my father was consistently employed as a warrant officer until his death when I was seventeen. Even after his death, the family survived because my mother received his pension from the army.

■ ■ ■

Anahita Theater was named after the pre-Islamic Iranian goddess of water. Both Mostafa and Maheen Oskoui had been working with Noushin's Theater for years. When the Tudeh Party—the Communist Party of Iran—was banned in 1948 (after its alleged involvement in an attempt to assassinate the Shah) and Noushin was arrested, the Oskouis went to France to study. Then, in 1950, they moved to the Soviet Union, where they were accepted into the Lunacharsky State Institute of Theatre Art in Moscow. In 1958, through the influence of Mostafa Oskoui's brother, the wealthy owner of a transportation company, the couple was allowed to return to Iran; with financial help from Mostafa's brother, they established Anahita Theater. Mostafa was the artistic director or, as he insisted, "head director," and Maheen was the director.

■ ■ ■

To my friends and me, members of a younger generation who had heard of the fame of the Saadi Theater and of its artistic reputation, the Oskouis seemed like the right people to study with, not only in terms of art but also politically. We admired them, both as individuals who were political and as actors in a legendary theater. We had a nostalgic image of the Saadi Theater as a stylistically and politically progressive theater that had flourished in the brief period of relative freedom during and immediately after World War II. After the 1953 coup, and the subsequent suppression of all democratic and semidemocratic activities, Anahita Theater seemed to us like a small window through which we could breathe. All the young actors and others who came to work there shared this view. Our generation of actors had nowhere else to express our feelings and thoughts, and no other place in which to grow to become what we wanted to be. Heavy repression loomed constantly; not only was there repression of arts and culture, but any type of gathering was closely monitored by the secret police. Freedom of speech, the right of assembly, and any sort of political activity were suppressed. Fear and caution ruled our social activities; even innocent gatherings at private homes to discuss life, literature, and art had to be carefully planned. Censorship was corrosive of independent thought. That was why Anahita was so important to us.

At that time, Anahita Theater was located in the north end of the city, part of a newly developed neighborhood known as Yousef Abad. Only one bus line went there. In winter, getting there was especially difficult. There was a very steep slope that the buses could not navigate when there was ice and snow. As a result, winter audiences tended toward the sparse. I remember one night when we were performing *A Streetcar Named Desire* for eight hardy souls. I played the part of the Mexican flower seller. "Flores para los muertos! Flores para los muertos!" ("Flowers for the dead! Flowers for the dead!") translated into Farsi as *"Gole baraye mordeh!"* The part was originally written for a female, but in the Anahita production I played the role out of necessity, because we had too few actresses. I would start applying my makeup at three or four in the afternoon in order to be ready to go on stage at eight. Each night I experimented with various looks—a scar on my face, a darkened complexion, anything to look as frightening as possible as I called out *Gole baraye mordeh!* In the scene, the character Blanche is alone, in a very dark mood and brooding on the past; then the flower seller shows up, and deepens her growing unease with *Gole baraye mordeh!*

That was the first line I spoke as a student actor in a professional theater and I intended to make the most of my debut.

4

WANDERING YEARS

All aspects of the theater inspired me. It was my first contact with an organization or group that linked me to a larger society. I was a simple person—perhaps a little naive, definitely idealistic. The sum total of my theatrical knowledge came from the two theater books I mentioned before, plus the plays I had seen with my father, a few plays I had read, and the staging of little plays for the neighborhood children with my brother.

At the time, there were few theater groups in Iran that staged significant modern plays. We had professional theaters that were doing commercial comedy, popular plays, the kind that are purely escapist entertainment, developing no meaningful themes. These theaters were located along one street, Lalehzar, which at the time was the entertainment and attraction center of Tehran. Most of the movie theaters were on or near that street as well. The golden age of theater on Lalehzar had faded badly. By the time I started doing theater, belly dancers imported from Turkey along with magicians, jugglers, and folk singers comprised the main attractions. These performers would take the stage as headliners, performing cheap, shallow comedies. Not surprisingly, the patrons of this type of entertainment enjoyed equally unsophisticated plays.

Another type of modern theater operated under the province of the Dramatic Arts Administration, a branch of the Homeland Fine Arts Administration, renamed the Ministry of Culture and Art in 1963 during the Shah's White Revolution.

To understand the attitude of the state towards the theater and the arts in Iran, it is necessary to understand the intent and context of the White Revolution. Instituted almost ten years after the coup of 1953, this so-called revolution was an all-encompassing economic and social program sponsored by the United States. The stated goal was to transform Iran from a feudal agricultural country into a modern industrial nation by breaking the political power of the feudal landlords as a faction—but not as a class—by redistributing some of their lands and reorganizing agricultural production.

Overwhelming pressure for land reform had grown for two interrelated reasons. One of the criticisms leveled against the Shah's regime was that Iran remained a feudal country without an industrial base. Feudal landlords, one of whom was the Shah himself, dominated the agrarian economy. After the oil industry began to flourish, the country's primary economic base became petroleum; oil production was controlled, however, by foreign-owned companies while the feudal agrarian economy persisted alongside it. There was also indirect pressure for reform from the example of neighboring Communist and Socialist countries that had already been pursuing antifeudalist land reforms and industrial development for decades. The Shah's U.S. backers wanted to make sure that Iran and its oil were developed along capitalistic lines as an integral part of the international capitalist supply chain.

By 1961, the pressure from political and social forces inside Iran for fundamental change was building up and threatening to destabilize the Shah's regime. The Shah attempted to control the situation through various political tricks but soon found himself in a quagmire. He was forced to dismiss parliament deputies who, in time-honored ways, had been fraudulently elected. He appointed a new prime minister to conduct new elections; however, top-to-bottom corruption proved impervious to reform. Dissatisfaction and disgust throughout Iran strengthened the voices of opposition to the Shah's ineffectual rule. Faced with widespread strikes and criticism, the Shah finally was forced to call on Ali Amini, a pro-American, liberal politician, to form a new government. Appointing Amini, an independent thinker with a legitimate agenda for reform, must have left a bitter taste on the Shah's political palate, but the despot had little choice if he wanted to appease his critics in and outside of Iran.

The Kennedy administration saw the Shah's resistance to reform as a possible obstacle to its strategy of developing Middle Eastern oil resources to serve American interests while at the same time denying them to the Socialist Bloc countries. Cold War political considerations demanded that the United States should not allow the Shah and his anachronistic view of absolute monarchy to make the Western model of development appear intolerably slow and inefficient compared to the Socialist model. Accordingly, the Americans, having first backed the 1953 coup in which the Shah consolidated power, now forced him to accept the pro-American Ali Amini as prime minister, and subsequently pushed for the White Revolution. The most important part of this "revolution" was land reform.

To kick off the reforms, part of the Shah's own lands, which had been forcibly confiscated by his father, were redistributed to the peasantry. The Shah peppered his speeches with slogans praising his own leadership in creating a modern industrial nation, but his continuing resistance to social, economic, and political reforms and his lack of respect for the rights of the Iranian people revealed his duplicity. It would ultimately cost him his throne and bring the Iranian people the tragic and sinister consequences of the revolution of 1979.

In a speech before a group of landowners in 1961, Prime Minister Amini laid out the plan for agrarian reform a few months before it was announced by the Shah. The program had actually been prepared a few years earlier but had not been announced because of strong opposition from high-ranking military landowners and especially from clergy who were benefiting from large endowments of land to mosques and shrines. The clergy also received a percentage of the harvest from holdings of any size; even landless peasants working fields rented from others paid a portion of their crops to the clergy. This was not required by Sharia law, but the mullahs and other religious institutions in villages made the peasants believe it was a religious duty.

There was nothing revolutionary about this so-called revolution. To many people, the programs sounded good on paper, but the government's execution of the plan proved the truth of the adage "the devil is in the details." The land given to the peasants turned out to be the least desirable, a fault made worse as these rural poor received no tools, no machines, no seeds, and no irrigation equipment. They had no other income, no way to survive than to work this nearly useless land. Meanwhile, the landlords, still in possession of virtually all the good land in the country, started to convert their holdings from producing food for local consumption to cash crops for export, following the capitalist model. The peasants, on their poor land, could not compete with the large landowners and their new, modern equipment, so they soon gave up and hired themselves out to their former landlords or migrated to Tehran to look for work. Being uneducated and generally illiterate, and possessing no industrial or professional skills, they worked as laborers, mostly in construction, making mud bricks (at the time, most contractors were using these rather than concrete or modern construction equipment for their buildings) and doing other heavy, unskilled work.

Tehran, like many capital cities in developing countries, was the only city in Iran that approached a kind of modernity. Urban areas in other provinces were mainly mercantile centers for the surrounding rural districts, or administrative outposts subsidized by the central government. They did not experience Tehran's rapid crowding. Without the capacity to absorb this overwhelming influx, Tehran witnessed the transformation of many migrants into Islamic warriors who supported Khomeini in 1979.

While the main thrust of the White Revolution centered on the supposed agricultural reform, another campaign was launched: administrative "reform"—establishing, expanding, or reorganizing different branches of the government. Some ministries were expanded and a few administrations were elevated to nominal ministerial status. This "reform" affected those of us in the theater most directly. The Homeland Fine Arts Administration became the Ministry of Culture and Art, and the Dramatic Arts Administration was expanded and renamed the Theater Programs Administration. The latter was a governmental theater office that had its own theater troupes whose actors and directors were government employees. Other groups were subsidized, under certain conditions. What all this amounted to, for us, was the tightening of restrictions on freedom of speech and artistic expression. For the first time in Iran the government developed an organized, official cultural policy that systematized and extended its control over all areas of artistic, literary, and cultural life.

Besides the Dramatic Arts Administration, there were, in the late 1950s and early 1960s, a few independent—or to put it more correctly, semi-independent—theater groups. They had no economic resources other than the dues paid by their members, and sometimes not even these. The government would not subsidize or help a group unless it pledged allegiance by printing its official affiliation with the government on its programs and posters, and by staging special performances for officials in Tehran and the provinces. Governmental support for independent artistic and cultural groups to promote art and culture was nonexistent, at the same time, the government required unaffiliated groups to pursue their art exclusively "for art's sake." The government used force, official censorship, and the threat of arrests to ensure that no independent group would engage in political artwork. The government's own cultural employees were bribed to create propagandistic political art in support of the regime. If you were an employee of the Ministry of Culture and Art, you were well paid but could not do any independent work. As a result, most groups who were committed to theater as a profession gradually became affiliated with or at least dependent on the Ministry of Culture and Art. In the mid-1960s, when I established my own theater group, it was the sole independent group left in Tehran.

When I began to work there in 1959, Anahita Theater was one of the few independent groups that seemed well organized. The company ran a repertory theater dedicated to producing artistic, noncommercial plays, mostly thanks to the many talented young actors who dedicated themselves to the theater. Other groups at that time possessed neither such dedicated members nor a clear artistic mission like Anahita's. The theater held these advantages even though financial support came exclusively from its members. The dedicated people working at Anahita managed to earn enough money from outside jobs to both make a living and run the theater. This was the situation when I joined Anahita. However, this state of affairs did not last.

Our self-styled "head director," Mostafa Oskoui, was neither a good manager nor particularly honest. Within two or three years he got supporters of the theater embroiled in messy financial issues. The most critical of these problems was Mostafa's failure to pay rent to the theater's landlord. At that time, we were performing a play every month for Iranian television's only private, nongovernmental channel. We had a viable financial plan and worked hard to meet our budget obligations. At first we did not realize that the money was being siphoned off. Mostafa loudly claimed to want his theater to compete with the most famous theaters in the world, but at the same time he wanted to run and control everything single-handedly and not share information or assign responsibility to anyone but himself. Nobody knew anything about the status of the budget or expenses or debts. We knew only that somehow the theater was failing financially. Finally, after struggling to straighten things out and getting nowhere, the members of the theater became disillusioned and disappointed and began leaving the group one by one. Five of us, including me, left at the same time after a futile fight with Mostafa about finances and various other management issues.

The problem was, when I left Anahita, I did not have anywhere else to go. At the age of twenty-three I did not have any goals beyond the theater, and no ready employment opportunities presented themselves. Seriously depressed, I pondered my limited options.

I did not want to go into the Dramatic Arts Administration because I did not want to work for the government. I was against the government, the establishment, and the whole system. I did not like the way the country was run. First of all, there was the harsh censorship; there were no free organizations, whether cultural, artistic, or political—a condition that militated against serving as an employee of the government or entering an artistic organization directly controlled by the government. For me, artistic activity was inextricably linked to freedom. My thoughts were guided more by feeling than by analysis—by a distrustful attitude toward the Shah's regime, including all government officials, whom I dismissed as puppets. The members of parliament (*Majlis*), for instance, were supposed to be elected by the people, but in reality they were preselected behind closed doors. Then the government would organize phony campaigns, and on election day government agents would bring illiterate peasants, seasonal workers, migrant marginal people, and some deluded or intimidated factory workers to the polls to stuff the ballot boxes. Officials would joyfully announce the unsurprising results of their "free, fair, and democratic election." It was a lousy scandal, a joke, a shallow farce performed by bad actors. The members of parliament in Iran were thoroughly tame caricatures, a bunch of obedient servants of the Shah. We did not have a single real, independent progressive among our representatives, a condition that has never changed during my lifetime.

Although those were my feelings, I could not imagine living my life other than on the stage, so I became more and more depressed. Finally, I got so desperate that I shamefacedly forced myself to appeal to the director of the Dramatic Arts Administration, Mehdi Forough. He knew and respected me as an actor, having seen me both on television and on stage at Anahita. He accepted my application to work for the administration, but he added, "But we have a policy here. I don't want anybody to criticize me for favoring you, so I have to adhere to our policy."

The policy was to require an audition, the performance of one scene for the administrative director (Forough himself) and for the stage directors who worked there. He gave me Antony's speech from *Julius Caesar* and told me to prep for a week, then come back ready to perform. It was a humiliating requirement for me. I was hurt and insulted, because I saw myself as an already established actor. They had seen me on television. Why should I have to prove my talent further? I was young and so proud of my acting ability, even though I had only two years' experience. Nevertheless, desperate to work, I took the proffered piece and returned a week later.

Forough had gathered four stage directors and a few employees of the office, including his assistant, a Mr. Ghoreishi, to observe my audition.

"OK, Mr. Rahmaninejad, we're ready," Forough said when I arrived.

The venue was quite small, probably around sixty seats, with a tiny stage. I went through a doorway into the backstage area, where I stood waiting behind the curtain on stage right. I finally came onto the stage, whirling, chanting, reciting, mumbling to myself, and blowing—performing a ritual in which superstitious Muslims exhale emphatically while turning around in a circle to clear away evil spirits. In the manner of a religious man coming out of his house in the morning, I spun around and mumbled from right to left all the way across the stage in front of the curtain before whirling backstage and out through the doorway that opened into the auditorium.

I looked at Forough, a very important, respected man with a Ph.D. in music and drama from an English university, and said, "So, how was my performance?"

"Well, Mr. Rahmaninejad, we were expecting something else, but you were good." I guess he did not want to embarrass himself in front of the others. "OK, welcome to our home." He was a very goodhearted man.

I did not stay more than a week. They gave me parts in two television plays, but before rehearsals began I left. I did not say goodbye to the administrative director; I just told one of the stage directors, Jafar Vali, whom I accidentally encountered in the courtyard on my way out, "I can't stay here—I'm leaving." And I left. The realization that I had become an employee of the regime I hated proved too bitter a pill to swallow—a young man's pride, I suppose. Could I be a lackey in the Shah's government? Never.

5

INTERLUDE

Brooding over what seemed to be a hopeless situation, I thought that the best thing would be to leave the country and go to Germany to study engineering, the plan my father had wanted me to pursue. I contacted a friend from school who had left Iran to continue his education there. I sent him my translated diploma and all the other necessary papers and asked him to make my application to the engineering school. After receiving a letter of acceptance, I applied for a passport from the Passport Office, a branch of the police department. Unfortunately, Iran's bureaucracy was slow and corrupt. After three months of coming and going, going and coming, back and forth to the Passport Office, the bureaucrats rejected my application without reason or explanation. The Shah's official minions knew well how to exhaust people and cause misery.

I had a very difficult time for a year and a half in 1963 and 1964. I did not see a future for myself anywhere in the country. I did not know what to do with my life. I had two close friends. The three of us spent most of our time together, reading books and discussing our common interests and our frustrations over our bleak prospects. A. D, who had been an actor at Anahita and left before me, was working at the National Bank of Iran. Eventually he came up with an adventurous plan to leave Iran illegally. I told him, "I'm with you. I want to leave the country. I can't do anything here." We took the plan to our friend Parviz, and although he was married he agreed to join us.

Over the course of six months, each of us was able to accumulate a few thousand tomans. We were ready to leave. But before leaving Tehran we decided to deposit all our money in one pocket, reasoning that making one person responsible for our expenses would help us spend more frugally. We all agreed that the best person for this task would be A. D, and he accepted the responsibility.

I told my mother and the rest of my family that I was going to Germany to continue my engineering studies. Of course I had no such intention, but when I left my family I acted like a student departing for Europe. I had purchased a new suit, shirts, shoes, and a suitcase, and I told my mother I had a bus ticket to Turkey and then to Europe. I asked them not to come with me to the station. "It is better to say goodbye at home. I don't like a goodbye scene in front of the others," I explained.

The first stage of our plan was to go to Shiraz, where one of A. D.'s friends was completing his military service. There we left our belongings with him and continued on to Zahedan, the capital of the province of Sistan and Baluchestan, near the eastern border. We planned to sneak into Pakistan and from there to go to India or wherever else we imagined might offer a better life.

In Zahedan we hired a guide to take us to the border and pass us into Pakistan. A. D. was in charge of all these intriguing actions as well as having financial responsibility.

We had devised a cover story for traveling close to the border, in case we were detained and questioned by the police. The story was that Parviz's brother-in-law, a teenaged boy, had fought with his single mother and had left home. His mother and family had searched everywhere and had gone to the authorities asking for help. They had received a report that the boy had gone to Shiraz to visit his uncle. When he failed to return, his family suspected he might have left Iran because during the quarrel with his mother he had threatened to leave forever. In retrospect I believe that the three of us thought this was a convincing story due to our own eagerness to escape our country.

We launched ourselves on this ill-conceived adventure and, predictably, soon encountered a major obstacle when we arrived at a border town called Saravan. This place could be reached only by a van that carried passengers from the neighboring county town of Khash twice a week. One short street comprised the entire community. We found rough lodging at a coffeehouse and planned our next step. As elsewhere in Iran, the proprietor served tea, not coffee; nonetheless, Iranians always used the term *qahveh khaneh* (coffeehouse) for such establishments. The town had one grocery shop, one public bath, and a general store that sold charcoal, brooms, blankets, oil, cigarettes, and almost everything else. The bath was not open all the time and stipulated limited hours on alternating days for men and women. Surprisingly there was also a very small liquor store, where we bought some drinks. Another surprise was a poolroom in a garage across from the coffeehouse. The pool table was a holdover from World War II, when the British had stayed there. The garage housed the vans that traveled to and from Khash.

Two days after we arrived we were arrested by border agents. It was afternoon, sunny and hot, and we were having tea in the coffee shop. A gendarme walked in, sat on the wooden bench right next to the door and ordered tea, which he slowly consumed. He appeared somehow strange and nervous, peering outside as if waiting for someone or something. He noticeably avoided eye contact with us. A couple of times he glanced our way but quickly averted his gaze when the three of us exchanged looks with one another.

After finishing his two cups of tea—in Iran it is the custom to have two cups of tea—and paying, he stepped toward us and, in an awkward, low tone, said, "You must come with me."

"Go where? What do you mean?" we replied.

"To the *marzbani*, the border station. The chief wants to ask you some questions," he answered.

It was clear that someone had reported us as suspicious characters. Fifteen minutes later we arrived at the border control station, where we were ordered to sit in the corridor on a wooden bench. Four doors lined the hallway. The gendarme disappeared through one of them. We stared at each other, then exchanged pale, skeptical smiles. Unprepared for this development and not understanding the seriousness of our situation, the whole business struck us as a dark joke. After a while, A. D, holding his hands together and leaning on his knees, sighed and, as if talking to himself, remarked, "Well, well, Mr. A. D.?" We got the implied message: he was going to give his real name when the questioning commenced. When creating our cover story for just such an event, we had agreed that each of us, except Parviz, would use a fake name. We had reasoned that since Parviz was the main character in our concocted tale, if he carried his identity certificate we would avoid serious trouble if arrested. Now A. D. was telling us he intended to reveal his true identity. Did I want to be the sole suspect offering a fictitious name? I was still pondering this unexpected issue when the gendarme stepped into the corridor and announced, "The colonel will see you soon."

Moments later we entered a room where we found a colonel sitting at a desk, a picture of the Shah behind him on the wall. The gendarme closed the door behind us. The colonel pretended to continue perusing a file while studying us, and then with a slight hand gesture pointed to three chairs placed against the wall opposite his desk and ordered, "Sit down."

We seated ourselves, me in the middle. After a brief pause, the colonel asked, "Why did you come here?"

A. D. spun our tale, emphasizing the sad plight of a single mother whose headstrong boy had left home and whose whereabouts were unknown. He explained how he felt a familial responsibility and accounted for the presence of Parviz and me as the sympathetic action of loyal friends. We interjected with bits of information on a couple of occasions when A. D. faltered.

"We knew that the boy left Tehran for Shiraz because his uncle was serving in the military there. But when we got to Shiraz we found that he had come there and not said anything about the fight he had with his mother, and after two days he wanted to go back to Tehran. He asked for some money from his uncle and left Shiraz, but he did not return to Tehran. After a few days, when the boy's family found out through the uncle that he did not come back to Tehran, the mother asked her son-in-law, Parviz, to help her and go after the boy. In Shiraz we checked all the travel agencies and finally found that when the boy was there he got a ticket for Zahedan. After checking lodges there, we finally decided that most likely he had already left Iran. So we thought that since we had come this far we would go all the way to the end of the road; who knows, maybe we could find the poor boy somewhere close to the border. We could not return to his mother without an explanation for his disappearance."

The colonel seemed visibly unimpressed by our joint effort. He ostentatiously opened one of the files resting on his desk, looked at the top left corner, then up at A. D., verifying his picture, then asked, "What's your name?"

"A. D ..." A. D. answered.

"What's your father's name?"

A. D. gave the information.

"What's your date of birth?"

Each time the colonel asked a question, he looked down at the file, pretending to check the answer for accuracy, an obvious attempt to intimidate a suspect. Closely monitoring the question and answer sequence, I was convinced that there was nothing in those files about us in this border area, which I later labeled "the cat's ass" because the map of Iran looks like a sitting cat and the province of Sistan and Baluchestan is located where, in fact, the cat's ass should be.

The colonel was obviously unaware of his incompetent interrogation technique, because after finishing with A. D. he started on me. Comfortable with my appraisal of the man, I relaxed and fed him the false information we had prepared. My first name was Taghi, last name Hosseini, born in Tehran the same year as I was actually born, and so on. After each answer, the colonel checked the information he supposedly had in his file, and it seemed he found that everything was right! He continued his pretend file checking while questioning Parviz, in an ineffectual attempt to startle us.

After the questions, the colonel gave us a short lecture. "Since you are educated young people from Tehran, from, I am sure, noble families, I think you're telling the truth. I am not willing to deliver you to the authorities, although I have a responsibility to do so." By the authorities he meant, we were sure, SAVAK, the National Organization for Security and Intelligence. He continued: "I am letting you go to stay in the qahveh khaneh tonight, but tomorrow you should leave and go back to Zahedan. We're going to watch you. Don't do anything wrong."

We assured him that we would leave on the first vehicle we could find. To allay any lingering suspicion, we emphasized that "we don't have anything else to do here; we now know that the boy didn't come here, we are sure." We thanked him for his understanding and forbearance, and walked back to the qahveh khaneh. It was late and the owner was asleep. We knocked on the door and he displayed surprise at our return.

The next day brought a peculiar turn of events. Our plan had been simply to wait out the day until darkness would cover our departure, at around seven o'clock, through the garden at the back of the qahveh khaneh and into the lane behind the garden. We would then follow our hired guide to another local guide's house. From there the two guides would lead us to the border.

At around three in the afternoon, having finished our lunch in the qahveh khaneh and after drinking our tea, we were lazily relaxing, half reclining on a wooden bed, leaning back against the wall, legs outstretched, when our repose was suddenly broken. A fiftyish, dark-complexioned man walked into the room lugging a big suitcase, followed by a young woman holding a baby and a young man toting a large bundle on his back. All three were sweating even though it was winter.

Parviz knew the older man. His name was Socrates and his business included organizing acting classes held in small rooms in the center of Tehran. Socrates and others like him were taking advantage of the brisk cinema business in Iran. Miserably poor in terms of story, plot, character development, technique, editing, and all the other elements that make a movie a movie, Iranian cinema nonetheless turned a handsome profit. Filmmakers tailored their product to appeal to the generally illiterate, unsophisticated masses. The plots were painfully predictable: a poor man, nearly always from southern Tehran, falls in love with a well-off woman, but true love does not triumph until the couple endures a series of obstacles that usually include a few fights and car chases and some songs and dances against a backdrop of subterranean restaurant-bars in Tehran. City police are portrayed as vigilant, alert, and never fooled by appearances. If one were to assign a message to this genre it would be that there is dignity in poverty and the righteous will win out.

Self-styled acting coaches like Socrates, themselves victims of formulaic cinema, persuaded naive young people that the world of cinema actors was both paradisiacal and profitable, in order to sign them up for three to six months of acting classes. Reality proved this claim to be a distortion: Iranian cinema was merely a cheap, miserable copy of someone's addled notion of Hollywood.

Parviz knew Socrates because he had once been one of his star-struck prey. Astonished at finding each other in this squalid village, the two cautiously exchanged greetings. Parviz introduced us to Socrates, who told us he was there to put on a show that very night at the Red Lion and Sun Clinic—Darmangah-e Shir-o-Khorshid-e Sorkh—which was operated by the Ministry of Health and provided basic and limited medical services. The unexpectedness of such a man on such an errand arriving unheralded in such a place seemed to us surreal and absurdist.

We asked Socrates to sit and have tea with us and rest a bit. We asked if he and his companions had any place to stay. With great pride he informed us that he had been invited by the governor of the district to stay in the Shir-o-Khorshid-e Sorkh Clinic and that transportation would arrive soon.

Shortly a Jeep did arrive. The driver helped them load their baggage and they took off.

Jubilantly we decided that the show would be a perfectly justifiable excuse for us to be out at night. The owner of the qhahveh khaneh would not be suspicious, and we could meet our guide as arranged. We left the qhahveh khaneh in the late afternoon, telling the owner we would be returning late because we were attending the show. We actually went to the Shir-o-Khorshid-e Sorkh Clinic to make the time go by. Socrates and the young man appeared busy, although their activities did not resemble show preparations. We told Socrates that we would be back for the show, and then we left.

We went to the garage and played pool until seven o'clock, when we left to meet our guide.

It was dark when we got to the arranged meeting place. Our guide was sitting next to a stream running through the middle of the lane. He led us through a series of muddy, narrow alleys. We finally entered a single room located on a dark side street. Inside, a large man welcomed us. The small room already had three other people in it: a woman of about forty, an old man, and a young man of about thirty, who we later learned was the second local guide. We all sat down, crowding in, while the woman cooked something in a corner of the room on a Primus camping stove. The men smoked and I thought we were going to choke, because there was only a small hole in the ceiling for ventilation.

The large man explained the situation: "We are going to have dinner here. We have plenty of time, so don't worry. The longer you stay here, the safer you will be."

The woman kept looking up from her cooking, glancing at us stealthily. The old man watched us as if we were sheep ready for the slaughterhouse.

The large man spoke again. "They will be coming after you when they find out you are not in the tea house. If you wait here three or four hours, they will give up searching and go back to the marzbani. There will be no one to see you leaving the village and crossing the border."

When dinner was ready, the woman handed the large man a *sofreh*, a tablecloth, which he spread over a tiny space between us. She brought him bread, then handed him an aluminum pot, and two aluminum plates that he placed on the sofreh. The man invited everybody to eat as the woman retreated to her corner. The dinner consisted of one fried chopped onion, one crushed tomato, a little turmeric, salt, and water. We were shocked, not by the sparseness of the meal but at the financial sacrifice this modest repast represented. Our guide was being paid for his help, but this gesture was still overly generous. None of us could eat much; emotionally it was impossible, and there was not food enough for us all. Parviz, A. D., and I feigned eating, consuming one or two morsels each.

We changed into traditional Baluchi costumes and departed after midnight, buoyed by the prayers of the woman and old man. The large man accompanied us for thirty minutes or so, until he was sure we were not being followed; then he left us with our two guides and instructions for the remainder of the journey. The narrow road was scarcely visible in the darkness of the night.

We found that our guide from Zahedan, Kheir Mammad, did not know the area well. After two or three hours of walking, we reached a place and rested. Miserably cold, we tried to gather some firewood, sticks, anything with which to build a fire. The tiny scraps of wood we gathered burned fast, producing no real heat. We jumped up and down, doing exercises to keep warm.

Our guides whispered together furtively for a few minutes, then the local guide from Saravan approached A. D. and demanded his wallet. When A. D. refused, the man began gesticulating vociferously, making threatening gestures. We protested this behavior and asked Kheir Mammad to send him away. Kheir Mammad insisted we needed the local, but he said we would get rid of him the next day. He talked the local into calmness, and we settled into an extremely uncomfortable night, exercising at intervals to keep warm.

Finally, in the early morning, we headed for the Pakistani border. We had not gone far before encountering a group of migrants composed of three or four families. Our guide said he would not approach local people because they might report us to government agents, but these migrants were not villagers. One of them called the local guide by name, so we approached them and were invited into their tent, where they prepared tea for us.

The tent belonged to a headman of some sort, who started asking questions: "Where do you come from? Where are you heading? What are you doing here?"

We told them, "We are looking for Parviz's nephew who fled Tehran. We think he wanted to go to Pakistan; that is why we are here." It was the same story we had told the border control colonel who had interrogated us.

Meanwhile, the guides and migrants conversed in Baluchi, which we did not understand. Although we were wearing Baluchi clothes, on the Zahedan guide's recommendation, the headman told us that at a distance he could tell we "were not walking like

Baluchis." This last bit of disquieting information fully convinced us of the inexperience and unreliability of our guides and the lessening likelihood that we would reach and cross the border.

Leaving the tent, we queried our guides about what the headman had said. Kheir Mammad replied that "the man told us the way we were heading was not safe. He said that just yesterday the border agents arrested three people near the village. He advised us to take another way, which is longer but safer." Kheir Mammad's tone expressed his chagrin. That was enough. We decided to return to Zahedan and find a competent guide.

Following the second guide's advice, we went to a nearby village to buy food and inquire about a safe route to Zahedan. In a small shop, we purchased meager fare—some dried-up dates resting at the bottom of a rusted metal bucket, and some grapes of dubious origin. We spent the night in an isolated, unfinished room outside the village. The room was doorless and had no windows, so we endured a second long, cold night.

Early the next morning we searched for directions to Khash, the next city on our way to Zahedan. The second guide knew of a road where we could catch a ride in a van or a pickup truck. He accompanied us to the road and, after consulting with Kheir Mammad, we gave the second guide some money and said goodbye to him when we jumped up onto the back of a pickup bound for Khash.

Once back in Zahedan we stayed in Kheir Mammad's house for the night. It was a miserable house built of mud and its rooms consisted of dugout holes surrounding a courtyard. These windowless hovels were entered through waist-high openings. If one wanted relief from the darkness, one could watch people sitting around a small hole in the center of the courtyard washing dishes and clothes.

Kheir Mammad told us, "I'm going to find a good person who knows everything. He can get you past the border." He returned with a knowledgeable man who was asking for a whole lot of money we did not have. At the same time, he was trying to frighten us with talk of police, prison, and other threats in order to push us to decide and give him a straight answer. We told the man to let us think about it, that we would contact him the next morning through Kheir Mammad and let him know our decision.

After the man left the house, we discussed the matter. The man's asking price for leading us to the border was more than we had left after the expenses we had incurred during our two weeks' absence from Tehran—not to mention that we would also need some money to cover expenses for the remainder of our trip. Our funds were nearly exhausted, although they should not have been, and that was confusing. Kheir Mammad entreated us to leave him alone and deal with the man on our own. He tried to convince us that this guide was the best and only one who could get us across the border. Under these circumstances we could no longer trust Kheir Mammad. The new man had been persuasive in his approach and it had seemed there was an urgency pushing him to go back soon. He had stood in the middle of the room the whole time while explaining the situation and his demands. He seemed like one of those dealers who are ready to do anything to grab some money, even pimping or selling people out to the police. After considerable discussion, we agreed that our only recourse was to leave Zahedan.

Discouraged, I told A. D. and Parviz that I wanted to return to Tehran. They agreed. "OK, we will leave Zahedan and go to Mashhad. There we can decide what to do." Zahedan, a small border city where the police were suspicious of strangers, did not afford us any anonymity.

In the morning, A. D. and I left the guide's house and headed toward the city center to purchase tickets for Mashhad. After we had walked about ten-minutes, a Land Rover pulled up next to us. The driver called out, "Hey, hey, fellows! Do you know where such and such a street is?"

Before we could answer, heavy hands seized us from behind and a rough voice ordered us to get into the vehicle. Two men shoved us in. They slammed the doors and the driver sped off.

Alarmed, we asked, "What's the story? What's the matter?"

One of our captors, a big guy, curtly replied, "You will see soon enough."

After a five-minute drive, the Land Rover turned onto a large secluded street hemmed in by high walls. I glimpsed treetops behind one wall. A garden? We stopped abruptly in front of a doorway and our kidnappers unceremoniously pushed us out of the car, through the door, and down three or four steps into a small hall. A door on our right opened and we were shoved into a room where, surprisingly, Parviz was already sitting. They ordered us to take off our clothes. We did and the men started searching us. Finding nothing of interest, one man demanded, "Where are the cameras? Where are the maps?"

"We have no cameras! We have no maps!"

"We are going to find everything," he warned.

The Land Rover's driver, who was searching A. D., suddenly asked, "What's this?"

I turned toward the driver and saw his hands groping between A. D.'s legs.

A. D. replied, "This is our money." Then he turned to us and explained, "Don't be surprised, guys. I saved this for *Rouz-e Mabada*"—an idiomatic expression meaning "the day we hope won't come" or "a rainy day." That revelation resolved a question

I had been turning over in my mind without finding a solution, namely, how we had spent so much money so quickly. I had been frustrated because I could not imagine that our friend A. D. could be dishonest, but here was irrefutable proof to the contrary. In Iran it was customary to give one person responsibility for family or group expenses. There is an expression for this: *maadar kharj*, "mother of expenses", because in a family it is usually the mother who takes responsibility for daily purchases. Husbands and other male family members give money to the women daily, weekly, or monthly, saying, "Here's the money for the *kharj*."

SAVAK—for it was they who had abducted us—kept us for a week in Zahedan, interrogating us about where we were going and why we were trying to cross the border illegally. They assumed we had committed some crime or some political act to cause our flight from Tehran. Every day we were interrogated for hours. They threatened us with torture, but they did not follow through. We stuck to our story as best we could, but a few pieces of information surfaced. In Tehran I had been learning Russian from an old communist. Learning Russian was a political crime. The Iran-Soviet Cultural Relations Society in Tehran organized cultural activities, including Russian language classes, but people usually did not go to them because SAVAK agents kept watch. I visited my Russian tutor quietly, always privately. Only a few friends knew that I was learning Russian. I had brought my Russian language textbook with me on the trip, but in Zahedan I had mailed the book back to a friend in Shiraz. On the third or fourth day of our incarceration the interrogator asked me, "Why are you learning Russian?" I was stunned at their diligence in uncovering my secret.

"You didn't tell us the truth, you hid this from us, so you will stay here until you tell us everything about yourself."

I told him, "I like Russian literature, Russian writers like Tolstoy and Dostoevsky. I wanted to read them in the original language. I am not a political activist; I don't know anybody—"

Actually, my love of Russian literature was part of the reason but not the full extent of my motivation to study Russian. For me at that time, Russia was the best place in the world, the best place to be. Because of censorship, we knew nothing concrete about Russia; we knew only that the Soviet Union was a workers' paradise. How could we know this? The Shah's anti-communist policies were an extension of the Cold War espoused by Iran's sponsor, the United States. The Shah imposed harsh censorship on every aspect of Iranian life. The regime did not allow anything, good or bad, to be published about the Soviet Union. We Iranians were wholly ignorant about the realities of life inside the Soviet Union. We believed in Socialism and we regarded the Soviet Union as the cradle of Socialism.

Further sessions featuring the same questions about my political activities followed, and I kept repeating that I did not know anything, did not do anything, and finally they realized that we were nobodies—just three stupid youngsters doing stupid things. They looked for maps and cameras, I am sure, because they had received a report from the border station near where we had tried to cross. SAVAK had also arrested Kheir Mammad, our first Zahedan guide, but none of us had committed any political acts in Zahedan. If we had been arrested on the Russian border they would have tortured us and thrown us into prison, but illegal Pakistani border trespasses mainly had to do with drug smuggling, rarely with political issues, until after the 1979 revolution.

After a few days they called for us one afternoon and transferred us to the Zahedan police station in the same Land Rover in which we had arrived. It was late afternoon and the office was already closed. An old man, an office clerk, was there and he signed a sheet of paper from SAVAK to show that he had taken custody of us. We were curious about the contents of the half-page-long report and tried to get a glimpse of it as the clerk perused it. After reading the report, the old man remarked, "I don't know why they sent you over here."

We said to him, "We were leaving Zahedan for Mashhad; we had tickets. We haven't done anything. We don't know why they sent us here. Probably it's a mistake."

The man replied, "I can't do anything. I am going to call the sergeant of *Agahi* (the investigation section of the police); he is the one who can decide." He placed the report on his desk and we stepped closer to read it. Affixed to the top of the document was a red rubber-stamped word: *SECRET.* The report stated that SAVAK had not found evidence that we were guilty of any political crime, and it directed the police to investigate any possible guilt for misdemeanor crimes. This disclosure reassured us, and we relaxed a little.

The clerk asked us to stay in the yard while he called the investigation officer.

An American man had also been arrested recently, and while we waited for the arrival of the interrogator, the four of us sat together in the enclosed yard enjoying the sunset. A. D. spoke a little English, so he asked the American why he had been arrested. The American explained that the police had found him in possession of some hashish while aboard the Quetta-Zahedan train.

Just before dark an officer arrived and events took a surreal turn. It was dusk and in the office, where it was much gloomier, he donned dark glasses to ask us questions. It was obvious that he could not see us well, but apparently he thought it would be more intimidating to hide his gaze with sunglasses, and for the same reason he adopted a very brusque manner. After reading the SAVAK report, he handed each of us a form on which we were to verify our personal identification information. Then he asked each of us some general questions. He summarized all the information we gave him in another report, signed it, and gathered all the papers into a folder.

He released the American—at least we did not see him anymore—but he ordered the guards to hold us while he checked our stories. We were kept separate from the general prison ward, next to it in a room about three meters by two meters that connected to the kitchen. The floor was filthy—greasy and dirty, almost wholly blackened, and bare except for a single army blanket. Sitting down was out of the question and we pleaded with the guard, "Please give us something to clean the room."

I don't know how but the news of our incarceration swept through the prison: "There are three guys from Tehran here! Who are they? What did they do?"

I guess we were a welcome relief from the humdrum of ward existence. In an alcove off the hallway, somewhat larger than our space, lived a celebrity inmate, the convicted murderer of a woman. He had appealed the verdict and had occupied the alcove for three or four years. A physician in civilian life, his small living quarters boasted a sizeable library. Altogether he was a respected figure in the eyes of the ward dwellers.

The other prisoners were so excited and curious to see us that they came to the ward door to the hallway to see if they could convince the turnkey to open the door so they could enter the connecting hallway and have a look at us. One of them, a short man in his thirties, came to our door. He wore a clean, white Baluchi shirt. He was handsome with large, beautiful black eyes framed by black eyebrows, and a mustache that covered his upper lip. "Hello, welcome. What have you done? Why are you here?" he asked us.

We invited him in and we all sat on the blanket. He seemed to exert some kind of authority, especially among the prisoners, who seemed to respect and rely on him. He told us he had murdered someone and was waiting for his execution.

At first we joked: "Yeah, we were in the desert. We tried to flee the country but we lost everything and we were hungry, so we killed a gendarme and ate him." After talking for a bit, we revealed what had actually happened to us.

The man reassured us, "OK, stay here and don't worry about anything. I'm behind you, I'll support you."

He left and returned ten minutes later, accompanied by a youth maybe sixteen or seventeen years old. They carried in three beds with clean white sheets and blankets. The man said, "Unfortunately we don't have any food left, but we'll bring everything to prepare tea and then we'll talk and relax together."

The teenager left and then returned and prepared tea with a Primus. We gave the guards some money for dinners, plus a tip, and they brought us some cooked food. In Iran at that time, if you had money in prison, you could get anything you wanted—drugs, food, whatever. The police, of course, had a hand in the prison drug traffic. After a while our neighboring prisoner, the physician, also invited us to visit, so we went to his side of the hallway and drank tea with him and he told us his story. Finally, at one o'clock in the morning we went to bed.

Before we went to the physician's room, I needed to relieve myself. The restrooms were in the courtyard and I had to go through the ward to get there. When the guard opened the metal door to the ward, I saw in front of me a long, dark corridor crowded with prisoners who were walking, sitting, leaning on the walls, and generally hanging out. Cautiously making my way along the corridor, I spied dark rooms on either side. It was a rotting prison. The plaster on the walls had peeled off nearly everywhere and they were black from smoke and dirt. The prisoners were dressed in rags. The floor of the courtyard was dirt, and a small, half-empty basin of muddy water stood there. The restrooms were execrable. I could not bring myself to touch the toilets and just peed and hurried back. Our greasy room seemed much more palatable by comparison after this excursion through the ward.

The next morning, we were escorted to the judicial court, where the public prosecutor questioned us. He found out nothing. We were held until lunchtime, when the prosecutor issued our release. The whole scenario had played out like an absurdist farce.

After our release we left Zahedan for Mashhad, because there was no way we could cross the border now. We spent one night in Mashhad. The next morning, I asked A. D. to divide the money and give me my share. He refused. He just kept repeating, "I'm not going to do that."

"Why? This is our money that you told us had been spent while you secretly kept it all. Why did you do that? We want to separate," I remonstrated.

He replied, "The situation is different now, and in this situation I have the right to save my own life."

I was angry and saddened; we had been close friends for years, sharing our ideas, ideals, hopes, and dreams for a better life. I could not find it in myself to fight him despite my disappointment.

Parviz told me, "I'm going to stay and get my money back."

Turning to A. D. I said, "OK, at least give me five tomans and I'll leave."

I wanted to go back to Tehran. I knew that a train ticket would cost much more than five tomans, but I thought I would buy the cheapest ticket from Mashhad to the next station and then try to stay on the train, talk to the conductor, explain the situation, and tell him I could get money from my family when I arrived in Tehran.

I went alone to the train station, where I purchased a ticket for the next station for one toman. Later, on the train, when two agents came around to check the tickets, one of them said, "You've passed your stop."

"I'm going to Tehran," I told him.

The senior agent told the other, "Issue a ticket for Tehran."

I said, "I don't have any money, but when we get to Tehran my family will pay."

"Do you have a gold ring, a watch, or any valuables?" he asked.

"I don't have anything like that," I told him. "I have only four tomans and I need to go to Tehran."

Neither agent looked especially impressed. "Come with me," said the senior agent.

He walked me down the aisle, opened the door to a compartment, pushed me in, and locked the door. Again I found myself in what amounted to a prison cell, albeit a moving one. After examining the compartment, I sat next to the window. After a few minutes the senior agent came back, unlocked the door, pushed in another fellow, and locked us both in.

The new arrival was obviously very poor. I myself looked disreputable; I wore a beard, a black cotton hat, some kind of a shirt, a cheap black cotton sweater, a pair of cheap, very thin cotton pants, and no jacket. This fellow wore a torn jacket, every part of it threadbare. His pants matched the jacket, and he had a week's beard. He sat down in front of me, smiling, and looked at me silently.

"Hello," I said.

"Hello," he replied with a Turkish accent.

I asked, "What happened to you?"

He tried to tell me using a mix of Turkish and Farsi. From what I gathered, he did not have a job and wanted to go somewhere to find one. "I can weave rugs," he explained, "but I don't have any money. But I have as much right to travel as any other Iranian. This train is operated by the Iranian government. I am Iranian and I am in Iran, so I have the right to travel on it."

He understood only a little Farsi, but I knew some Turkish words and could understand the gist of his conversation.

I told him, "I'm in the same situation as you. We are together. Don't worry." After a pause I asked him, "Do you have any money at all?"

He drew out of his pocket one *dah-shahi*, worth approximately a penny, and placed it on the small table under the window; twenty dah-shai equaled one toman, and seven to eight tomans equaled one dollar, at the time.

I told him I had four tomans.

Again the door opened. This time a woman was pushed inside. She was wearing a *chador*—the traditional full-length, shroudlike garment for women—that was dirty and worse than threadbare; it had holes in it everywhere. It was unbelievable. It looked as if she had been wearing it for a hundred years, a length of time that might have passed since she had bathed. Her hands and face were filthy. Nonetheless, she spoke and hesitantly shared a little of her story with us.

She was originally from Kerman, a city in the southeastern region of Iran. I recognized her regional accent. Somehow—she didn't explain exactly how or why—she had become a prostitute. She had come to Mashhad, a religious city, to work but she could not find customers because she was so dirty. That is what she told us. She wanted to go to Tehran. Like us, she had boarded the train with no money. I suddenly realized that I could have saved my one-toman fare and boarded the train without spending anything at all.

When the train stopped in Neyshabur, a city in the same province as Mashhad—Khorasan—we were ordered out and turned over to the station police. The train agent instructed the police to "hold them until the train leaves the station."

We—the Turkish man, the woman from Kerman, and me—walked from the station to the police office across a snow-covered thoroughfare in the freezing cold. Once we were there, an officer asked us, "Why did you take the train without having a ticket?"

I told him, "We lost our money and we have to get back to our hometown somehow." The other two did not say anything, because the man could not speak Farsi and the woman was virtually scared speechless.

The officer threatened, "You know, I can throw you all in jail here!"

He made some other vague threats, which I thought were obviously nonsense, so I answered back, "You can't do that! We haven't committed any crimes. You are responsible for returning us safely to our hometown!"

After the train pulled away, the station officer called another policeman and ordered, "Take these two fellows and send them to the city police station in the carriage."

The two of us stood up, but the woman just sat there in her torn chador. I had a bad feeling, so I stopped at the door, turned, and announced, "This lady is also with us."

The station officer made a threatening move toward me from behind his desk and said, "Son of a bitch! This is none of your business!"

There was nothing I could do. and the second policeman told me, "Come on, let's go," and took us outside to a small square in front of the train station, where a horse and carriage waited in the cold. There were no cars, just horse-drawn conveyances, as if it were a nineteenth-century city. The policeman ordered us, "Go in! Go up into the carriage!" and instructed the driver, an old man sitting hunched up in the frigid air, "Take them to the police station!" The policeman himself did not bother to come with us—a sign, I realized, that we had little to fear.

Ensconced in the carriage, we rolled into the city. The driver pulled up across the street from the police station and gestured, "This is the police station you're looking for." We started to cross the street, but the driver shouted, "Hey! Your fare! The money!"

I turned back, bewildered, and told him, "We don't have any; that's why they sent us here. You should get it from the train station police."

He protested, "No, no—you are the passengers!" The poor old guy could not do anything and obviously did not want to ask the police for his fare, so I gave him five rials—half of one toman—from my dwindling cash.

We crossed the street to the police station, not to turn ourselves in but to ask for help. A guard was standing in the sentry box. I told him, "We want to see the chief of police or the officer on call."

He replied, "What for?"

I said, "The train station police sent us here to ask for help to get back to our hometown."

From inside his box he stretched his head out and called for someone to come. An officer, a short, chubby man in his fifties, came out of the station and asked, "What's the matter? What is it?" I told him our story. He was eyeing us as if thinking, "I'm looking at two very naive or very stupid guys." He looked into my eyes for a few seconds, then took us to the office of the *keshik*, the duty officer, and explained why we were there. I remember he had a moon-shaped brass plate hanging around his neck. It said, *Afsar-e Negahban,* the officer on call.

The keshik looked at us, then turned to the policeman and proclaimed, "We can't do anything for them! We can't help them —get them out of here!"

The officer led us out and suggested, "Go to the teahouse, a few doors up on your left; wait there until the bus for Tehran comes. Then ask the driver to take you to your hometown. All the buses and trucks stop there to pick up or drop off passengers."

Naively I believed that he was really helping us, that a bus would actually stop there and take us to Tehran. So we walked to the teahouse, where I asked one of the people who were serving tea whether a bus was coming to take passengers to Tehran. He nodded and answered, "Yes, if you are passengers, stay here until the bus comes."

It was around four o'clock in the afternoon. I had not had breakfast or lunch and I knew the guy with me had not eaten either. I had three and a half tomans left, or thirty-five rials, so I ordered two cups of tea for us and purchased fresh *taftoun*—a loaf of bread—from the bakery next to the teahouse. We shared the bread and drank the tea. The waiter brought a second round of tea for us. In my mind I was counting money. Altogether we had spent five rials, and now I had only three tomans left.

Just before dark, buses and trucks started to arrive, and the passengers came in for tea. I went to each bus and truck to plead our situation to the driver and ask him to take us with him. None were willing to help. I remember one of the bus drivers indignantly asking me, "Why should I take you to Tehran for free?"

"Because I'm poor. I have no money," I answered truthfully.

He looked me up and down. "YOU are poor?" he questioned skeptically.

I did not have proper winter clothes and my attire was cheap and dirty from a month of wear; nonetheless, compared to many others, I was recognized as an educated person. Thus I ought to be a man of some means.

At last one bus driver said he would take us to the next city, Sabzevar. "I'm not going to Tehran, so in the next city you will have to find something else," he said.

I thought to myself, "At least we'll be one *manzel*, one stop, closer."

When we got to Sabzevar, it was after midnight and we were well and truly stranded on cold, dark streets lined with shuttered buildings. I decided to look for a policeman making the rounds. Eventually we found one and I told him our story and obvious plight: no shelter. He needlessly explained, "Right now every place is closed." But he finally relented: "OK, come with me. I can probably find someplace for you."

We walked a few blocks until we reached the door of a teahouse. The policeman knocked and called someone by name.

Inside we heard noises, then somebody poked his head out the door. The policeman said, "Take these two guys in. In the morning they will leave."

The man answered, "But we're full. There's no space for them."

The policeman said, "That's OK, just take them in. It's cold outside; just let them sit somewhere until morning."

So the man stepped aside and opened the door. "OK, come in."

We thanked the policeman and went inside. It was quite dark but I could sense there were a number of people sleeping in the room. The man closed and locked the door, then showed us a low, short bench, less than one meter long and totally wet. "This is the only place we have," he said.

Gradually my eyes adjusted to the gloom and I could see a high platform next to the bench. There was no mattress on it, just a *gelim*, a cheap cotton floor covering used by poor people. Several people covered with *lahafs* (quilts) were sleeping on the gelim. The teahouse worker quickly jumped up onto the platform, got under his own lahaf, and pulled it over his head to trap his body heat. My Turkish traveling companion looked around, then he, too, jumped onto the platform, where he pushed himself between two men who were sleeping there. One of them grumbled, then fell back asleep immediately.

I stood there in the middle of the small teahouse, my natural shyness preventing me from following my Turkish companion's example. Reluctantly I decided to lay down on the wet wooden bench, folding my legs to keep them from dangling. For warmth I had only my *loang*, a piece of fabric that one wraps around oneself when visiting a public bath. Curled up, wet, and cold, sleep eluded me. I stared through the teahouse windows into the freezing night, waiting for sunrise, watching the color change from dark midnight to morning's faint glow. I thought about my traveling companion. Maxim Gorky wrote a powerful short story entitled "My Traveling Companion". I always conjure it when rethinking the journey with my Turkish companion.

At dawn the teahouse worker woke up and began his morning chores. He created quite a din, rattling pots and kettles. I was amazed at his ability to go from sleep to energetic toil with an effortless transition. He opened the door wide and attached the string tied to the doorknob to a nail on the wall. Minutes later a boy delivered a stack of *taftoon* bread and the teahouse worker wrapped them in a sofreh. I had just shifted my position and sat up on the bench when he told me he had to put a pot of water where I was sitting. I realized that the bench was the place for washing his teacups and saucers. When people finished their tea, he would wash the cups in this big pot of water, necessarily splashing the bench. In daylight I could see that the worker was much younger than I had thought the night before, and I perceived a friendly mien as he carried out his tasks.

One by one the other sleepers woke up, some of them getting tea and some going off to work without breakfast. My traveling companion awoke, and I bought us a small breakfast of fresh bread and tea. I asked the teahouse worker, "Where can we get the bus to Tehran?" I explained our situation, including our lack of money.

He advised, "The best thing is to go to the city gate." (There was no gate, actually, but that is what they called the area where the city clerk had an office and collected tolls from buses and trucks leaving the city.) "All the people who don't have money go there and ask the city clerk to help them return to their hometowns. The clerk will ask the drivers to take anyone they can."

Immediately after breakfast we walked down to the city gate. I thought that because we were early we could get a bus or a similar vehicle; but when we arrived I saw a long line of people standing or sitting or leaning against the wall, starting from the doorstep of the ticket office and winding around the building. I went up to the clerk, explained our situation, and asked for help. The clerk said, "OK, just get in the line and wait your turn."

We moved to the back of the line and began to talk to others in the queue. We discovered that some people had been waiting for as long as three days, not leaving the line and sleeping outside in the cold. We waited about an hour, watching as buses and trucks stopped, paid their tolls, and rolled on without letting anyone board. Their excuse always was, "No empty seats."

After a while I realized that those with money ready to bribe the clerk eventually found seats. Many of the buses did have empty seats, but they were saved for people who could pay at the next stop, half a mile down the road. I realized that waiting there any longer would be useless; our remaining few rials would not gain us passage. I thought about my meager possessions: a tarpaulin shoulder bag, a shirt, and pajamas. Maybe I could sell them to raise the bus fare. Leaving my traveling companion to hold our places in the line, I left. I asked some locals for directions to the secondhand market, which proved to be only a short distance away. The clothes dealers were not interested, even though my pajamas were made from cloth superior to any available in the town. The problem was their pattern—not suitable for their local tastes. One buyer asked me, "These pajamas are really yours? Or for a woman?" The price they offered was insufficient for our fares, so I toted my bag back to the queue at around noon. We were not making any progress.

I knew that a friend of my father's lived in this city. He was an army sergeant who had stayed with us in Tehran when he was posted to a military facility there. I did not want to ask him for help, but at this point I had no other choice. I started asking people, "Where is the military base in this city?" I told the Turk, "I will go to borrow some money from this man—you stay here until I come back."

I walked to the base, which was outside the city. At the gate I told the guard, "I'm here to see Sergeant Torshizi."

I waited about ten minutes, and then saw him coming toward me. When he saw my condition—dirty clothes, beard, and black cotton hat—he was shocked. He asked, "What happened to you, Nasser?"

I told him, "It's a long story. I just need money to get out of here and back to Tehran."

He answered, "No way! I'm not letting you go back like this. Stay here—I'll be right back."

When he returned he told me he was taking me home with him. I told him, "Someone is waiting for me. I have a traveling companion."

"After you have lunch with me you can go," he insisted.

We went to his home, where his wife prepared food. I did not see her; she never came into the room. We two ate lunch together. The sergeant was a very conservative, traditional man, but he was also a musician and played a few instruments, including clarinet, his favorite. He was director of the town's military band.

Soon after lunch, I told him that I had to leave. I did not feel good about eating warm food while my Turkish friend stood in line. Sergeant Torshizi gave me forty tomans, just enough to take both of us to Tehran. I took the money, thanked the sergeant, and walked back to the city gate. But when I got there, I could not find my traveling companion. I asked the man who was in line ahead of us, but he did not know anything about him. I stood there waiting for him, but he never returned. I walked to the secondhand market in case he had wandered there looking for me, but no one remembered him. Finally I gave up and asked some people, "What is the best way to get to Tehran?"

One of them replied, "Get a bus to the next city, Shahroud. From there you can get a train that will take you directly to Tehran."

I did exactly that and arrived in Tehran early the next morning. My whole family—mother, sister, brother, and all my other relatives—thought I was in Germany. They had no idea what I had been up to. From the train station to my aunt's house was a ten-minute walk. I did not want to go home in my filthy condition; better to go to my aunt's first. Then maybe she could tell my mother and sort of soften the shock. As I drew closer to my aunt's house, my heart beat faster as my steps slowed. How could I explain my foolishness?

Walking as slowly as possible, I shuffled to my aunt's door and rang the bell. I heard her coming down the stairs. When she opened the door, she pulled back, horrified, and just stared at me. She could not utter my name. She managed only "Na—" before fainting. I stepped into the house, knelt, and held her while yelling for my cousins. Everyone woke up—the cousins, my aunt's husband—and for a few blessed minutes I was ignored as they rushed to my aunt's aid. They carried her to another room and tried to revive her. Finally she opened her eyes and looked at me—I was right next to her—and I felt as guilty as if I had committed a crime. I was the cause of her fainting. One of my cousins brought a glass of water for her while another patted her to comfort her. She gradually regained her color and equilibrium, and her relieved family members turned their attention to making breakfast.

As they made tea I began my story. I told them about my friends and our plan to flee Iran, and about all our subsequent misadventures. They told me that Parviz had actually arrived in Tehran the day before and had already told my mother the essentials of our escapade. I asked my cousins to tell her that I had arrived and to ask her to come to my aunt's house. I did not want to go home, because I was afraid that SAVAK might be after me, a surmise that proved accurate.

Mother came before noon, looking pale and disturbed, staring incredulously at me. At first she did not say a word, then every few minutes she repeated, "Why did you do that? Why did you do that?" without really expecting an answer. She was just surprised and stunned that I had involved myself in such an insane, ill-advised endeavor. I could only say, "Well, I did it anyway, but it's over now." Then I added, "It's better that I stay away from home for a while, until everything is safe."

As it turned out, Parviz had warned my mother that SAVAK was looking for me, because his brother-in-law was working for SAVAK as a driver, a fact I had not known previously. Parviz had found out that the SAVAK office in Zahedan had sent a report to the Tehran headquarters. They were searching for the three of us because they still suspected we might have been involved in something political. Parviz was safe; thanks to his brother-in-law they had not taken him in for interrogation, but he warned Mother that they were still looking for me. I decided to stay at my aunt's house and to look for a job.

Through Parviz I found employment in a print shop. I set type, both in Farsi and in the Latin alphabet. For a year I worked there and maintained a very low profile.

My Turkish friend often intruded on my reveries. What had happened to him? Unlike the prince in Gorky's "My Traveling Companion," who purposely cheats and abandons his friend, I could not shake a feeling of guilt over my inadvertent leave-taking from my companion. The notion that I had not done enough to find him haunted me for years.

6

IN SHIRAZ

After a year at the print shop, I started thinking that I should resume working toward living a more meaningful life. My heart yearned for *theater!* I renewed my friendships in the entertainment business. One of those friends, Mohammed Reza Keykavousi, formerly with Anahita, now worked for a ceramic company as a licensed representative for the province of Fars, with his own sales office in Shiraz. He was also an independent contractor for the creation of frescoes and the reproduction of ancient ceramic patterns copied from historic buildings. Reza was one of the Qajars—the descendants of the Qajar dynasty, which controlled Iran before the Pahlavi dynasty.

Knowing that I had drawing and drafting experience, Reza proposed that I take a position with him in Shiraz. He also held out the possibility of some theater work that he had already started with some young students in the Youth Palace of Shiraz. At that time, the government's cultural policy was aimed at gathering young people into youth clubs to guide them toward the types of programs that fit the government's agenda. The clubs in the cities were called *Kakh-e Javanan,* or Youth Palaces.

I moved to Shiraz, where for the first time in my life I lived by myself. My first task for my friend was to reproduce all the tile patterns from a six-volume history of ancient art in Iran—three volumes of text and three of pictures—written by Professor Arthur Pope. To augment Pope's work, we traveled to different cities, where we took photos of extant ancient tiled buildings—color pictures in order to get the exact combinations used in the original designs. Most of the tiles we used were square, but some required cutting, such as the many-pointed star shapes called *moaragh* in art history, an Arabic word. To create curves, we had to cut the tiles individually. Most of the frescoes we created were commissioned for the homes of the wealthy. I think we were the first such commercial effort since ancient times. Reza had brainstormed this endeavor but lacked the necessary skills to carry it out by himself. He had engaged me to cut the tiles and he later hired a young talented local and I trained him to learn how to work with tools and ceramic. Reza and I worked side by side for nearly two years.

I enjoyed the work but my passion was still reserved for the theater. Luckily Reza shared my enthusiasm. We organized a theater group with young people from among Shiraz's Youth Palaces and I taught an acting class for three months, training them, before we started to prepare a one-act play by Eugene O'Neill, *In the Zone*.

A member of the Tudeh Party named Nasser Khodayar originated the idea of Youth Palaces. After the CIA coup of 1953, most high-ranking cadres of the Tudeh Party, including its head, were imprisoned and forced to denounce their communist activities and join the Shah's regime. Nasser Khodayar was one of them. He took the Soviet concept of cultural clubs for youth and put it at the service of the Shah in the form of a nationwide organization working directly with the office of the prime minister. Each Youth Palace included a literature committee, a sports committee, a theater committee, and so on. All Youth Palace activities were under SAVAK surveillance; agents observed the youth, evaluated their activities, and identified those they considered suspicious. Despite our prior knowledge of this situation, Reza went ahead with our plans because the local theater committee had the only available stage facilities. I worked with the youngsters until the play was ready for the stage; then the entire theater committee, influenced by Reza and me, resigned. We did not want to be affiliated with the Youth Palace in any official or unofficial way. This embarrassed the Youth Palace director, Khajeh Nouri, a wealthy and influential individual in the city. He confronted Reza and me, and when we refused to bow to his will he worked his revenge by making sure that we did not receive a permit to stage our show. We had not realized that he was also the head of the city's Theatrical Commission working under the office of the governor.

Fortunately, when Reza had first set up his ceramic business in Shiraz, he had been introduced to the governor himself by his father, who was the latter's friend, and who had asked for the governor's support of Reza's business. After we received notice that our permit application had been rejected, we visited the governor's office. We explained how awkward it would be for all of us if the show did not open, because we had already invited all of the local authorities and dignitaries to attend the play. Besides, we told him, there was nothing politically questionable in the play; therefore, Khajeh Nouri's objection must be personal. "The only reason this play was rejected was that we quit the Youth Palace," we added.

The Governor called Khajeh Nouri and told him that the mayor, General Minbashian, and many other dignitaries had already been invited to the show, and he requested that the play be reconsidered. This request proved sufficiently intimidating and Khajeh Nouri reversed his decision. The governor attended the opening-night performance, saw that there was no adverse political content, and gave us permission for an extended run.

For the programs, I had written a short text offering my own interpretation of the play. The print shop we engaged sent the program to SAVAK for a permit, because all printers had been given notice by SAVAK obliging them to clear all books, pamphlets, and fliers with them. The printer failed to mention this initially, saying only that our program would be ready a day later due to heavy demands on his shop. I took off my jacket when he told me and asked to set the type myself. He was surprised but willing to let me help in order to expedite the job. After I finished the typesetting, he said, "OK, but now I have to get the permit."

The next day I got a call from the SAVAK office in Shiraz. I went there and was ushered into a room where I waited about fifteen minutes. A SAVAKi entered and I was startled to discover I knew him slightly. He was a popular local singer named Nariman, whom I had met once before, in the company of the son of a wealthy feudal landlord, Joekar.

In the early twentieth century, after Reza Khan, the Shah's father, took power in a coup, a new regulation was instituted that required the issuing of birth certificates for all citizens. If one had a profession or possessed a skill, he would take the name of his profession as his surname. *Joe* means barley and *kar* means grower, so the combination "Joekar" means barley grower. I had met the SAVAKi singer with Joekar's son.

Nariman did not show that he knew me. Very officiously he asked my name, profession, and address, then handed me a copy of my program, in which certain phrases had been underlined, and asked, "What is the meaning of what you wrote?"

I had tried in the program to explain in an allegorical way that the relationships among the characters in the play represented something that has existed since the beginning of humankind's existence. I had tried to express these ideas as simply and clearly as possible, avoiding any intellectual commentary. After thirty minutes, Nariman indicated I could leave and assured me that SAVAK would send the program to the printers. When the program arrived, I saw that the text had been severely censored; incomplete sentences and missing words now rendered it nearly unreadable. At first I was furious and thought of not distributing the programs at all, but I changed my mind. What better way to show the public SAVAK's heavy-handedness?

After the second successful performance, Reza and I went to the governor's office again to see whether he could assist us in future theater projects.

"The first thing you should do," he suggested, "is register your theater group. You are not registered and this is the problem that the authorities here have with you."

We knew whom he meant by "the authorities": SAVAK. The procedure for registering a cultural or artistic group was daunting—complicated and tedious. After gathering the required information, I wrote a cover letter containing a very simple, neutral mission statement to submit with all the pertinent documents to the local labor office, a state branch of the national office in Tehran. Thanks to Iran's corrupt and inept bureaucracy, five months passed, during which I repeatedly visited the state office about our submission's progress. On the last visit, an old man approached me in the courtyard and said, "I'm going to tell you something as a father would tell his son. Don't pursue this file, young man. They won't let you work here in Shiraz. They don't need art; they don't need theater. They didn't even let Ali

Mahzoun work here, so they won't let you either, because you don't even have the advantage of his reputation." Ali Mahzoun was one of the most famous theater actor-directors of the generation previous to mine. He was not a leftist, just someone producing apolitical comedies. Apparently he had tried for years to establish a theater in Shiraz but had finally given up and moved to Tehran, where he worked as an actor in plays and films. After the old man's revelation about Mahzoun, I realized that staying in Shiraz any longer would be a waste of time.

■ ■ ■

There was a lady, an Armenian-Iranian actress named Loreta, the wife of the renowned Iranian stage director Abdol Hossein Noushin, mentioned earlier. Loreta had been in exile in the Soviet Union for many years until she was permitted to return to Tehran. Her husband had been a member of the Tudeh Party. The members of the party's Central Committee, including Noushin, had been arrested and put on trial. They were able to escape from prison and were successfully smuggled into the Soviet Union—except for Noushin, who stayed in hiding in Tehran for about a year and a half. During this time, until he too escaped to the Soviet Union, he was able to maintain communications with his theater and with some of the actors. While he was still in prison, Loreta had reorganized the group in the newly rented Saadi Theater, where they performed until the coup of 1953, when she, too, had to escape the country. Now Loreta had returned to Iran and wanted to do theater again. When I heard the news I was very excited. Because of her background, I thought that working with her would be an invaluable, exhilarating experience.

I traveled to Tehran to meet Loreta. With the help of an actor friend, Taghi Kahnemoui, who himself had been a member of the Saadi Theater, a meeting was arranged at Loreta's house on Manouchehri Street. She received me so kindly, without any formalities, that the tension I had felt as a young actor meeting a revered veteran actress eased almost instantly. I explained about my background and my enthusiasm for theater, and especially my interest in working with her. She asked a few questions about my experience, and invited me to join her theater group. She explained that the play she was currently working on was already cast, but she would definitely include me in the next play. I left and did not see her again until she was on the stage in Alexander Ostrovsky's play *Guilty Without Guilt.*

I was in Shiraz when the play opened and I read all the reviews about it. I was anxious to return to Tehran and see a performance. When I did, my dream of working with the legendary Loreta was crushed. Her acting was so conventional, so old-fashioned, and I could detect no creativity in her direction. The cast, although talented, utilized exaggerated gestures and dated mannerisms. Disappointed and disillusioned, I returned to Shiraz, where I stayed a month, mulling over my situation. I decided to return to Tehran, because all avenues to theater work elsewhere were closed.

7

THE MEHR THEATER GROUP AND THE IRAN THEATER ASSOCIATION

In Tehran I came to the conclusion that if I were to have a theater career it might be better to organize a theater group of my own.

I began to contact friends I had worked with at Anahita Theater to find out if they wanted to come together as a theater group. I did not have a clear idea exactly how a theater group might work. I had no set agenda; I just wanted to do theater and stage socially conscious plays that also entertained.

One friend, Manouchehr, from the Anahita acting class, joined me in some brainstorming, which led to the first step: finding a doable play. There were obstacles to overcome. First, finding women who were socially free and independent enough to work in theater, and uncaring about the negative notions held by Iranians toward female artists, would be difficult. This task would be rendered even harder because we were unknown, just starting out as a group, with no funding for actresses. Accordingly, we decided to find a play with only male characters. I ransacked the Iran-America Society's library, as well as the Abraham Lincoln Library, but I could not find a play that suited all our purposes—having no female parts, with a subject or theme unrelated to Iranian politics, and not requiring complicated and/or multiple sets, which would be impossibly expensive for a young theater group.

Desperate, I sought out Franklin Publishing Company, known in Iran as the Pocket Books Company, which used to publish American literature in cheap pocket book format. I went there thinking they had a library. I knew that Iranian intellectuals, especially leftists, were suspicious of this publishing company. They saw it as a governmental company that published only American literature. As a matter of fact, Franklin Publishing Company was indeed part of the CIA's worldwide program to promote the American way of life during the Cold War. Nevertheless, the director of the company at that time, Najaf Daryabandari, was a knowledgeable, literary man and a former member of the Tudeh Party. Imprisoned for a while after the 1953 coup, he had left the party and started his life as a man of literature. Manouchehr and I visited the publishing house, where I met with Daryabandari about our difficulty finding a play compatible with our unique needs. When asked, he informed us that the company had no library, then added, "I'm sorry I can't help you with a library, but I have a play by Arthur Miller that I purchased on a recent trip to the United States. I can give it to you to read if you like."

The play was *Incident at Vichy*.

I gave it to a friend of mine, Rahim Asgharzadeh, who was a translator and physician. We set up a time and he read the play for me in Farsi in one sitting. I found it intriguing and well written. Although the cast of characters was lengthy, they were all male, and the play utilized a single set. Energized by this discovery, I began contacting friends and friends of friends to recruit a cast.

Needing a venue for rehearsals and performances, I went to the Iran-America Society and told them, "I have this play and I would like to do it in Farsi for an Iranian audience."

The American director of the society, a woman, replied, "We can help you. We'll give you a place for rehearsals, provide the theater for performances, and help you financially as well."

Because the society operated one of the best theaters in Tehran and we had no money, I was elated. We rehearsed the play for three months and staged a two-week run in November 1966. All of the twenty-one cast members were amateurs. Many worked at day jobs and were unable to commit to full-time acting, so when our booking was completed, most of them returned to their various employments. This meant that casting for our next project would start from scratch.

I submitted the next play to the new Theater Division of Iran National Television, INTV. The play we had chosen was an adaptation of a short story by a famous Iranian writer, Sadegh Hedayat, called *The Mohallel*, which translates as "The Problem Solver." There is a Shiite Islamic law that says if a woman has been divorced by triple *talaq*, or "triple divorce", in which the husband formally registers his intent to divorce three times—her ex-husband cannot marry her again unless the ex-wife first marries another man for a short time—usually for a single night. It is a deal made between the men to allow the ex-husband to remarry his ex-wife. The mohallel is the middleman with whom the husband negotiates this scheme. In this story, the mohallel refuses to divorce the woman because she is young and beautiful. The woman has no right, under Islamic law, to apply for divorce, so she is stuck with a man she does not want. Years later, when the two men are old and lonely, they accidentally meet. The play is about the tragic effect of Islamic law on the lives of these two men and the young woman.

We did this play for INTV, which aired it a few times.

Iranian National TV had a fairly good reputation in the beginning. As time went by, INTV added divisions as needed and more importantly, created a policy and strategy suited for a dictatorship bent on appearing benevolent. One of the divisions of INTV was the Theater Division.

Although I was trying to focus on stage plays, I naively thought I could do television plays to support the theater group financially.

■ ■ ■

After two years with this group, which I called Mehr Theater, I realized that if I wanted to continue in theater, I had to do some serious preparatory work. I decided to look for people who would fully understand the situation and the role of theater in our time and be able to develop a social concept of the theater. Those fitting this description were people I knew from Anahita Theater who were no longer working there. I contacted them one by one and explained what I wanted to do. After two or three months I organized a meeting with all of them. The meeting place, arranged through one of the young actors who was a high school student, belonged to the Teachers Association and was rented to us by one of its senior members who was responsible for the site's administration.

The first meeting drew slightly more than twenty people, all male, some of whom had worked with me during the previous two years, along with some newcomers. We had a few follow-up meetings at which we discussed different aspects of our work in terms of the rights and responsibilities of the individual within the group. Some of the new recruits were at first reluctant to join because they were concerned that we might harbor ill will toward Anahita Theater. None of us were bitter toward our former associates, but by the third meeting, five participants had dropped out. The remainder continued in our discussions, which centered on principles and policies and selecting a play for our first presentation.

We decided to open with Miller's play *Incident at Vichy*. It was a powerful drama and the timing was right. The first time I had produced it I had not been satisfied with the results. This time, however, with adequate and mostly professional actors, we hoped for a successful run.

Another issue, brought up by one of my friends, Said Soltanpour, and some others, was finding a name for our group. The majority settled on the Iran Theater Association (ITA).

We were able to use the Iran-America Society for our first play and received very good reviews. We had planned to extend the run at another venue, the Faculty of Fine Arts theater, but two of the actors who still had issues regarding allegiance to Anahita left the company. Ironically, one of them ended up acting in some of the most reactionary movies made under the auspices of the Islamic Republic of Iran.

Our group did not have statutes or specific regulations. We decided that anybody who believed he or she could direct might propose a play and the group would do everything necessary to produce it. Said Soltanpour proposed Ibsen's play *An Enemy of the People*. I had known Said for years and I knew he had tried once before to direct this play, when he was a theater school student in the Faculty of Fine Arts of Tehran University. I posed no objections, especially as no one else stepped forward with a project.

Said began preparing the Ibsen piece for the next season. For this play we knew the censors would be an obstacle. We decided to eliminate all scenes that could conceivably prove problematic. We had done the same with *Vichy*—submitting an abridged script to the censors but performing the original, unabridged script.

Ibsen's play offered greater challenges. First, the very name of the play, *An Enemy of the People*, would raise a red flag for the police. Said changed the name to *Dr. Stockmann* and painstakingly eliminated all sensitive dialogue. Although the play was already published in Farsi, we typed a new version and submitted that script to the censors. It was still a very risky piece given the incredibly harsh censorship, but we were committed to producing a socially conscious play.

Submissions for approval were read by a standing committee, one of many censorship committees and groups established at the time to control cultural and artistic activities at all levels. This committee, composed of five individuals, worked for the Theater Programs Administration. The most important member was a SAVAK agent. Normally he would read the play first and offer his opinions, which were almost always slavishly seconded by the other committeemen, who wanted to avoid even the appearance of opposing the secret police. Even if another member of the committee read the play and had the temerity to disagree with the first rendered decision, votes for approval or denial of a permit were not valid unless they reflected the SAVAK agent's vote. Consequently, a combination of feelings of hopelessness and fear dictated a minimal role for the non-SAVAK committee members.

It was not likely that anyone else on the committee would have been inclined to challenge the SAVAK agent's decisions anyway. The second member was an official from the Ministry of Information, who was charged with ferreting out suspicious political messages in script submissions. The third member was always an Agahi officer, from the information section of the police department, which shared the paranoia of all of the Shah's officialdom.

The fourth member of the committee was the head of the Theater Programs Administration whose appointment was primarily a fig leaf. He was the one who would ultimately sign the official permits, and if anybody had a complaint he would try to justify the decision. The fifth member was chosen from among the senior stage directors of the Theater Programs Administration, and this poor fellow really had nothing to do with the issuing of permits beyond the dirty work of signing the papers. He received a little money as a bonus for his committee service.

The committee's makeup—representing all parts of the Iranian administration—had more to do with the Shah's growing anxiety and fear of losing power than with anything else. He did not altogether trust any agency, even the SAVAK, and instituted separate, competing groups of political police to keep watch over each other. The agencies' chiefs reported directly to him.

Astonishingly, despite a stacked bureaucratic deck, we got our permit. We performed the play cautiously, according to Ibsen's text, with one notable exception. In the original, after Dr. Stockmann fails in his struggle against the corrupt authorities who deceive the masses and turn them against him, he decides to stay in his hometown and educate street kids, whom he calls "curs" or "regular little punks." We did not agree with this ending, on the basis of our interpretation of Iranian society at the time. We were looking for a more revolutionary conclusion without straying too far beyond the existing political limits.

After lengthy discussion within and outside our group, a very close friend, Amir Parviz Pouyan, suggested a viable solution. His idea was that Dr. Stockmann fails because he uses poor strategy in approaching the people. Educating "boys off the street" was an idealistic strategy with no real revolutionary content. In our version, Dr. Stockmann, after thinking for a suspended moment, sitting in the middle of the stage under a spotlight, suddenly stands up and excitedly announces his decision to his family: they will stay in the town and continue his struggle there. Rather than speaking the original play's final words, "The strongest man in the world is the one who stands most alone," our Dr. Stockmann reaches out to the masses for help and understanding.

In those days, words like *people, masses,* or *"the poor"* held sacred meanings for us. With the benefit of historical hindsight, particularly the events of the 1979 revolution, we now know that catch phrases such as "the solid majority" can be twisted by authorities and hypocrites to manipulate people. We Iranians, ordinary people and intellectuals alike, suffered as a result of our naive notions in that revolution.

The reaction of audiences to our play was unforeseen, and not a little intoxicating. The show was interrupted by prolonged enthusiastic applause time and time again. All too soon I discovered that these types of reactions by an audience, possessed and triggered by mere agitation, are not necessarily constructive. Such audiences get as excited by a Bertolt Brecht production as they do by cheap but colorful vaudeville. The play, as we performed it, was a success, but in a country like Iran, an intellectual or cultural achievement of that kind would sooner or later become problematic. SAVAK was eternally watchful and sensitive about any such "excessive" displays.

Meanwhile, outside our group's production, independent theater was limited nationally. Anahita functioned for the most part merely as an acting school, putting on a single play at three-to-four-year intervals, mostly in the provinces. There were provincial theater groups, but these were strictly amateur, usually students performing for small, mostly student audiences.

Because the main theater activities took place in theaters sponsored by the government's Theater Programs Administration under the Ministry of Culture and Art, SAVAK kept close watch on our association, the only major independent theater group attempting to reach large, diverse audiences.

■ ■ ■

Once again I was looking for the next play that, by our group's agreement, I was to direct. The only suitable play that surfaced was a piece written by a friend of ours, Mohsen Yalfani, which we renamed as *The Teachers*. The original script required considerable reworking. The play, except for some beautiful Chekovian scenes, proved monotonous in terms of inner development. It needed clearer motivation for the dramatic action. We almost gave up and even did a desultory search for an alternative, but Said expressed his strong interest by starting rehearsals.

Customarily, before opening a play we would show it to some of our friends to gain their input. All of our friends criticized the play, from different aspects: insufficient character development, insufficient development of the theme, and so on. These were pertinent, well-founded critiques with which I agreed. The teacher characters seemed indifferent toward their situation, especially toward the politics behind the system of education. The play needed some major reworking to become a true statement about the necessity for change.

Mohsen, who at the time was teaching at a high school in Rasht, in northern Iran, had a part in the play and had been coming to Tehran every week for two or three rehearsals; however, he decided to stay in Tehran to work on rewriting the play. After two weeks of hard work we had a play that was substantially rewritten, to unanimous approval. Rather than resubmit the altered version to the censors, who had already approved the original, we simply wrote the committee a letter asking permission to stage the play under a new title. The ruse worked—temporarily.

The Teachers turned out to be a big hit. For the first time in our brief history, large numbers of reservations were made days ahead of the performances, all of which played to packed audiences. The play was especially popular among teachers. Our performances coincided with discussions taking place among actual teachers who were planning to strike for certain demands.

On the eleventh night, the play was abruptly canceled by SAVAK.

Fortunately, while still in rehearsals for *The Teachers*, I had chosen the next play, intending to direct it myself. Written by Said Soltanpour and called *Hassanak-e Vazir*—Hassanak the Vizier—it offered an opportunity for social commentary. The story of Hassanak, a vizier to the powerful ruler Mahmud of Ghazni, who was executed in the eleventh century, is a classic story of Iranian history, but the play was set in modern times. Every afternoon before performing *The Teachers*, we would rehearse *Hassanak-e Vazir* in a building across the street from Tehran University. Formerly a prestigious art gallery named after famous contemporary Iranian painter Mansoor Ghandriz, it was transferred to us by the head of the gallery, Rouin Pakbaz, himself a modern and progressive artist. One afternoon, while we were in the middle of rehearsal, the door opened and one of the actors, Hassan Askari, called for me to come outside. When I came out, Hassan told me, "I was going to the Iran-America Society [where *The Teachers* was being performed] and saw some men put Said into a car and drive away. I went to the Iran-America Society and asked what had happened. They told me that SAVAK agents had come and insisted that the play had no permit. They showed the agents the permit but they said, 'This is a forgery!' then left the office.

The agents waited outside until Said arrived and then arrested him. I thought I should come over and let you know about it so we can figure out what to do."

I went back into the rehearsal room and asked the whole group to sit down while I relayed the bad news. We discussed these events and finally decided that I should go to the theater and make sure we had received an accurate account of SAVAK's intrusion. I was to stand outside the auditorium and turn away playgoers, letting them know that the show had been cancelled. We also decided to inform Mohsen, the playwright, and warn him not to come to the theater. We did not want Mohsen to be arrested in Tehran, because he had only unofficial permission from the principal of the school where he worked to be absent during the performances in Tehran. The members of the group were hesitant about letting me go, because they were afraid I too would get arrested. I reassured them, "If they are going to arrest me, they will do it anyway. It makes no difference—tonight or tomorrow—so it's best to let the audience know what is happening." One of the group's members, Mahshid, said she would come with me so that if I was arrested she could inform the group as well as my family.

The two of us made our way to the Iran-America Society. We talked to Mr. Light, the director, a nice, calm gentleman who talked slowly in a friendly manner. He said, "I sympathize with you. We understand your situation here in Iran."

I put a sign on the ticket table that said, "Due to technical difficulties, tonight's performance has been canceled." By this time, my brother, Mansour, our ticket salesman, had arrived. I asked him to stop selling tickets and to refund the money to those who had already paid for the show. Between seven o'clock and seven-thirty, people began to arrive and asked what had happened. For that specific showing we had set aside fifty tickets for teachers and fifty more for students. As eight o'clock approached, more and more people arrived, and many became upset and agitated over the play's closing. Some students came to me and said, "If you say it's OK, we'll burn the society building." They were against American backing of the Shah and SAVAK and viewed the occasion as ripe for a demonstration.

I begged them, "Please don't start anything, because we don't know what Said is charged with. We only know it's because of the play. If you burn the society building, it might make Said's situation worse."

The people lingered until late that night and I stayed on to talk with them. Very late, as the people were finally leaving, I went to Mohsen's home to discuss what we should do. He thought it best for him to return to Rasht. If the authorities were determined to arrest him, they could arrest him there.

It was a Thursday night when they closed the play, and on Friday morning Mohsen left for Rasht. On Saturday morning, SAVAK appeared at his school and arrested him. They brought him back to Tehran, where they took both him and Said to court. The two were convicted of an "act against national security" and sentenced to two months in prison, the usual term for defying the censors. They could have been given sentences from one day to three years. Probably SAVAK felt some pressure to give Mohsen and Said light sentences because everyone, even outside of Iran, knew what had happened and why.

8

SEAN O'CASEY ABORTED

Unsurprisingly, obtaining permits for future plays became more difficult, and our daily lives were subjected to disruption. Each of us worked second jobs. I, for example, was the editor of a publishing company that produced literary and artistic publications. I did not have a license to run regular monthly serials, but we put out unlicensed publications, following the established Iranian tradition of publishing unlicensed, irregularly appearing journals. These publications were closely watched by SAVAK. Also, all of us moved in a social milieu that included numerous individuals habitually targeted with suspicion by SAVAK.

Given this situation we decided that we should apply for permits for several plays rather than submitting single scripts, hoping that one or two would receive favorable attention. This strategy was adopted due to my experience in sending Sean O'Casey's *The Shadow of a Gunman* to the censors right after *The Teachers* was closed. For that play, we went into rehearsal, costumes were sewn, part of the set was built, and we still did not have a permit. Every time I went to the Theater Programs

Administration I was informed, "Everything is fine. Only a signature is needed, but the person isn't here right now. Come back tomorrow," or some such vague and meaningless excuse. Finally, when we announced the opening, we were told, "Unfortunately, we don't have good news for you. It's a pity but the play has been rejected."

Stubbornly, I approached two censors and tried other avenues of inquiry. I realized that my efforts were going nowhere, but I created a file for the letters I wrote, along with the official replies, because I wanted at least to explore the mechanism of censorship. I recall asking one of the censors, "What does this play have to do with Iran? This is an Irish play and it's about the Irish people. Why don't you issue a permit?" He did not bother to answer. He just looked at me and smiled. I pushed further. "Do you think Iranian audiences would identify with the Irish in the play and see the English in the play as substitutes for the Americans in Iran? Do you think the audience would see that relationship in the play?" He just looked at me and said nothing, offering only meaningless gestures by way of dismissal.

Following that meeting, I wrote a letter to the head of the Superior Council of the Arts, a Mr. Rohani, in the Ministry of Culture and Art. I explained all the problems I had had from the beginning with the Theater Programs Administration. I complained in detail about how the censors had dealt with the case, and I requested a meeting with all parties involved in the permit process. I was determined to use this case to create a file about Iranian censorship applied to the field of theater.

Failing to get results from the Superior Council, I wrote directly to the Minister of Culture and Art. I still have most of this correspondence. In Iran, when you wrote a letter to a government official, you had to use some adjective like "the honorable," "the respectable," and so on. These titles offended me because of my antagonism for the "modern" dictatorship of the Shah, but they were doubly offensive because they were remnants of the old feudal system. Finally, I decided to dispense with adjectives altogether and simply address the position that the official occupied. I had just written one letter without using the customary honorifics when I received a missive from the Superior Council of the Arts stating that, after thoroughly investigating the case, no wrongdoing on the part of the Theater Programs Administration could be perceived, thus there remained no need for a meeting. When I sent this letter to the minister with copies of all the other responses I had received, no further correspondence was forthcoming. As far as the government bureaucracy was concerned, the case was closed.

■ ■ ■

Soon after, I was arrested and detained for a short time. When I was released, I felt I had gone as far as possible working through channels and documenting my lack of progress. I started to prepare multiple plays for submission, hoping that one would pass muster and earn a permit.

Oddly, the actual charge for which I was arrested had nothing to do with the plays and the permit issue. In February of 1971, in the small town of Siahkal in northern Iran, a group of guerrillas attacked the local gendarmerie to secure the release of a comrade who had been arrested. After this attack the entire surrounding area was besieged by government forces determined to wipe out this previously unknown guerrilla group. In an armed clash, approximately a dozen guerrillas were killed and an unknown number were taken prisoner and tortured to death.

This was the beginning of a sustained armed struggle, and the guerrilla force, previously nameless, spread to become the Organization of Iranian People's Fedai Guerrillas (OIPFG), otherwise known as Fadaiyan-e Khalq. In a massive government counter-attack carried out before they were wholly prepared, the group suffered greatly. During the crackdown, a lot of people were arrested and interrogated and gave up the names of the theoreticians and founders of the group. One of these founders was a friend of mine, and after a follow-up investigation, other persons, including me, were arrested for questioning.

They came for me at the publishing company right after I returned from lunch. I was taken first to the central police station in Tehran. The prison cells in the basement were full to the point of overcrowding. Some prisoners, including me, were held in administration offices on the building's first level. In the room where I was held, desks were pushed against the windows to block access to them. That [that night] night I was given a blanket and told to sleep on a desk—a strange, incomprehensible arrangement. A policeman seated on a chair next to the door was on guard. At midnight, another policeman entered and led me to a different room. There a man sat behind a desk with a fan belt cut like a whip laying across it. I was ordered to sit on a chair opposite him. The moment I sat, I could smell vodka. He was drunk and I could see from his features that he was also addicted to opium. He looked straight at me, picked up the fan belt with both hands, and said, "OK, Mr. Rahmaninejad, if you tell the truth and cooperate, you'll soon be back home. If not, I'm here with you until morning." He started asking questions, gradually getting louder, verbally abusing me with outrageous nonsense. "The Shahbanu [the Shah's wife] has spoiled you motherfucking intellectuals! You could have a good life, good job, good money if you lived like Parviz Nikkhah," one of the former leftist-activist intellectuals who had become an apologist for the regime. Later on, I found out that the interrogator was Niktab, one of the most cruel police interrogators, who had inflicted humiliating and painful torture on any number of prisoners. To offer just one disgusting example: he stripped one young woman, Ashraf Dehghani, and pretended he was going to rape her, then urinated into her mouth.

He wrestled with me for about an hour, mostly shouting insults and trying to humiliate and upset me. At one point he taunted, "Who do you think you are? Do you think you know better than Parviz Nikkhah? He's working for the government now. Many intellectuals who are bigger than you are working for the government; but you, you fucking shithead, are too stupid."

He was jumping up and down as he walked back and forth across the room, continually shouting. Eventually he ran down, exhausted. He could not continue, and ended his tirade with the threat that, if I did not cooperate with the police, they would keep me in prison forever. Then he summoned a policeman and said, "Take him back."

I spent a month in detention and was interrogated four times, but they did not beat or torture me. They had arrested me for being a friend of Amir Parviz Pouyan. They knew that I knew him, and I acknowledged that, but I vehemently denied all their false political accusations, steadfastly insisting that I was only an acquaintance of Pouyan's. They were trying to locate him by browbeating and threatening all of his friends.

After I was released, my sole focus was still on doing theater. If it had not been, I could have become one of those guerrillas. Twice I was asked to join them, both times indirectly, for obvious security reasons.

I felt a strong sympathy for the armed struggle that I believed was justified and necessary, but I also believed my contribution to the cause would come through furthering progressive theater.

Once again I sent plays to the Theater Programs Administration, seeking permits. Two of them were Brecht pieces, one a series of sketches and short plays about Nazi Germany entitled *Fear and Misery of the Third Reich*, and the other was *The Visions of Simone Machard*.

This time we approached the censors differently. I was almost certain that the censors would not give us a permit, because my group was being carefully monitored by authorities already suspicious about our work. In addition, Brecht, a communist, had been blacklisted by Iranian authorities. Counting on the censors' ignorance of the arts and their limited abilities to think critically, I asked the translators of the plays, Shareef Lankarani and Abodol Rahman Sadrieh, to apply for the permits themselves. Both fully understood the situation and cooperated willingly. This was an unprecedented ploy, which proved successful. We obtained the permits.

I had just begun scheduling rehearsals for *The Visions of Simone Machard* when, a few days after the first preliminary meeting with the actors, I was arrested again.

Agents knocked on my door at night, entered, and arrested me without explanation. They beat me for three days. This had never happened during previous arrests. I was repeatedly interrogated. No one would tell me why all this was happening and I did not want to risk asking them, given their relentless questions about my relations with political activists and my own involvement in political matters.

I repeatedly insisted, "I have no political activities. I am an actor and a director of theater, and I work at a social research center to make a living."

On the morning of the fourth day, a guard came to the cell and called me out. He escorted me to the torture chamber, where the interrogator waited. He told the guard, "Tie him to the bed,"

This was an iron military bed frame, totally bare, with no mattress. Usually they tied the prisoner's hands to the head of the bed and his ankles to the foot, and then beat the prisoner with an electrical cable. The interrogator left, and after the guard had tied my hands and feet, he too left the room. I was there by myself for about half an hour. I lay there thinking that anything could happen. I wondered about the reason for my arrest. I had a few possibilities in mind, but of course, I could not ask, not only because my own case could become more complicated, but also because more people might be arrested. Gradually my hands numbed and my fingers became heavy because the straps tying my wrists severely restricted my blood flow. The numbness turned to pain that spread through my arms, and I imagined that my hands were twice their normal size and turning blue.

Suddenly the door opened and the interrogator came in and asked, "OK, you are not going to admit your connections? Now I'm going to show you!"

He covered my face and head from the nose up with a piece of paper, and told me, "Don't say anything! Don't make any noise! Just listen!" He then called out, "Guard! Bring him in!"

I was all ears, straining to hear everything. I heard someone slowly shuffle in and stop in the middle of the room. The interrogator said, "Just answer me, yes or no."

I sensed the person move toward me, and the interrogator asked him, "Do you know him?"

I heard a noise, just a noise, like "eh."

The Interrogator demanded, "Yes or no? Do you know him?"

The prisoner quietly said, "Yes."

The interrogator asked, "What is his name? Tell me his name."

I tried to recognize the voice. I had a vague notion, a guess, and then the unknown person identified me: "Mr. Rahmaninejad."

I finally recognized the voice: a man I knew, a very nice fellow. Later, when I saw him in Qasr Prison, he approached me and apologized for naming me. He was very ashamed, so embarrassed that he had submitted to the electric cable. I knew him through his uncle who was a close friend of mine, a physician who had left Iran for the United States. He had wanted me to take care of his nephews, who were much younger than me. The man whose voice I had recognized was the younger nephew, a university student at the time and member of a group of about twenty people composed of students and others who were trying to organize themselves and acquire weapons in preparation to join the armed struggle against the Shah. They had been trapped and arrested.

Before we met in the prison, this young man had visited me to talk about political issues, sometimes bringing fliers distributed by his group. He was passionate about the political situation both in Iran and outside the country. Once I gave him a book about the Chinese revolution, but that was the extent of our political relationship. I did not know any details about his involvement with others in his political group. I did not even know that his older brother, Reza, had been arrested because of him, until a few days later when I met Reza in the prison restroom. That was one of those rare encounters that could happen in the interrogation center.

The Center had a name—an infamous name; it was called Komiteh, or "committee", from its official name *Komiteh-ye Moshtarak-e Zedd-e Kharabkari*, Joint Committee of Anti-Subversive Activities.

The occupants of each cell were taken to the restroom three times a day, whether individually or in groups of two or three people. I was in solitary confinement, so I was taken alone, but as I entered on one occasion, the young man's elder brother was leaving. As he passed me, he whispered, "We don't know each other!" I had never mentioned him. During the interrogation, after the younger brother identified me, I had admitted that yes, I knew him through his uncle. I explained that our meetings had been few, and that he had brought me a flier distributed by a professional organization, something about a student event, not political at all. I noted that I had loaned him a book available at any bookstore, without adding that it was a banned book written by the Russian journalist Konstantin Simonov about the revolution in China. I did not mention his older brother at all.

During a search after my arrest, SAVAK had taken from my house some political writings—books and essays—written by a friend of mine. These writings, plus items seized in previous searches, rendered my case more complex and suspicious, resulting in longer interrogations and harsher tortures. I justified my possession of these political writings by pointing out that, as a publishing editor, I received many unsolicited manuscripts. "I don't know these writers. All kinds of people submit all sorts of things and it is my job to read them and let them know if we can publish their works or not." I remained steadfast and stuck to this story, which I now believe saved me, at least for a time.

After I spent a month at the Komiteh, SAVAK wrapped up my file and transferred me to the Qasr Prison, which held both political and criminal inmates. Qasr—a Farsi word that translates as "palace"—was one of the many residences built during the Qajar dynasty. During the first visit from my family, I told my sister, "Let Said know that I am in this time for a longer stay, and that he should start the rehearsals for *The Visions of Simone Machard* without me."

9

THE PRISON COMMUNE

The prison environment then was totally different from any other time in Iranian history. The majority of prisoners were Marxist Fadaiyan and Muslim Mojahedin—two guerrilla organizations involved in armed struggles in the 1970s that culminated in the 1979 revolution. They viewed prison as a continuation of the struggle against the Shah's regime. Because of their numbers and their political authority in the prison, and because of the general sympathy toward guerrillas at the time, they were able to alter traditional prison conditions.

The Commune, the organization formed inside the prison by the political prisoners from the two groups, immediately became part of the prison experience for new inmates. For the first time in the history of Iranian political prisons, Marxists and Muslims lived together and shared everything with each other—everything except their ideologies. Anyone unaffiliated with either of these two organizations could be accepted as a member of the Commune if they could satisfy two conditions. First, they had to come out clean from interrogation. That is, if they had betrayed someone or given up secrets under torture, they were not accepted into the Commune. Second, they had to accept the legitimacy of the two organizations in leading the Commune. Those who were previously unaffiliated or from another political organization could be accepted as long as they acknowledged the authority of the Commune. As long as they accepted the Commune's discipline, they could retain their own ideas about the correct line of struggle and their own political principles. For example, members did not have to personally subscribe to a strategy of armed struggle as long as they acknowledged that this was the position held by the Commune. If members did not personally know a new prisoner, he would be kept out of the Commune for ten days or more while his past was investigated, after which he would be either accepted or rejected for admission.

Every two months the Commune held elections for positions whose occupants ran the daily life of the Commune. One person was responsible for seeing after the daily well-being of Commune members, another was responsible for the Commune's financial issues, and a third person, the Commune speaker or representative, served as liaison to the prison authorities to discuss problems raised by prisoners that required the cooperation of the prison personnel. Issues ranged from the very simple, such as providing needles and thread or string for sewing or patching clothes, to the politically potent matter of books, which were kept in the prison office and were subjected to the vetting of the censors before distribution. Because of its political aspect, the third position was an especially sensitive one.

The prisoners' physical needs were met by a number of fellow prisoners whose responsibilities included distributing breakfast, lunch, and dinner and twice-daily tea or fruits, at 10:00 a.m. and 3:00 p.m., after two-hour rest periods. When I was in prison, conditions were so crowded that ten prisoners were required to serve as Commune workers. They were known to the prison population as *shahrdar,* or "mayors." Each day their tasks began at 6:00 a.m. and lasted until 9:00 p.m.

The mentality of the Commune reflected a guerrilla ethos. You had to train yourself to live with minimal creature comforts. There were prisoners, for example, from Fadaiyan who were living like *mortaz*—those Indian Buddhist ascetics or yogis who live on one almond a day. I remember one of the prisoners, a very pleasant fellow, whom I liked a lot. We talked incessantly, especially early on, when I was initially accepted as a member of the Commune. My acceptance had been swift, because sympathizers of the Fadaiyan knew me, both for my theater work and for my friendship with Amir Parvis Pouyan. For some time I thought my new companion had been assigned by the Commune to befriend me, but we soon became real friends. He was very idealistic, almost to the point of asceticism. He shaved once every week or two, changed clothes once a week, and ate very little; he was bony, pale, and shrunken. The word *mortaz* described him perfectly. Oddly, after the revolution I saw my old prison mate and failed to recognize him. We talked for two or three minutes in the street and only later did I realize who he was, because of his changed appearance—handsome, clean-shaven face, and clean clothes covering what appeared to be a healthy, well-nourished body.

The prison housed an impressive number of readers. Their topics of choice were primarily political; rarely did one find someone perusing novels and poetry. The few who did prefer fiction and who were observed actually discussing literature were often subject to ridicule or simply not taken seriously. It seemed an unlikely atmosphere in which the arts would flourish, yet during the next eleven months I directed ten short plays.

■ ■ ■

In prison I could sit and read works of literature, but I knew something more was required. I contemplated the different poets, writers, and artists who had struggled against despotism, against dictatorship, in the history of Iran. Among the Fadaiyan imprisoned with me were poets and writers, literary people who had become involved in the armed struggle against the Shah. Amir Parviz Pouyan, for example, was an excellent writer whose style I admired. Additionally, he read extensively, and whenever we discussed a novel or a play he invariably was the one who could really analyze and articulate its literary merit as well as its shortcomings.

Another Fadaiyan, Behrouz Dehghani, who was killed under torture, had been a talented writer and translator who combined politics and art. He introduced Sean O'Casey to Iranian readers through an analysis of his plays, and translated two of them, *The Moon Shines on Cilenamo* and *The Plough and the Stars*. He had also done a vast amount of historical and social research on the folklore of the Azeri people of Iran. Alireza Nabdel, a poet, had been trapped by the police and had tried, unsuccessfully, to kill himself. He was arrested and sent to a police hospital; there he tried to kill himself a second time by tearing his stomach stitches open, but the guards and nurses caught him, and doctors restored the stitches. Again, during a second of the guards' negligence, he threw himself from a third-floor window, but he collided with a pole and only his stitches were torn. Still alive, he tried to tear up his colon, but the guards stopped him. He was subjected to severe torture, succumbed, and finally was executed. I also pondered the fate of another poet, Farrokhi Yazdi, whose lips were sewn shut in prison during the reign of the late Shah's father, and who allegedly was killed by air injection. All of these men refused to abandon their art, even while struggling politically, and I intended to do the same by continuing my theater work in the midst of the politically charged atmosphere in which I found myself.

Two actors were imprisoned with me. I approached them about doing some plays for the other prisoners, but I was rebuffed. One of them, Manouchehr Yazdian, a member of the Commune who had studied theater with the Faculty of Fine Arts at Tehran University, was frightened at the prospect of acting in prison. At first he tried avoiding me altogether, but I cornered him and he finally told me, "Let me be frank with you. Honestly, the comrades in the Commune don't accept these kinds of activities in prison. They will judge us negatively."

The other actor was from Mashhad, in Khorasan province. He had chosen not to join the Commune and was living with the members of another political organization, SAKA, which translates into English as the Revolutionary Organization of Iranian Workers. He expressed no strong feelings against participating in theater pieces, but he explained that he was busy translating David Magarshack's essay *The Stanislavski System*.

Pushing aside this lack of cooperation, I decided that a comic-serious approach might be best to announce my theatrical intentions. There is an old Iranian style of performance used for telling comical stories—a peasant piece and a staple in villages. A storyteller stands before the audience with his hands clasped behind his back. A second person stands behind him, hidden, so that the audience, at first, does not notice him. The person in the back reaches forward beneath the armpits of the storyteller and moves his arms, gesturing as the raconteur speaks, as if his arms belong to the storyteller. The audience gradually realizes that something funny is going on, because the visible hands of the man in back aren't synchronized with the story, and they are a bit short. Initially the audience is a little confused, guessing that somebody is in the back but not completely sure what is going on and intrigued, trying to figure it out. This absurd situation inevitably triggers snickers, then outright laughs.

The Commune usually gathered for an hour on Fridays at 8 p.m., after dinner. At that time we usually shared tea or some fruit, if we had any, and the prisoners sang regional songs—Kurdish, Turkish, Lori, Bandari, and so on. *Bandar,* for example, means "port," so the Bandari songs originated among people who lived along the Persian Gulf. The songs usually depicted the plight of the people in those areas and their struggles against the injustice of despotic rulers.

I found a fellow prisoner to act as my arms. One Friday night he hid behind me as I stood in front of the Commune members and began, "Hello, Comrades. Tonight I'm going to tell—," and interrupted myself with a sneeze. "I'm sorry," I continued as my partner's hands went into my pockets searching for a handkerchief and bringing out different items from different pockets. I proceeded to explain how each item related to our daily lives in the prison. All smoking prisoners, for example, who were members of the Commune made do with limited rations, so I joked about the cigarette rationing. I continued in this manner for a few minutes, trying to cheer up the audience, who gradually relaxed and began to laugh. I shifted my spiel to literature, art, and culture in an attempt to tie these aspects of life to society as a whole, and ultimately to the political struggle. I offered specific examples to illustrate the pervasive influence of literature, theater, and art, and the inspiration they had given to many Iranian political figures. Gradually I adopted a more serious mien and tone of voice and named all of the poets, writers, and artists the prisoners knew only for their heroic political activities and martyrdom. The laughter was replaced by intent concentration, the audience listening with serious faces. My partner slowed his arm movements as my stories grew more earnest. Finally, he just clasped his hands quietly in front of me. Our simple collaboration broke the ice and served to introduce theater, art, and literature as meaningful parts of the prison Commune.

Apparently my partner and I had given an acceptable performance, because I was able to enlist other prisoners to train and rehearse for more plays. A few of them turned out to be quite competent actors; some were very good. After the revolution I had occasion to cast one of them for a play in a professional theater.

Some of our first plays were adaptations of short stories, such as "The Chameleon" by Chekhov. Others were inspired by daily prison routines. One of them focused critically on the management of the Commune. As noted earlier, every two months there was an election to choose responsible officers and a few extra men to act as substitutes as needed. The officers were reluctant, or negligent, to share information and their experiences with the substitutes. The latter would query one another, "Have you heard anything? Is there a meeting?" A fellow prisoner, a Kurdish comrade named Sheikholislami, and I wrote a play called *All Substitutes of the Commune, Unite!*—calling on them to rebel. In the play, the actors played the substitutes, showing up at meetings with banners and protesting their exclusion. After the play, the Commune officers modified their behavior and began including the substitutes in their meetings. We staged everything from Chekhov to *All Substitutes of the Commune, Unite!* with good success and some small influence on the prison population.

One day in early winter of 1972 (1351 of the Iranian calendar), when all the prisoners were eating their lunch in their rooms, a group of SAVAK agents suddenly launched a raid of prison number three, one of the sections for political prisoners at Qasr at the time. Members of the Commune were in rooms eight and nine. I was in room nine. Four SAVAKis abruptly appeared at the door. Most of these agents were interrogators and torturers already well known and familiar to us. I was sitting in the back of the room, where I could see the door and part of the corridor. The unexpected appearance of the agents quickly changed the whole atmosphere. The shahrdar, who were going in and out of the other parts of the prison, had spotted them and were whispering warnings, but they had not yet reached our ears.

One of the SAVAKis announced, "Continue eating your lunch. Don't stop, finish your lunch. We'll want to speak with you after." If this comment was supposed to allay our fears, the effort was completely unsuccessful. The faces of our former tormentors resurrected dark thoughts we had all tried to stifle on sleepless nights. Our apprehensions were made worse by the knowledge that some of our political writings, normally kept secret, had been distributed to interested prisoners. I myself had a short pamphlet in my pocket. At that moment I was wondering how I could quickly dispose of it before we were herded out of the room. Pretending to continue my meal, I scooped a shallow depression in the thick prison bread, took the pamphlet out of my pocket, pushed it into the half-emptied bread, and covered it with the gouged-out portion, hoping that the result would pass as an insignificant leftover. The shahrdar came in to clean up the scraps as we left the room.

The agents ordered all prisoners to go to the courtyard. At the door of the corridor leading to the courtyard, two agents searched us, confiscating any suspicious items, including all written materials. My cautious fear had given me a minor triumph against the SAVAK.

■ ■ ■

Before my one-year term was over I was transferred to another prison, Ghezel Hesar. There, we had more artistic freedom because the staff had less experience dealing with political prisoners than with common criminals. I directed two plays in that prison. For one of them we needed a rifle. With a piece of wood and a piece of one-inch pipe, a Commune worker, Asghar, a member of SAKA, crafted our prop. From a distance of three or four meters you would not have recognized his handiwork as fake. At one point in the play, when an actor playing a partisan entered onto the stage with the rifle, one of the prison guards suddenly turned pale and froze in place before realizing that the rifle was a mere prop. After the play, one of the guards, who usually behaved in a friendly manner toward the prisoners, approached me and admitted, "I was really scared! I just want to see how you could make this rifle!"

Since I wanted him to relax, I handed him the rifle and told him, "See, it's really fake. You can dispose of it now; we no longer need it." I knew they would not let us keep it anyway.

10

RELEASE AND
REIMPRISONMENT

In the summer of 1973 I was released after a long year in prison. I wanted to know what had really happened to create the mismanagement and confusion that had occurred in the theater group while I had been confined. Through my sister, who had come to visit me during my incarceration, I already knew something of what had occurred during rehearsals of *The Vision of Simone Machard*. A month after rehearsals had begun, Said was arrested by SAVAK because of the publication of his pamphlet *A Kind of Art, A Kind of Thought*, about the state of the theater in Iran. The pamphlet was published without Said going through the censorship procedure to get a permit.

After Said's arrest, rehearsals were directed by Mohsen Yalfani according to his own interpretation of the play. He thought that while SAVAK would most likely hold Said in prison, the show must go on. Said was released from prison about a month later and came back to continue the rehearsals. He did not like what Mohsen had done with the play, and they had had some heated discussions and a few clashes. After my release, I met with my two friends, Said and Mohsen, who had developed different notions about how the play should be interpreted and how actors should be directed. I needed to understand their differences first-hand. Afterward, I called for a general meeting of the entire cast. The meeting quickly revealed that almost all of the actors were dissatisfied with Said. They felt unappreciated, especially after the play had finished its run and he had curtly dismissed them, as if they were not really part of the group, just hired actors. They also accused him of behaving unprofessionally in rehearsals.

Most of their criticisms did not really surprise me. I tried to comfort the actors and explained that their complaints were well-founded, that the group's problems were not due to our guiding principles but, rather, emanated from Said's wrongheadedness. My words were designed to soothe the company's members, but we lost some of our actors anyway, including several who were young and quite talented, the kind of people a theater group hopes to recruit and retain.

Nevertheless, the play must indeed go on. Our next play was *The Petty Bourgeois*. This was a Farsi translation of Maxim Gorky's play *The Philistines*, also known under various other names such as *Scenes in the House of Bessemenov* and *The Smug Citizen*. We chose to use the title employed in the published Farsi version. Because of continuing legal and financial difficulties, we could stage only one play each year; as a result, we felt that play must highlight the most important social and political issues of the time, or else we would waste a whole year's invaluable time and effort.

Gorky's play, according to our interpretation, offered an excellent opportunity to comment on current Iranian issues. Our society was in a phase of development in which capitalism and capitalists were rising as the dominant socioeconomic force. The capitalists were gaining more and more influence, assuming an increasingly effectual role in shaping Iranian society. Simultaneously, the working class was not well organized and not yet able to stand on its own feet, even though it was undeniably emerging as a potent rival sociopolitical force.

Somewhere in the middle were the intellectuals, who were critical of their parents' traditionalism and posed as antiestablishment. It was not always clear how this group would react in difficult situations; nonetheless, in Iran at the time, intellectuals comprised the largest part of those who were actively struggling against the oppression of the Shah's regime. Progressive political organizations, Marxist and non-Marxist alike, were composed primarily of activists from petit bourgeois families. These intellectuals—educated activists—comprised an important force in society.

As a theater group, we often displayed dismayingly characteristic weaknesses. I felt that our play provided the best text for showing certain aspects of ourselves to our audiences, who were mostly fellow petit bourgeois intellectuals. Part of the process involved self-criticism. At the same time, we wanted to show historical and social aspects of our mutual antagonists, as well as the class character of the solid core of the revolutionary force that we thought would ultimately arise out of the working classes.

Gorky's play is about a traditional, fanatically authoritarian father, and a mother who commands absolutely no significant power. She has no influence in family affairs involving the couple's son and daughter. The son is constantly apologizing for his participation in the student struggles and demonstrations. The daughter, crushed under the heavy authority of the father, is completely pessimistic, always talking about the dark side of life, about failure and disaster. She sees no light, no horizon—only, at best, a severely restricted future. The siblings' friends, students and nonstudents, gather in the house and talk and talk. By contrast, their father's stepson, their half-brother, works as a train conductor. Work has taught him to view society differently; unlike his privileged siblings, he understands the place he occupies in society and knows his enemy. All of these characters were familiar to us; they portrayed not only prerevolutionary Russian culture, but also our own society.

For the first few weeks of our preparations, we read and analyzed the play. Everyone in the group participated in the discussions. At one point I felt a little discouraged. It seemed the actors held the notion that we, the cast members, were somehow chosen, exceptional intellectuals who were going to correct the problems of our audiences without recognizing our own issues. I did not want our company's attitude toward the audience to be aloof and preaching, "Look at your problem; you need to correct yourselves!" I did not see us as fundamentally separate from and immune to society's ills; my position was, "Let's learn from the play, and let's learn about ourselves too." I remember using the Farsi expression, "We are not *tafteh-e joda bafteh*," that is, we are not made from a different and better cloth, woven separately from the rest.

We opened the play in northern Iran, in the city of Rasht, where we had a history of drawing enthusiastic audiences. Abedin Zanganeh, the head of the branch of the Ministry of Culture and Art in Guilan province was a sincere supporter. It was dangerous for him to back a theater group such as ours, which had been officially labeled as leftist; nonetheless, he sought and obtained a permit for the play from the local SAVAK office. With his patronage, we were allowed to stage our play for a five-night run in the new theater built by the Ministry of Culture and Art, rent-free. But SAVAK remembered his actions, and Abedin was detained when we were arrested the next year.

When we returned from Rasht, I decided to shorten the play from four to three hours. Also, Said and two other actors had left the play, so we needed to rearrange the cast. In addition, we had to overcome a major problem: we had no place in Tehran to stage the play. For a long time I had dreamed of having a theater of my own in a part of town that could attract working-class audiences. I thought we could use our abbreviated play to move beyond the mostly intellectual audiences that had been our mainstay in the past.

Lalehzar, the home of Iranian commercial theater, was a possibility, albeit a risky one. At that time, most of its theaters presented variety shows with Turkish and Arab belly dancers, accompanied by cheap popular music, magicians, and broad comedy. These theaters opened in the morning at around ten o'clock and, like movie theaters, would push out the audience every two hours to make way for the next show. If the management saw that there was a long line outside, they would shorten the normal two-hour performance, cutting short the play, not the acts of the dancers, singers, and magicians. Lalehzar audiences were never exposed to lengthy dramas about social problems. Years later, after the revolution of 1979, the new Islamic regime insisted that all singing and dancing be removed from the theaters, which were then forced to rely on plays and, in a few places, magicians.

Lalehzar audiences were composed largely of people from the provinces, poorly educated small-business people, and, especially on Thursday nights and Friday mornings, mostly soldiers, along with a fair scattering of lower office clerks and service workers. After considerable hesitation I decided to rent one of the Lalehzar theaters, the Dehghan, which was one of two theaters belonging to a Mr. Vala, a longtime theater entrepreneur. He also played a very important role in Lalehzar by booking the attractions for a number of commercial shows.

We rented the theater for the fall season, which gave us the spring and summer months for preparations. I organized some meetings of our group and told them frankly, "If we want to survive as a theater group, every one of us needs to get involved, financially and in every other way."

We decided to establish a common fund—a *sandough*, or coffer. Everybody contributed what they could. We rented a four-story building for our company, in Vaziri Alley, off Pahlavi Avenue; the first story was set aside for acting classes and our office, the second was reserved for rehearsals, and the third was rented as living quarters to one of our members who had given up his own apartment in order to rent from the group so that his rent money would go into the group's funds. The fourth floor was our workshop for building sets and our storage space. One member of the group who was also a student of puppet theater used the space to make puppets, costumes, and sets for the group he was working with.

During rehearsals, one of the actors, who I knew had sympathies with the Tudeh Party, brought up the question of whether we were really doing the right thing by performing this play. Most of us had no problem with it, especially after our experience in Rasht, where the play had been warmly received. The actor did not articulate his objections substantively; perhaps he was hesitant because he knew the rest of us wanted to do the play. We invited some of our friends who in the past had shared our political views (although some had since developed alternative views) to watch a rehearsal and offer their opinions. After seeing the play, these friends discussed Iranian politics and the changing condition of all the social classes, and they identified which classes they thought were most revolutionary and who was currently supporting progressive politics and revolution most fervently. They talked about our task as intellectuals among these progressive forces, and they asked us if we understood that it might be perceived that we were attacking some of these progressives by staging this play. As soon as I heard their doubts, I realized where they were heading. Finally, they stated their views more bluntly: "The people you are attacking in the play as petit bourgeois, like the student who is angry and the other characters in the play, are exactly the same young people who are right now in prison, struggling against the dictatorship. These young people's families are similar to those you are attacking in this play."

Our answer was equally forthright: "We are actually targeting a very important issue. In this play we are defending working class people, and to us the working class is the only thoroughly revolutionary class, although in Iran they are not yet fully aware or active, which is understandable because they are not allowed to organize themselves. We don't want to defend the behavior of those petty bourgeois activists, who are inconsistent and wavering in the struggle. And even though the petty bourgeois activists are in the forefront now, our concerns stretch beyond the immediate situation. There is a permanent struggle against petty bourgeois weaknesses within the movement. We are attacking the weaknesses, not the people themselves, because we know many of them are committed to the struggle."

Our old friends departed with unhappy faces, even though I thought we had made it clear that we were attacking class weaknesses, not individual people. Some of those who left were famous among the intelligentsia. We knew they were affiliated with the Tudeh Party and promoted the Tudeh Party's line. After the revolution, when the Tudeh Party in exile came back to Iran and everyone's politics were out in the open, these friends of ours went back to their own party and were no longer friendly with us; their political position was distinctly different then and they extended their contempt to the social milieu. They considered us counterrevolutionaries and lumped us together with all other people and organizations who were against the Islamists.

■ ■ ■

In the summer of that same year, Said was arrested just as he was preparing to leave for Europe. One month before our play was to open, Said's brother, Masoud, who had a part in the play, was also arrested. He was detained for about ten days and then released. We were quite worried that our entire company was under suspicion. At the first rehearsal after Masoud was released, we anxiously questioned him: Was his arrest related to our theater activities? Masoud assured us that the arrest was related to his brother and had nothing to do with the theater group.

Ten days later, at eleven o'clock at night, after rehearsal, when most of the actors had gone, my sister and I, along with my close friend Mohsen Yalfani and one of the actors, Yadolah Vafadari, left our building by way of the alley. When the four of us turned onto Pahlavi Street, I realized that an unusual number of cars were parked there. We walked north through the Shah intersection to catch a taxi for home, as usual. Soon after we passed the Mahtab Movie Theater, I heard a car's engine start, and then a white Paykan passed and stopped about fifty meters ahead of us. All four of its doors flung open and four people emerged, one of them carrying an Uzi. We stopped, not knowing how to react. Two men approached us from our rear, pushed us forward, and said, "Don't make any wrong moves! Just go ahead and get in that minibus!"

They herded us forward about twenty-five meters to a waiting prison van. As they shoved us inside, I saw that we were joining some of the other actors, who had left the building earlier. We exchanged wry smiles. I moved toward the back of the minibus to sit with them, but the commander, one of two men behind us, ordered, "You sit here, in front." Another agent sat next to me in the seat just behind the driver.

The commander demanded, "Give me the keys to the building."

He confiscated my keys and briefcase and left. Cars in front and back of us escorted the minibus to the interrogation center, the notorious Komiteh.

When we arrived, it seemed that they were expecting us, because we were greeted by the infamous interrogator Rasouli. He was well known among political prisoners because he considered himself an intellectual's intellectual and smarter than the rest. He would boast, "I know better than any of you fucking intellectuals! You don't know your own history! Your own literature! You don't know that we were the nation that for the first time in history had women warriors!"

As we stood there in the office, Rasouli called to me, "So, you are Nasser Rahmaninejad."

"Yes."

He turned to Mohsen and said, "You are Mohsen Yalfani."

"Yes."

He turned to the warden and said, "Put them in the cells, one by one."

The warden said, "The furnace hasn't been lit. The ward isn't warm."

"OK, tomorrow we'll heat it. Give each of them one blanket."

One of the actors, Hassan Askari, said, "Mr. Rahmaninejad has heart problems. He can't stand the cold."

Rasouli shouted, "Fuck you and Mr. Rahmaninejad! Give him two blankets!"

They took us to the cells, and I found that we were the only ones in that ward.

I remained sleepless most of the night, pondering why we had been arrested. Many of my friends were "political," but under the Shah's regime that covered a multitude of possibilities, many deemed guilty because of the possession of the "wrong" book or pamphlet.

I personally knew all of the actors and actresses who were working with me on the play and they were not political activists; most of them were apolitical. Many were educated, and all were devoted to theater that produced high-quality plays dealing with meaningful subjects. None of us supported the Shah's regime because of the obvious injustices it perpetrated, but we had not schemed to overthrow the government.

All these ruminations, plus being exhausted physically, worked against sleep and the cold penetrating my blankets did not help either. I was awake at six o'clock when the guards began opening the cells and distributing breakfast, which consisted of a piece of bread and butter. I sat up and waited for the guard to bring tea or escort me to the restroom. Finally, the cell door opened again and a different guard appeared and led me out to the courtyard.

The building we were in was called the Komiteh, but it was not the same building in which I had been detained and interrogated in the summer of 1972. That Komiteh had been a women's prison that had been turned into an interrogation center for political activists. The present Komiteh had previously been the Police Provisional Prison; it had been turned into the Komiteh because they needed space for more detainees. It was a three-story building with offices, a torture chamber, a big bath with solitary showers, and six large wards built in a circle around the central courtyard, or *falakeh;* we were on the ground floor.

As I stood there I was joined almost immediately by two of my friends, Ahmad and Javad, and by an interrogator with three or four guards. The guards each were holding a black electrical cable. The interrogator, who I later learned was called Manouchehri—a fake name, of course—shouted at us, "Lie down!" and ordered the guards to remove our socks. They grabbed our feet, took off our socks, and, holding our feet between their legs right there in the courtyard, they started to beat the soles of our feet with the cables. They asked no questions and offered no explanations; they just beat us.

We protested, shouting, "Why are you beating us? What have we done? We didn't do anything! We did nothing!"

The interrogator stood over us screaming insults. At one point he asked Ahmad, "Are you the son of Hassan H.?"

"Yes, yes I am."

"From that father, how could a son turn out like you?" He then turned to the guard and ordered, "Beat this one harder!"

As the guard resumed beating Ahmad, the interrogator yelled, "Do you know where you are?" And he ordered the guard, "Beat him harder!"

But Ahmad could not answer coherently; he could only scream because of the pain.

They beat us with the cables for about half an hour.

Finally a few other interrogators appeared and the guards stopped beating us. The interrogators talked among themselves and there was much coming and going between their administrative office and the courtyard. Eventually the guards escorted us up to the second floor, where they took me into one of the offices. After a while a big man named Azodi, the head interrogator and supervisor of the others, came in with another man whom I later found was Shaheen, my formal interrogator. Azodi looked at me and said, "Mr. Rahmaninejad, you have not only destroyed your life, you have destroyed your family's life as well, your sister's life, and all those people who were working with you. You are going to tell us everything. If you tell the truth, we'll spare your life and the lives of the others. Now it is up to you."

He exited the room and Shaheen who had been standing like a soldier, went to a desk where I was sitting next to it, and sat behind it. He took a stack of paper out from a drawer, wrote something on the first page and handed it to me, with these words: "Mr. Rahmaninejad, your identity is certain to us. Are you going to answer all the questions truthfully?"

It was written in the kind of formal Farsi used in legal documents. Usually, with this type of document the first question is insignificant, merely a means of encouraging the captive to be forthcoming—a seemingly civilized legal procedure. In reality, the document is a testing maneuver, a feeling-out process to gauge how resistant the detainee is.

The document's second question was, "Explain in detail all political activities you have been involved in, and all those in which you are currently involved."

I replied, "I have not been and am not involved in any political activities." He asked me again to sign it, and reached out to grab the papers.

The veneer of legality ended abruptly as the interrogator angrily shouted, "Let's go, motherfucker! Hosseiniiiii!"

I recognized that name all too well. Hosseini was an infamous torturer.

I was blindfolded and led to the torture chamber, where the interrogator pushed me inside and tied me to a famous huge wooden chair that the prisoners had named "Apollo." Occupants of the chair could only feel it, not see it, because they were invariably blindfolded, and the torture chamber was dimly lit by one feeble bulb. The torturers would stretch out the prisoner's legs on the capacious chair, loosely tie his ankles, and beat him with an electrical cable.

While Hosseini was so occupied, Shaheen, the interrogator, questioned me about my political activities. After a number of blows, he ordered Hosseini to stop because I was insistently yelling, "I am not involved in any political things! I haven't done anything! I'm an artist and I'm only doing theater! We have permits for our play!"

They did not take me back to my cell for four days but held me in an entranceway with a guard. My hands were cuffed under one raised knee while I stood on my other leg. When, inevitably, I fell, the guard would kick me with his military boot and yell, "Get up, motherfucker!" This proved to be a very painful and effective means of sleep deprivation. Days were reserved for questioning and a variety of imaginative tortures. I was forced to run in place on a concrete surface, which was agonizing to the soles of my feet, already swollen from daily applications of the cable.

During the late afternoon of the second day, they took me to the third floor, where I was put into a room with two of the actresses from our group and two interrogators, one of them the much-feared Rasouli. I tried leaning against a wall to relieve my swollen feet. A young interrogator addressed me, "Listen to me, Mr. Rahmaninejad! I'm going to ask your friends some questions. You listen to them, and then I'm going to ask you if what they say is true."

He then asked Azimeh, "Where did you see the caricature of the Shah for the first time?"

Azimeh reluctantly replied in a soft voice, "Mr. Rahmaninejad had the caricature."

This caricature was not something I had drawn. An actress had brought it to me and said that the artist, whom I did not know, wanted me to have it. The large poster caricatured the Shah wearing a paper crown emblazoned with the Shell Oil Company's logo. His face looked evil and disgusting, and he wore a military tunic on which were pinned medals in the shape of a gallows.

The interrogator turned to me and asked, "So, is this true or not?"

I said, "I think she is mistaken. I've never seen such a thing."

The interrogator jumped up from behind his table, slapped me hard, and shouted, "You motherfucker! Denying everything! She's saying right in front of you that you had the poster!" He pointed to the other actress and said, "Mahboubeh also says you had the poster!"

Rasouli moved toward the young interrogator and said, "Don't beat them in front of each other. They have a sentimental relationship." What he meant was a romantic relationship, a very civilized way to describe such a thing considering the surroundings.

The young interrogator continued: "You destroyed the life of Mahboubeh! The sister of Manoucher N.! How could you do such a thing?" Mahboubeh's brother was a popular radio actor in Iran.

Sensing that the young interrogator's attempts to shame me were not working, Rasouli motioned for a guard to return me to my alcove on the next floor down.

During the second week of torture, my left foot sustained three broken toes and bled without stopping. The director of the Komiteh, General Zandipour, visited my cell. He asked me how I felt and said, "I want to help you. This way, you are going to kill yourself. If you tell the truth, I will send you to the hospital. They will take care of you and then you can go home. You should realize that we know everything. In your theater building the agents found porn magazines and panties. If you don't tell the truth, we'll publicize these discoveries in the media and destroy your reputation. The only way you can save yourself and your friends is to come down to the TV station and tell the truth—that you are not against the Shah, that the country is progressing under the Shah's leadership. That the Shah wants to develop the country, while the Western powers want to keep us undeveloped and dependent."

I told him, "You know better than anybody else that the members of our theater group can be proud of our moral and ethical principles. You know that we don't do such things. My sister is working in the theater group and all the other women are like my sisters. Our relationships are strictly professional. You know this and you know that our theater group doesn't engage in any political activities, so I don't know why we are here."

In Farsi we have the expression, "He looked at me as a wise man would into the face of insanity." The general's gaze epitomized this expression as he calmly replied, "I don't want to argue with you. I'm just advising you. Just think about it."

The general opened the cell door and left. The guards followed him out and closed the door. Blessedly, I was alone.

Just before noon the next day, the cell door opened again and a guard called me to come out. It was a slow process, because since the fourth day I could no longer walk normally and employed a scooting motion to get around, using my hands and heels to avoid having my soles make contact with the floor. The tops of my feet were swollen and infected from Azodi repeatedly crushing them near the toes with the heels of his shoes, every day. He would push the same spots while looking into my eyes, waiting for me to beg him to stop.

The guard monitored my crawling down to the courtyard and into a room they called the clinic, which was really just a small space containing basic first aid items—ointment, a few bandages, and some painkillers. Across from this room was the office of General Zandipour, who was waiting for me. I was led in and said hello. The general offered me a chair next to his desk and told the guard, "Bring us some tea."

In a fatherly tone the general said to me, "As I promised you, I'm going to send you to the hospital."

I replied, "Thank you very much but I don't need tea." That was the mentality we had then: don't take anything from them, the enemy.

"No, you need it," he said. "You're weak." Then he repeated, "As I promised, I'm going to send you to the hospital. There you'll have time to think about all of this. And when you come back, I hope everything will be OK."

The guard brought in big glasses of tea and the general pushed the sugar bowl across the table toward me and said, "Put in a lot of sugar cubes—make it sweet. It will be good for you because you've lost a lot of blood." I tried to ignore his offer but he kept insisting, so I finally put some sugar cubes in my tea, stirred it, and gradually drank it, but not without feeling guilty. After I finished it, he called the guard and sent me back to my cell.

Later, in March 1975, I found out that the Marxist faction of the Mojahedin had assassinated General Zandipour.

■ ■ ■

When I returned to my cell it was meal time. The guards distributed lunch, and sometime around two o'clock a guard opened my cell and called me out. He took me down to the prison office and turned me over to two other guards, who escorted me to a prison minibus and drove me to the police hospital on Bahar Avenue. This was the hospital where Alireza Nabdel, one of the Fadaiyan, jumped from a third-floor window, and it was there, at the end of a corridor where partitions had been erected to create two makeshift rooms for the prisoners, that I was left. The room in which I was placed held three other prisoners, two of them from my theater group, and a third, Mohsen Makhmalbaf, who later became one of the most famous movie directors of the Islamic regime. When I made his acquaintance he was not yet seventeen, a boy from a very poor area of the city spread along an old wagon road—a pilgrimage route—leading south from Tehran to the religious city of Rey. The neighborhoods on both sides of that road were nearly destitute; the inhabitants were toilers, mostly uneducated but very religious. The children from these neighborhoods were typically rough; many grew up to be good people, but some turned out bad. The majority of the members of Hezbollah (literally "the party of God," like the organization with the same name in Lebanon, but here meaning Khomeini's followers) originated in such areas. They also served as recruiting grounds for fascists, police agents, and the like. In Tehran, people refer to the area surrounding this route as *Pa-Khat*, meaning "at the foot of the railroad tracks" or "below the tracks." *Pa* usually means "foot," but in this case it means "below" or "at the foot of." Makhmalbaf grew up in Pa-Khat, a term that, for Tehrani people, connotes "rough, shrewd, hooligans."

When they put me in bed the SAVAK agents guarding the prisoners placed a partition between my bed and the others so that I was segregated and unable to see the other detainees. A nurse came in and removed my pants in order to dress my wounds. She hung my pants over the partition, and when my friend Ahmad saw them, he realized that I was occupying the next bed. One of the agents walked in, watched us, walked out, then came back in again. Four agents were always there and their presence was felt even when they were sitting in the corridor.

After a while I heard Ahmad calling out, "Is it you, Nasser?"

I was shocked. I had not expected anyone I knew to be there, and certainly not Ahmad. Later I discovered that Akbar also shared our room. After two weeks of isolation from my comrades and fearing the worst, all I could think about was how to communicate without alerting the guards.

It was Thursday afternoon and nothing could be done for me other than dressing my wounds. The next day, Friday, was the beginning of the Iranian weekend. Not until early Saturday morning did a nurse appear and tell me, "Get ready, we're going to take you to the operating room now."

Then a doctor entered the room and examined my feet. He reassured me, "Don't worry, we're going to take care of you." They took me to the operating room, where the doctor told me, "We're going to give you a general anesthetic."

I told him, "I can't have a general anesthetic," and explained I had a heart condition that had caused seizures and fainting spells when I had received a general anesthetic in the past.

He said, "OK., I will consult a heart specialist." He left the room, then returned after a short while and announced, "Dr. Heyat is coming now. You can tell him what you've experienced."

Dr. Heyat was a famous heart specialist in Tehran and I was fortunate that he was working in the police hospital that day. I explained to him the problems I had experienced with anesthetics and he asked me what kind of heart condition I had. I told him that the wall between the chambers had a hole in it—a birth defect.

Dr. Heyat instructed the surgeon, Dr. Sedghi, who was also a police officer, "Don't give him a general anesthetic; instead we will use an ampoule of liquid nitrogen to freeze the area long enough to do the operation."

It was a dreadful experience. I could feel the knife cutting the infected flesh, and I shouted and cried. At one point, Dr. Sedghi paused and whispered in my ear, "I'm not a torturer; I'm trying to heal you. Please try to resist the pain as quietly as possible; it is too unnerving to work like this."

So I bit my lip and tried not to make any more noise. Both my feet required attention, the right foot especially. I do not know how long the surgery took—certainly more than an hour. Back in my room I was given a painkiller and other medications. Each day the dressings were changed, and at regular intervals some kind of wet dressing was applied to my corrupted flesh so that when the dressings were removed the wound would not be damaged. Before they changed the dressing in the morning, I was given a shot of codeine or morphine or a barbiturate or something. When the nurse asked me if I was feeling the drug, I signaled that the injection was taking effect and she changed the dressings. But even with the painkiller the procedure was excruciating.

At the prison, before the guards took me to the hospital, the interrogator had given me some paper and a pen and told me, "In the hospital you'll have time to write about your political activities from birth up to this date." There was a term for that type of document—"details writing," or something similar. They wanted everything: where you were born, what schools you went to, who your friends were, and so on. Before being transferred to the hospital, I had written a few pages, which Azodi tore up. "These are bullshit!" he shouted. "Don't write a story for us! Write down what you have done politically!"

In the hospital I did not write anything at all, not even my usual evasions. I knew that simply writing denials of the interrogators' accusations and insulting the interrogators on paper like a hero in bad resistance literature might demoralize my friends in the adjoining beds; not knowing what I was writing, they might have thought that I had broken under torture and was cooperating with the interrogators. I did not want to risk their possible mistrust, so I refused to write at all. Few of our number cooperated, even after enduring prolonged torture. The very appearance of possible collaboration with our tormenters could well undermine the resistance of others'.

While I was recovering, the hospital staff moved my bed near the room's sole window and added a fifth bed. Then they brought in another friend, Mohsen Yalfani, for surgery. His feet were also infected and in very bad shape. Most of our time in that room we talked, telling jokes and stories, avoiding serious conversation to thwart the ubiquitous SAVAK agents, who continually warned us, "Don't talk about political stuff."

After Mohsen's operation, he was returned to the bed next to mine. We had been warned by friends that after surgery, as one gradually awakened from the effects of anesthesia, one might unconsciously mumble possibly revealing secrets. All of us in the ward guarded against such an eventuality by trying to lead their postoperative ramblings in a safe direction, particularly when the agents hovered too closely.

In Mohsen's case we need not have worried. He did not respond when I first spoke to him. He looked out the window and uttered a few words that seemed to have no rational meaning, but I could understand him. He was saying *shure, shure*. In Persian music there are different *dastgah*, or moods, for expressing various emotions. *Shure* is used to evoke a tragic mood. Mohsen gazed steadily out the window at the falling snow and repeated "*Shure, shure, shure,*" and then "Snow, snow, snow." Finally, he looked at me and confided, "I destroyed everything." That was the guilt they had drummed into his head, the same guilt they had tried to give to me: "You destroyed your family, you destroyed your friends' lives, you destroyed everything."

That same day I was not fully at ease because another friend occupied the bed on the other side of Mohsen. This person, an architect, had worked with us as a set designer, starting not long before our arrest. I had met him through a friend when on tour in northern Iran, at Rasht. During my interrogation I had begun to sense that somehow, somewhere, information was being leaked. Adding to my suspicion was the architect's condition. He appeared physically fit, with no sign of having sustained a beating, yet he claimed to have a broken jaw, despite seeming to speak painlessly. Before we were arrested we had enjoyed a close and trusting relationship, even studying some political texts together which, he told me, he had acquired from a friend. Trusting him, I had revealed some of my political relationships, including my friendship with Mostafa Shoaiyan, one of the struggle's theoreticians and an influential person in the movement, who had gone underground, pursued and hunted by SAVAK.

Shoaiyan was independent of all groups and was trying to negotiate a united front between the leftist Fadaiyan and the Islamic Mojahedin. I had known him since the Honarestan, my school, and years later we had worked on a project concerning *hashieh neshinan,* marginal people, or squatters, at the Institute of Social Studies and Research at Tehran University. We were still working on the project when Mostafa was forced to go underground, and he gave me all he had written to that point for safekeeping and made a few carbon copies for other close friends as well. A few months later he called and we arranged to meet at a bus stop where we were to queue up. Mostafa was ahead of me in line when the bus came, and at the last moment, just before boarding the bus, he gave me a package containing his writings. These were confiscated from me when I was arrested before. I had lied to SAVAK about them, saying they were just unsolicited writings sent to me because I was an editor and publisher.

The architect sharing my hospital room knew this story and, I was certain, had informed on me to SAVAK, which was why they had tortured me so diligently and at length. I stayed in the hospital for a month, and I was nearly healed when guards appeared to haul my protesting body back to the Komiteh.

■ ■ ■

The daily interrogations began anew and numerous excuses to beat and torture me were added to my torment. One day, in the early morning, right after breakfast, three guards opened my cell and told me to come out. I could not walk so I crawled out and watched as they searched my cell. It contained only two military blankets and a plastic cup; nonetheless, one of the guards shook the blankets, searching for anything hidden in them, then turned his attention to the gelim, the cotton floor covering. Turning over a corner of the gelim he suddenly shouted, "What are these?" He held out his hand to show me some pins, the kind used to pin papers together before we had staples. "Why do you have these in your cell? Let's go to your interrogator!"

They took me down to my interrogator's office, and the guard who had the pins handed them to Shaheen and announced, "We found these in his cell. He was hiding them under the gelim."

Shaheen looked at me and shook his head. "So, you want to commit suicide, yah? You don't want to give us your information. Now I'm going to take that information from you."

He called Hosseini and they took me to the torture chamber, where they beat me and hung me by my wrists from a pipe in the ceiling, a process we prisoners referred to as the crucifixion. Then Hosseini beat me with electrical wires braided together, all the while shouting the most vile insults. After fifteen or twenty minutes he left the room, leaving me hanging there. My nerves burned inside the muscles of my arms.

This was the third time they crucified me. They had done it twice before, sending me to the hospital. The first time they had hung me from a bar on the balcony directly in front of Shaheen's office on the second floor, overlooking the circular courtyard, or *falakeh*. It was snowing on that occasion and flakes landed on my back as Hosseini beat me with that braided electrical wire until I fainted. The second crucifixion had occurred inside the torture chamber after the first beating in that huge chair we called Apollo.

SAVAK has to be credited with insidious ingenuity. One device, a simple clamp, was used to press your fingers together by tightening an attached screw. Most of the time they chose the left hand, hoping you would use your right hand to write a confession. As he tightened the screw the torturer would say, "Whenever you want me to stop just tell me, or raise your finger, raise your hand."

After my hospital respite, the interrogator introduced me to the *akhor*, or manger, the word for the place where livestock are fed. There, prisoners were instructed not to bend their knees as they were forced to bend over as far as possible, close to the floor, where their neck was tied with a rope, belt, or strap to a bar embedded in the floor. A guard was posted to ensure that the prisoner did not bend his knees. If he did, the guard kicked any part of the prisoner's body that struck his fancy.

I was subjected to a visit to the akhor and was made a target of opportunity for any guard who happened to walk by. One of them kicked me from behind, successfully aiming at my genitals, a blow that elicited such a scream of agony that my guard summoned Shaheen, who untied me and told the guard, "Take him to the restroom so he can pee." They mistakenly believed that urination would ease the pain.

On another occasion I was sitting in the interrogation room where I was supposed to write about my political activities. My prison blouse—we called them blouses but they were actually gray prison jackets—was pulled over my head so I could not see, a common practice in interrogation rooms. At first I could feel that nobody else was in the room, but then I heard the soft footsteps of someone slowly entering. Suspicious, I shifted inside my jacket and spied Hosseini's feet stepping toward Shaheen's desk, close to where I was sitting. He slowly opened the desk drawer, then suddenly shouted at me, "You sisterfucker, are you trying to steal the blade from the drawer?" He jerked the blouse off my head, thrust a blade before my eyes, and said, "I was watching you from outside, motherfucker." Then he called out, "Shaheen!"

Shaheen appeared in the room so quickly, I knew this scene was prearranged. They dragged me to the torture chamber, tied me onto Apollo, and beat me while demanding, "Why are you trying to kill yourself?"

I do not recall exactly but, after forty or fifty blows of the cable, they returned me to the office, where Shaheen told me, "You know, motherfucker, I'm not letting you go before you give me all the information you have. Don't imagine that you can get away. I myself am going to kill you. Don't think that there would be any problem if you were killed here. If I kill you, they'll give me a prize, they'll give me a promotion, so you might as well tell me whatever you're hiding from me."

There were occasions when I almost wished he would carry out his threats. My thumb had become badly infected, and the prison nurse decided to do something about it. After a few days he had made no progress, so Hosseini announced, "I'll heal your thumb." He used his cigarette lighter to heat an oversized needle, which he employed to attempt to pierce a hole in my thumbnail, ostensibly "to let out the infection."

His wife was a prison guard in Evin Prison; in fact, they themselves lived in Evin, which I considered appropriate, because one could not imagine him dwelling in any normal place. A tall, heavy man, Hosseini possessed an abnormally small head. He drank a lot and exuded a noxious body odor; you always felt as if you were being attacked by a monster.

Years later, during the revolution, Evin Prison was raided and Hosseini attempted to flee. Cornered, he shot himself, though not fatally, and was placed in the prison hospital, where he eventually died after suffering prolonged agony.

The new Islamic government employed *Zajr kosh,* a Farsi expression that translates, "We kill you with torment." They proceeded to do just that to Hosseini, and no one grieved his ordeal.

It got to the point where they could not torture me anymore without risking killing me. My feet and left thumb were infected, and I had sores and cuts everywhere—hands, face, chest—and I could only crawl, so they sent me back to the hospital.

■ ■ ■

Two weeks later, Azodi showed up at the hospital along with some other interrogators and some prison guards. Furious, he shouted at me and another prisoner whose back had been broken under torture and who was sleeping on a wooden plank in his hospital bed. He and I were the only ones in that room.

Azodi said, "You have been well pampered here." He walked over to my companion's bed and unceremoniously lifted the plank and flung him onto the floor, where he lay screaming with pain while Azodi shouted insults at him. Then he turned to me and asked, "Who sent you here, motherfucker? Who sent you to the hospital? Why are you here?"

He already knew that nobody could send prisoners under interrogation to the hospital without his permission, which made a mockery of his query.

He loudly ordered the guards, "Take these motherfuckers back to prison."

The other prisoner could not walk, much less stand, so they dragged him to the elevator. I could not walk either, but I could crawl, and in that manner I made my way slowly to the elevator. After we descended to the ground floor, we exited the hospital building to the parking lot, where the guards started to kick and insult us, saying, "You motherfucking cop killers! You're killing our *ham ghatars!*"—a military term for comrades or colleagues. They continued to kick and beat us as we crawled to the van. They opened the back door and threw us in. As the van pulled away, I saw a woman prisoner crawling across the parking lot. She was Masumeh Shadman, a famous member of the Mojahedin, and the mother of a Mojahed. As she vanished from my sight, I turned my gaze onto my surroundings, and saw a pile of bloody hospital sheets. The floor of the van was also bloody.

The previous night I had not been able to sleep. After midnight I had heard footsteps approaching in the corridor and people whispering. I could not make out their words but I could tell that the speakers were agitated. They entered a room across the hall. Moments later I heard Manouchehri, one of the head interrogators who used to interrogate the Mojahedin, asking urgently and repeatedly, "What is your name? What is your name?" Perhaps ten times he asked for a name, and then urgently said, "Do you hear me? Do you hear me? Count with me: One! One! One!"

There was a pause, and then he repeated, "Say one! One! Two! Two! I am telling you, count with me: One! Two! Three! Four!" His efforts continued until dawn, when everyone left and there was complete silence.

Riding in the back of the bloody van, I thought about the night before, wondering what had happened, I constructed a story in my head: There had been a fight, a gunfight, between the guerrillas and SAVAK agents; in the fight, one guerrilla was captured and they were trying to get him to talk but he had died. Probably one or more of the SAVAKis were killed, or maybe police, because they were calling us "cop killers." And that's why they came to the hospital to take us back to the prison, because they had lost one or more of their own.

■ ■ ■

A few days after I returned from the hospital the second time, my sole means of locomotion was still crawling. One morning a guard took me for interrogation and as I crawled over the threshold of the interrogation room, I saw five people standing in front of me. I craned my head to look up, and saw Azodi in the middle, flanked by two other interrogators, Kaveh and Arash, on his left, and Ostad, not officially an employee of SAVAK, but an old, wretched interrogator, and Shaheen, my usual tormentor. I was so frightened that without thinking, I said "Hello."

They all stared down at me coldly, and Azodi's face held an expression of absolute hatred. I could see in his eyes an intent to ridicule and humiliate me, but he started calmly, nodding, and said, "Hello, Mr. Rahmaninejad. So, the foreign radio says you have been martyred." He stopped, then said, "Look at me. I said martyred. You have been sacrificed to my cock"—an expression of extreme contempt in Farsi. "We've already gotten a bad name for killing you, so now we're going to actually do it. We are going to kill you, motherfucker!"

He stepped toward me, grabbed me by the shirt, and pulled me up to my feet. He brought his knee up into my stomach, and repeatedly hit me before passing me on to the next man. All five took a turn, then they all stood together in a semi-circle and attacked like soccer players, passing me to one another as if I were a ball. At one point I bounced off a wall and fell onto an electric heater. One of the men pulled it away by its cable and I fell to the floor. They continued kicking me for several minutes, until tiring of their sport. Azodi told Shaheen, "Keep this motherfucker here until he tells you everything."

They started interrogating me again but changed their approach. They renewed their previous efforts to force me to write my "life story," meaning my political activities, and to name activists with whom I was connected, except now they insisted on details. They demanded descriptions of every political scene or milieu, including what kind of actions my friends and I had taken against the government. They would take me from my cell every morning, bring me to the interrogation room, put me in a chair, and threaten to punish me this way or torture me that way. Sometimes they made good of their menacing threats by beating me right there in the interrogation room, not bothering to take me to the torture chamber. They would look over my shoulder, shouting and cursing, to see what I was writing in response to their questions. Then they would change the questions around or ask the same question over and over. Keeping me in that same room and badgering me relentlessly proved to be an exceptionally punishing method of interrogation.

I tried to save myself by writing autobiographically without any mention of politics; I did not make anything up, I just left out everything they wanted to know. I tried to buy some time by pretending to agree to write my true life story, then churned out a narrative laced with irrelevant detail.

I had concluded that there were two possible strategies to employ in responding to interrogation. One, the way usually recommended by experienced political activists, was to say nothing or respond with a brief uninformative answer; to try not to talk at all or, if you said anything, to make it a denial. There is an expression, "To be under interrogation is to have a dagger held under your chin. If you say yes, the dagger cuts your throat. If you say no, you save yourself." The alternative strategy, which no one recommended to me, was to seemingly cooperate without actually confessing or revealing anything incriminating about yourself or others. When the interrogators said, "Write everything about your activities," I took pen in hand and wrote and wrote about all of my artistic activities, casting them in a generally liberal context, wordily expostulating about art, literature, theater, and so on, in effect stating, "Here it is: this is my life. I am an artist! A man of the theater!" I would even go so far as to write about my difficulties with the censors, as an intellectual and a sophisticate, though I would add, "Of course, people like myself have difficulties with the censors; that's a matter of public record."

The interrogators already knew about my long friendships with Amir Parviz Pouyan and Mostafa Shoaiyan. We prisoners referred to such information as "burned" or "dead" information, because it was irrefutable. When the interrogators pressed me about these men, I did not pretend not to know them; instead, I characterized our relationships as purely personal and apolitical. "We were friends, yes," I wrote, "but regular friends, not political friends. We may have discussed social issues along with theater, but we shared no political activities. I don't know anything else about them."

I am not sure if this strategy really benefited me, but it did lead them to think that if they just kept pressuring me they might get some information. It certainly did not benefit me in the short term; it did not forestall beatings and torture as the interrogations continued. But maybe it benefited me in the long run, because they got no information out of me and did not kill me outright. My ploy certainly gave me some hope of survival for the near future, and of possible freedom eventually.

The interrogations may have been extended because of the architect, Akbar. When the interrogators confronted me with the fact that the two of us had studied politics together, I insisted that our joint efforts were purely personal literary studies; that if we talked sometimes of social issues, it had to do with their relation to literature and theater. I actually was not prevaricating, because that is how I had thought about our studies—not that they were purely literary, but that they were strictly between the two of us, with no connection to larger events, and definitely unconnected to any sort of political activism. Unfortunately, Akbar did not look at it that way. During his interrogation, he talked about my political beliefs and my sympathy for armed struggle. He confessed to exactly that in his written statement, a copy of which was put in my file. In his confession, he begged for pardon based on his cooperation in turning me in.

During the last sessions of that period of interrogation, Akbar was almost always in the room. Our interrogator, Shaheen, was playing with me, bringing Akbar in with me to erase any suspicions I had about him, showing that they were also tough with him by beating him on occasion. Twice Shaheen asked him questions, then flew into a rage, shouting at Akbar and calling a guard to take him to the torture chamber. After a while they brought him back and Shaheen said to him, "Now, you sit and write everything!" But I could see that it was only a show, a charade staged for my benefit. Nothing very bad had been done to him. To my eyes, as a man of the theater, they simply were all bad actors, and I took the liberty of using "bad actors" as a double entendre in characterizing these would-be thespians.

Much later, when one of the high-ranking members of Fadaiyan asked me to join the organization, I replied, "You know about this guy Akbar; he is one of yours." He answered, "Yes, we have other difficulties too; that is why we need people like you to help clean up the organization." I declined the offer, commenting, "Clean it up yourself."

At one point, I was taken to the interrogation room on three consecutive nights around ten or eleven o'clock, where I was confronted by a new interrogator, an obviously intelligent man dressed in a nice suit and tie who spoke in a civilized manner. He was more subtle in his approach than the others, deriving his questions from my daytime interrogations. He would constantly ask me questions about other questions, or reframe questions within questions, for hours. Under the guise of civility, he utilized misdirection to take advantage of my mental exhaustion from the daylight sessions with their incessant intimidations and beatings.

I recall quite vividly the last time he interrogated me. In the middle of the session, as he was sitting and waiting for me to write an answer, I heard a shot that seemed to come from outside the prison. More shots followed and I noticed my "good cop" interrogator suddenly stiffen. I tried to appear calm, pretending I had not heard anything. I finished my response and gave the paper back to him. He stopped the interrogation, put the paper in his briefcase, and called the guard to take me back to my cell. When the guard came, the interrogator left. I could see that he was completely discountenanced, frightened. Most experienced interrogators would have concealed their unease, but this man was so scared he did not even want me to finish writing my responses; he just wanted to leave.

A few months later, when I was in Qasr Prison, after the interrogations, I heard about the assassinations of General Zandipour and the interrogator Niktab. I think the shots I heard that night were connected to one of those assassinations.

■ ■ ■

During my last month at the interrogation center, I was transferred to a room with some other prisoners, including Akbar.
The atmosphere in our cell was very tense. Every morning after
breakfast we lit cigarettes, and the entire ward fell into a deathly
silence. Everyone awaited the call to go to interrogation, which
very likely meant a round of torture. Every noise, every footstep,
every click of the ward door was a sign, a frightening sign, that
your time had come. When the lock of the ward door actually
did click, one could visualize the keys turning in the lock and
the iron door moving on its hinges, and the silence became even
more profound. Nobody wanted to show any sign of fear. We
could each sense the other's apprehension, which echoed our
own. When the guard stepped through the main door into the
ward, all the prisoners were alert, counting his steps to ascertain
whose cell had been reached. Whenever the guard stopped, the
inmates in the other cells would hold their breath. The most
frightening moment occurred when the guard paused in front
of *your* cell door; surely your heart would explode from sheer
anxiety. The noise of the latches being released was unbearable,
but when the door opened and you were called, you felt something akin to relief: your fate was no longer an unknown, which
was always the worst possible torture.

After nine o'clock, those who were left in their cells gradually
began to feel a sense of relief, however dubious and shaky. There
was no guarantee you would not be called later, but that rarely
happened. In retrospect, it is surprising that no one among our
tormenters hit upon the notion of random torture sessions; respite would have been impossible.

As time passed, relief became more tangible. You could
feel the atmosphere easing as the whole ward relaxed. Even the
way the guard paced up and down the ward changed. If you
were alone in a cell, depending on what stage of interrogation

you were enmeshed in, or how complicated your case was, you thought about the responses you made to questions about the people you knew, whose names the interrogators were trying to pry out of you, and about how you must continue to resist their efforts. You also thought about your family, parents, sisters, brothers, and friends. You thought about the places you had been, about the people of your city walking freely under the sun. And if you loved someone, you thought about your beloved, and you wondered if she had been arrested, if she was in prison, if she was surviving the interrogations, the tortures. You drove yourself crazy wondering. When you were alone in a cell, you thought through your life again and again, without being able to be an active part of it.

In my case, I was worried about Havva, the Farsi equivalent of the name Eve. I had met her through her brother, who was working with our theater group. She was a professor who had participated in one of our summer acting classes in preparation for a class she would be teaching. Just before I was arrested, the two of us had talked about living together. I was going to move in with her after I put our play onstage. I was thirty-six at the time and a virgin. The interrogators had mentioned her name a few times during questioning and had referred to pictures they had taken of us together, standing next to her car. I had been frightened and angry when on several occasions the interrogators threatened people I knew, but this time was different. My relationship with Havva was so dear to me that I was ready to defy to the death any attempt to harm her.

They could not coerce anything from me to justify arresting her, but I knew they could apprehend her at any moment on trumped-up charges. I took some comfort from her family connections. Her father was a very respected man, the vice president of the government department that filed and preserved land titles and other important documents. Additionally, he was the department's chief executive for northern Iran. Azodi hailed from the same town as Havva's father and knew the whole family. He was a strange man. Despite holding a high position in SAVAK, with a sizable income, when he led the raid on Ahmad's apartment in our theater group building when we were arrested; he confiscated everything for his personal use, including a valuable and expensive edition of the *Shahnameh* by Ferdowsi, whose reputation in Iran matches that of Pushkin in Russia or Shakespeare in the English-speaking world. Ahmad's family tried to get him released and also tried to retrieve his belongings, but they could not pry this rare edition from Azodi's grasp. Those who are evil are not always punished, at least in this world; the odious Azodi survived the revolution and was able to leave Iran before he could be held accountable for his crimes, large and small. He was living in Los Angeles when death came for him in early 2000.

Alone in a cell, even the toughest intellect is subject to occasional flights of fancy. During one day's interrogation, snow had fallen, and that night my imaginings conjured Tehran blanketed with the cold whiteness. What if they decide to free me tonight? I mused. I could walk home in the snow without shoes or socks. This notion required considerable late-night naivete because my feet were infected and badly swollen. Perhaps we all are desperate to go home to our mothers; I know I was.

I knew she was ceaselessly searching everywhere for information about my whereabouts, begging people to tell her where her son was or at least that I was OK. On the other occasions when I had been arrested, she waited outside the prison gates, trying to find out what building I was in, trying to send messages, and asking to see me. One day, soon after I came back from the hospital the first time, the director of the prison, Major Vaziri, came to my cell. He handed me two items of clothing and a bag of pistachios and said, "These are from your mother. You are going to kill her. What sin has this woman done that you are doing this to her? If you won't take pity on yourself, take pity on her." Then he added, "I couldn't refuse her this time. For two months she has been coming here every day, sitting outside behind the gate. By the way, don't tell anyone that I brought these in for you." I never doubted my mother's love and devotion.

Having a cellmate in prison eases the loneliness, especially if you trust each other. Some of the larger cells held as many as five to ten inmates. Besides talking, the most common way to kill time was playing backgammon or chess. We would fashion game pieces by gouging out the soft centers of standard issue military bread and softening it with spit and sweet tea, and we would draw game boards on a blanket. Although we enjoyed the games, our minds never wholly relaxed; we were all prone to fixating on our individual fates. The more phlegmatic and rational among us could summon the necessary concentration for chess, but most of us settled on backgammon. I was puzzled that people occasionally cheated at these games. How could somebody cheat companions in this gulag? There was no money or prizes at stake. We were all prisoners at the mercy of a monstrous system, yet some would cheat a fellow victim.

After the Iranian New Year of 1354 (March 1975), they transferred me to a large cell with five other prisoners, and later as many as eight occupied the space. Akbar was also transferred to the cell. By that time I was aware of his perfidy and I knew why he had been placed in that particular cell, but I pretended ignorance and greeted him cordially.

Among us were four religious Muslims, a leftist teacher, and a northern Iranian suspected of guerrilla activity. The teacher was a pleasant man with an acute sense of humor. He continually teased, but in a good-natured way. We did not talk about our cases much, and usually prisoners did not ask unless they knew and trusted one another completely. When there were numerous prisoners in a cell, conversations about politics almost never occurred, due to the increased possibility of informants. I spent nearly three months in that cell, enduring interrogations and tortures almost daily before being transferred to Qasr Prison.

I I

QASR PRISON AND
A BELATED TRIAL

Akbar accompanied me to Qasr, where we were assigned to a room in a ward for common criminals. We called it Quarantine, a kind of temporary limbo for tortured political prisoners before they were moved on to a political prison. Normally, political prisoners are placed in a separate room, to segregate them from the ordinary prisoners, who were usually eager to have contact with us. There was a third political prisoner in our room, an agricultural engineer whose prolonged tortures had rendered him mentally unbalanced. After a week, the three of us were sent on to the political ward of the Qasr Prison, a mere five-minute walk from the criminal ward.

When we stepped into the prison lobby, we entered what in Farsi is called the *hasht,* like the word for the number eight. In a traditionally designed Iranian house, one enters through a vestibule or entryway that leads to the rest of the house. In the residences of the wealthy there is an outer area where guests are received and an inner space where only family members are allowed. The outer, transitional space is called the *hashti;* you are inside the building, technically speaking, but you are not really in the living area until you are admitted through a second door. In the hashti there are often niches built into the wall, where one can sit. In the prison hasht were the offices of the director, the officer on call, the receiving area for checking prisoners in and out, bedrooms for the guards, and doors that led to the wards.

Entering the hasht, the first thing I spied was a particularly vicious guard whose acquaintance I had made when previously arrested. Akbar, the engineer, and I were standing in the middle of the hashti with our little bundles when the guard Abdi slowly moved toward me, a sneer on his face. "Welcome, hello— the great leader! So, what happened to you?" he asked, pointing at my crushed feet, on which I had limped into the lobby.

I said nothing, thinking it was useless to waste words. The supervisor of the guards, Officer Karimi, wearing the uniform of the police department, walked up to me and said, "Hello, Mr. Rahmaninejad," in a very neutral way, with neither apparent hostility nor friendliness. He asked, "What happened this time? Why are you here?"

Again I said nothing.

He looked at me with disbelief, as if to say, "Nobody is here for nothing." He instructed me, "Go to Mr. Ghadimi's office and sign in."

I laboriously navigated the four or five stairs to the office in question. His logbook was open on the desk and alongside it lay our papers. He entered my name into his log and at the same time whispered to me, "Mr. Rahmaninejad, don't answer back. Don't talk to them. The situation is different than the last time you were here." I emptied my pockets and unbuckled my belt, and as he searched me he said, "That's it. Be careful."

I thanked him and descended the stairs back to the hasht. I could see into the guards' room at the southeast corner of the hasht. Although most of them were still wearing only their underwear, they were obviously awaiting orders to beat us. After the crackdown on prisoners in 1973, whenever political prisoners were brought in, they were beaten in the hasht before being moved to the wards. Akbar, the engineer, and I stood against the wall, waiting.

Abdi came up and started to *band kardan*—a Farsi slang expression meaning "to mess with"—the agricultural engineer, pushing and crowding him back into a corner of the hasht. He then used his baton to strike the engineer on the head. He was quickly joined by four or five other guards, still in their underwear, who rushed from their room and assaulted the engineer until he cried and slumped down in the corner, unconscious on the floor. Abdi then turned toward me and I braced myself to receive his blows, but Supervisor Karimi slipped between the two of us. Without a word being spoken, Abdi turned away. I waited there while two other companions were processed, then Karimi announced, "Every one of you is assigned to a specific room. You will not be allowed to go to other rooms. You will be allowed no contact with other prisoners."

He turned to me and said, as had Ghadimi, "Mr. Rahmaninejad, this prison is different now than it was before."

A few weeks before I transferred into Quarantine at Qasr, while I was still at the Komiteh, I saw in a dream one night that I was being sent to Qasr. I was waiting behind the ward door for the guard to open it, and I was thinking that my prison friends were standing on the other side of the door to welcome me as it always used to be. When the door opened, the first person I recognized was Bijan Jazani. He was looking at me with a smile and I rushed to him, but before I could embrace him I suddenly saw that his face had no natural color. It was reddish grey and his hair was lighter and looked like ashes. I woke up horrified.

Now, in reality, Abdi opened the door and we stepped into the ward that was specifically for prisoners who were waiting to go to court. Here everything was different than in the dream. Abdi guided me through a narrow corridor whose one side was lined with iron bunk beds. The first prisoner I saw rushed past me and whispered "Hi" in my ear. It was Said. Abdi turned into a second corridor, where he led me into a room smaller than two by three meters, with one small window positioned high on the wall and a cell door.

It was seven months since I had been arrested, seven months under interrogation, with no visitors allowed and of course no lawyer. To request a lawyer would have been as ridiculous as asking to telephone the Royal Court Ministry.

It was late afternoon and as I sat in the cell with the door open, another prisoner came in and said hello with an Azari accent. He introduced himself and welcomed me. Apparently when the guards said we would not be allowed contact with other prisoners, they were just trying to intimidate us. The cell doors were left open day and night; they only locked the door to the courtyard at night. The Azari sat and talked a little, and after a while Said showed up. We hugged and kissed each other. It was more than a year since I had seen him. We had parted on less than friendly terms, but after a year it was as if nothing negative had transpired between us.

Said explained, "Because of the situation, I have to leave, but I just came to say that I'm here, don't worry, if you need anything just tell me." Then he left.

I told my new Azari cellmate, "I want to go out to the court-yard before it gets dark."

I walked down the corridor and out into the yard, thinking it was better to stay next to the door, lean against the wall, and observe the situation before mingling. I watched other prisoners walking around the courtyard. Some were washing dishes beneath a tap that poured water into a concrete tub on the ground. I sensed rather than saw someone approach and stand next to me. I turned and saw Sattar, an Azari guard whom I knew from a previous arrest. He had always been ridiculed and joked about by the inmates because he was slow-witted, forever misunderstanding orders, but he had undergone a change, becoming vicious and cruel. During my previous stay in Qasr he had been new to the prison and would turn red with embarrassment every time he wanted to say something. I had been a prisoners' spokesman for the commune then and had dealt with him and several other guards directly.

Now Sattar was next to me and asking in his Azari accent, "What happened?"

I didn't want to talk to him, so I said, "Nothing."

After a pause he asked me, "Where is Bijan now?"

At first I did not understand what he meant, so I asked, "Who?"

And he said, "Bijan. Where is he now?"

I replied, "I don't know. Probably in one of the Qasr prisons." I really did not know what had happened to Bijan. But moments later I learned that this vicious guard knew that Bijan Jazani, along with eight other prisoners, had been killed on the hills of Evin Prison.

Sattar's question was meant to intimidate and torment me. When I told him I did not know anything about Bijan, he laughed at me and said, "You don't know where he is now!"

I walked away from him, joined some of the other prisoners, and told them what Sattar had said. They asked, "Don't you know what happened to Bijan?" And they told me about the executions.

■ ■ ■

During the next few days I spoke to several of my friends I had not seen since the night of the last rehearsal. I also saw Ahmad, who had been badly beaten and who had been with me in the hospital. Another was Heshmat, who had translated the Gorky play.

In a prison like this one, where there are prisoners with diverse histories and widely varying backgrounds of political ideologies and involvements and all are waiting for trial, daily life is not as regulated as it is in other prisons. After people are convicted and sentenced, they are assigned to different wards according to the length of their sentence. Normally prisoners have a daily schedule based on their own interests—different subjects of discussion and study; however, in this prison, where people have not yet been to court, the prisoners are more careful about their activities and their connections to other prisoners. They do not want to do anything that would negatively affect their court cases. Also, lingering fears from interrogations and torture haunt them, and paranoia reigns.

Now that we were through the seven-month period of torture and interrogation, families were allowed to visit twice a week for fifteen minutes. Some people were allowed visitors during the interrogation period, but I had not been that fortunate. On the first visiting day at Qasr, my mother and sister arrived. The visiting hall was a large, long, bare concrete hall with two entrances—one leading from the prison through the hashti, and one for visitors coming in from the outside. Two parallel rows of bars spaced about a meter and a half apart separated the prisoners from their visitors. Two or three guards stood in the space between the bars at a short distance from the prisoners, monitoring the conversations. When the doors on either side were opened, visitors and prisoners alike rushed to the bars so as not to waste a single second of their fifteen minutes. Coherent conversations were nearly impossible with the near-deafening cacophony of many voices echoing from the concrete walls. Predictably, visitors and prisoners were barely able to hear one another and responded by shouting louder and louder. These mass visits resembled demonstrations with no recognizable slogans. I never knew whether or not this was a deliberately planned exercise.

I was still experiencing pain in my left foot at the time of that first visit. Still limping, I tried to walk normally to show my mother and sister that I was alright, but I knew my effort was futile. When I reached the bars, I tried to project cheerfulness, pretending that everything was fine and there was nothing to worry about. It was a ridiculous, sad ploy because my mother spied my infirmity immediately and exclaimed, "Why are you limping?"

I demurred, unconvincingly, "No, I'm not limping, I'm fine!"

I asked about my brother and we stuck to the mundane, our entire conversation shouted at the top of our lungs. Most of the time my mother just looked at me worriedly. She spoke only a few words during the visit, and I was happy to see that my sister had been released and reunited with her first baby, now seventeen months old.

After that visit I arranged with Ahmad that both our families would come together on visiting days so I could see Havva, although strictly speaking I could not talk to her because she was not officially my visitor. Nonetheless, sometimes Ahmad and I were able to find spots next to each other so that our families would be together on the other side. At least Havva and I could look at each other, using simple eye contact to express our deep feelings.

More than a year passed from the time of my arrest before I was summoned to court. All political prisoners were tried in military court, which wasted no time convicting me and handing down a twelve-year sentence. An appeals court, also a military court, upheld my conviction and sentence. A friend, the writer Ali Ashraf Darvishian, who had been arrested four months after me, appeared with me in the original court proceedings. We were familiar with the procedures of the military court. We knew they would appoint a retired military officer, ostensibly to defend us. The only hope we had was that he might stay neutral, because most of these retirees "defended" you in a way that actively helped the prosecution. They had no motivation to explain the facts to the court, much less make an honest effort on our behalf. There was always an assumption of guilt. They were unconvincing actors in a farcical procedure. If we were to put one of these so-called trials on the stage as a play, the audience would burst out laughing derisively. These old officers would strain to appear neutral as they tried to please the court. When talking to the defendants, they pretended they were their advocates, a transparent falsehood. "We are trying very hard to defend you," they would insist, especially if they were "chosen" by the helpless family of the defendant. Sometimes the family would choose from the court's list of lawyers and—naively believing that the court lawyer would actually try to help—would actually pay him to save the prisoner.

In nearly all instances, convictions were predetermined by SAVAK. The military courts simply carried out SAVAK's orders, which possessed a higher authority than the judiciary. The members of the court, if in fact they even bothered to read the court papers pertaining to the case, simply followed the conclusions written up by SAVAK. Prior to the opening of the sham trial, the accused and their actions would be subjected to a legal fiction labeled an investigation. The defendant would be taken to a room where, with the assistance of a lawyer, his denials and complaints of torture would be listed and then cavalierly disregarded. Many of the defendants' families were unaware that the legal structure was completely anticonstitutional, even according to the dubious law of that era. The entire hypocritical process was there to deceive the credulous into believing there was some substantive democratic check on the power of the Shah and the other officials.

Hoping against hope, many families thought that hiring a lawyer, even a retired military lawyer, would help their kin to be proven innocent or at least receive a lesser sentence. My poor brother, who was a scrupulously honest man and a member of the military himself, contacted the military court and did his best to convince them, on the basis of his own service to the military, that I was innocent and should be set free. The court convinced him that his only recourse was to engage a lawyer from their list.

During prison visits, I told him, "Don't waste your time. It won't change anything. These lawyers will not help me."

He disregarded my words and hired a lawyer, because the military people had scared him, saying, "Your brother's case is very bad. He's in a very dangerous situation."

Although I did not approve this choice of an attorney who claimed to be my lawyer, he took it upon himself to give me advice. He read the statement I had written in my own defense and tried to convince me to "correct" it, but I argued with him until I realized that he was going to do whatever he wanted. At our first meeting held in the military legal office, as Darvishian and I were reading our files, my lawyer, who was also going through my file, suddenly exclaimed, "It looks like you have a fifth column—an informer—among you." He held up a piece of paper.

"Let's see—what's that?" I said.

It was a record of the last interrogation session of Akbar, in which he begged for his freedom. The interrogation was conducted by Shaheen. According to the transcript, Akbar had written, "As I have tried to convince you during my interrogation, because I know many intellectuals, I can prepare valuable information for you." Later in the document, Shaheen tells Akbar, "Tomorrow you are going to be transferred to Qasr prison with Nasser Rahmaninejad. In the prison you will watch his movements, his connections with the other prisoners. Later we will call you to the Komiteh to inform us of his activities."

This revelation was scarcely a shock; I had long suspected that Akbar was spying for the interrogators. I told the lawyer, "I am not sure why this is in my file—it's not mine."

I did not want to say anything that would induce further curiosity in him about my case. I passed the paper to Darvishian to read because I wanted a witness, someone besides me who would know about Akbar in case verification was needed. After Darvishian read it, he looked at me and in his Kirmanshahi-accented speech he whispered, "Ay, Baba! Ay, Baba!" (which literally translates, "Oh, Papa!" but means something more like, "Oh, my God!"). "Who was that guy?"

After the revolution of 1979, Akbar called four or five of our mutual friends together for a meeting. Later, one of these friends called me and told me about the meeting. He said that Akbar had begun with an introduction justifying his life, rationalizing everything. With a little tear, he had confessed, "I sacrificed Nasser to save some important information for the organization," referring to the Fadaiyan. Years later I met another one of the people who had attended the meeting, and he confirmed what I had heard previously.

When Darvishian and I went to the Court of Appeals, he was sentenced to eleven years, one year less than me. The primary crime for which I was found guilty was "Forming a communist organization under the pretext of a theater group," for which I received the ten-year maximum sentence. An additional two years were tacked on because it was the second conviction for the same offense. The other members of our theater group received sentences ranging from one to six years, for a total of more than sixty years.

Our days in court coincided with the Shah's claim that his administration was forging the "fifth most developed country in the world." He boasted that Iran was "the gate of great civilizations."

This was the same government that Jimmy Carter later credited with creating "an island of stability in the Middle East." Obviously the American president understood nothing of the Iranian people's hatred of the Shah's government and its vulnerability, because the revolution overthrowing the despotic regime took place just months later.

■ ■ ■

The political divisions within Qasr Prison aligned with the prison's eight wards, which were arranged in clusters. Before going to court I was in the section comprising wards two and three. After my conviction I was transferred to the cluster of wards numbered four, five, and six. When I entered there, I believed I would be staying for eleven years, since I had already served a year from the time of my arrest. Based on my previous prison experience, I prepared a plan to survive my incarceration. I would study art, especially the history of art, partly because books on these topics were available, a legacy of previous inmates. Additionally, families brought books that we could receive if they were approved by the censor, an officer from Agahi.

In addition to art and literature, I also studied more general historical works, history being a subject in which most political prisoners understandably developed an interest, and the kind of books that most often fell into our hands. My friend, movie director, Reza Allamehzadeh, and I studied together a volume I had longed to read for years, *The Social History of Art* by Arnold Hauser. For two hours every day before lunch, Reza read to me and simultaneously translated for my benefit. That period of studying Hauser with Reza, learning a historical materialist view of art, remains among the best experiences I had in prison.

About two years into my sentence, one afternoon in February 1976, they called my name from the prison office by loudspeaker and instructed me to come to the hasht.

Such an order was not a good sign. It presaged either another period of interrogation and torture or transfer to some other prison, usually in the provinces, far from family. When I went to the hasht, a guard escorted me out to the main gate, where a military van waited. Entering the van, I found Mohsen Yalfani, Said Soltanpour, and Mahmoud Dowlatabadi already sitting inside. We exchanged looks, uncertain and fearful about our destination. We thought they might be taking us back to the Komiteh. After we signed some papers, the van pulled away and indeed headed in that direction. Upon our arrival, they separated us, placing us in separate cells. I sat there pondering the possibilities of the near future. Nothing suspiciously unusual had occurred recently, but considering how much I was concealing, the secrets my mind harbored, might this turn of events not mean another round of interrogation and torture to pull them from me? And why had we four been brought here together? Funny, every prisoner dreams of an end to his prison life, yet when the daily routine is interrupted, one cannot help wishing to be returned to that comforting, predictable existence. Truly, fear of the unknown is among the most troubling of human emotions.

At eleven that night, a guard opened the door and ordered me out. He took me to a room on the third floor of the falakeh, the circle. I had always been tortured on the second floor before, so my spirit rose slightly. Within seconds, other guards brought in Said, Mohsen, and Mahmoud and seated us in chairs facing a desk. While looking at one another with sidelong glances, we mumbled questions, fearful of being overheard, communicating mostly with our eyes and facial expressions: "What's happening? Why are we here? What do they want from us?"

All at once we heard the voice of Rasouli, the interrogator I had met before down in the courtyard. We knew that Rasouli sometimes called famous intellectuals, poets, writers, artists, and the like into his office late at night to challenge them about their understanding of politics, literature, and history, trying to prove his intellectual superiority. His inevitable conclusion was that "all of you so-called intellectuals have proven you are idiots by struggling against the government." Then he would recite all the great things the government was doing.

He arrived reeking of alcohol, a common pattern with him—to get drunk and then have some intellectuals sent in for the sport of insulting and humiliating them. On this occasion, Rasouli greeted us sarcastically—"All of the high intellectuals are here tonight"—accompanied by his usual sneer. Sitting behind his desk, he surveyed our little group, turning his head slowly from left to right, and asked, "So, how is everything? I don't think your situation is that bad. I told the guard to make tea so we can have tea here all together and chat a little."

A few minutes later, two guards came in, one carrying a tray with cups of tea on it, the other carrying a big box of cream puffs and other assorted pastries. We looked at each other, consternated, our lips curled in half smiles, not knowing what to say.

Rasouli said, "OK, have some tea! Eat some pastry—these are good! We know your situation is pretty good right now, but we are going to send you somewhere else where you will have it even better. I hope you can appreciate it." His manner clearly conveyed what his speech did not: "We're doing you a great favor and we expect you to reciprocate."

Then he asked each of us personal questions, such as, "What have you been doing?" "How is it going?" and again urged, "Please, have some tea." So we drank the tea and ate the pastries. Then, in the old hectoring style he so often employed, he said, "I really don't know for what reason you would stage a play of Gorky's. Hasn't anyone told you that Gorky doesn't have anything to do with us? You intellectuals! Instead of reading your own history, you read Western literature, Western history, Marxism. Those things have absolutely no relevance to us, to our lives, to our country."

He tried provoking us and involving us in discussion, but we well knew it was useless to try to discuss anything with this man, or with any other officials in this kind of situation. Then he tried to provoke us individually. Each one of us cautiously replied to his questions, always saying something softly neutral, as if we harbored no strong feelings on these subjects. The wily bastard fully realized that we were in no position to take issue with him, that we were trapped, reduced to listening passively while he spouted his dubious theories. Our passivity prompted his agitation to a new height: "You should go and read the Shahnameh! Instead of putting on Gorky's play, there are hundreds of potential plays in the Shahnameh! Read it and make plays of it! Do you know that we Iranians are the first nation in history to produce women warriors? The first in the history of the world! I'm asking you: Who is Gordafarid? She was the first woman commander in the world! Nowhere else can you find this!"

He continued this drunken tirade as we sat there listening, eating cream puffs, and enjoying our tea. Finally he ran out of breath, finished his own tea, and said, "Alright, I'm going to call the guards to take you back to your cells, and tomorrow you are going to your new home." But he did not say where.

The next day, after lunch, the guards loaded us into a van, blindfolded us, and delivered us to Evin Prison. They would always blindfold prisoners if Evin was the destination, mostly for psychological reasons, because Evin, like the Komiteh, was not an ordinary prison but an interrogation center.

At Evin they separated us and placed each of us in solitary confinement, and I resigned myself to whatever fate Evin Prison might bring me.

■ ■ ■

The next morning, the four of us were assembled and led to an office where we met a man introduced as Manouchehri, a name that turned out to be a pseudonym. He looked like the prototypical bureaucrat, attired in a neat, clean suit and an equally immaculate shirt and tie. He spoke and acted in a polite, relaxed manner after we had been seated in his little office. Using ordinary, civil language he asked, "I hope you are all doing well." He then cut to the chase: "The reason you are here is that we have been given a list of nine prisoners that a lawyer from Amnesty International has asked to interview. No one other than the Shah had the authority to grant this request, so I hope you understand the favor the Shah has done you in giving his permission. I think you understand the significance of this benevolence and will fully appreciate it. We know that we have made some mistakes and that sometimes a few people have gone too far, but this is not our official policy and we are no longer condoning certain practices. You know that the policy the Shah has been pursuing for years and years is the building of a country that can compete with the Western countries. Of course these Western countries oppose His Majesty's policies; they try in different ways to keep Iran down, to keep it underdeveloped ..."

He continued in this vein, politely enunciating what was obviously a carefully prepared speech. It was clear to us that embedded in this friendly address there was a threat. In a careful, subtle way, he was letting us know that there would be harsh consequences if we failed to cooperate. When he finished, he spoke directly to each one of us, trying to elicit our thoughts in order to gauge the effect of his speech. Each of us tried to be brief and to phrase our responses carefully; to be, as far as possible, honest, yet not take what could be perceived as a radical position, and at the same time not to show fear. We could see that SAVAK had no choice but to let us meet the Amnesty International lawyer; however, we did not know what we could say to him without running the risk of being tortured again. We did not know that Amnesty and the Red Cross would be coming regularly to Iranian prisons after this initial visit—thus our caution in answering our politely threatening bureaucrat. All of our responses were variations of the same theme: "We are a group of artists, writers, and theater people who had nothing to do with political organizations, yet SAVAK has treated us as if we were armed guerrillas who attacked the government militarily. We have all been harshly tortured, and there was no reason to torture us because we had nothing to hide."

That was the position we took with him. When the discussion grew heated, he tried to defend SAVAK's treatment of us. Again he characterized their policy as positive; they had merely made a few overzealous mistakes. He said, "We are all like a family. Every family has its problems and its issues. There are some problems that should not be spoken of outside the family. You can say anything you want to say about your difficulties in your professions, and even about censorship, about everything, except one thing." Here his words took on a threatening tone: "*You cannot talk about torture!*" He then added, "This is something that is very important for our country, for our situation in the world." He continued talking, trying to appeal to our patriotism, going on about the Western powers as if we were all ignorant of the fact that the United States had put the Shah in power and had armed and backed him ever since.

Finally he concluded: "We transferred you here because here you can have better living conditions. You will have better facilities and, really, you can have anything you need. Here we don't have all those regulations and limitations imposed on you at other prisons. We will send you into a ward where there are good people, no overcrowded facilities. In fact, there is an artist in this ward. Later on," the bureaucrat continued, "we'll have time to talk again. Now you can go and discuss all this among yourselves. I don't need your final answer now; we will talk more later."

He summoned the guards, who guided us to ward number one in the new prison within the Evin complex. The first floor was totally empty, and we were housed on the second floor. Four members of the Iran Liberation Organization were in the ward, including two of its leaders, Manouchehr Nahavahdi and Akbar Izadpanah. These men occupied the first room in the ward. Another prisoner, introduced by the bureaucrat as an artist, was Salimi Moghadam. His room, the second in the ward, resembled a painter's studio, although he was no longer an active artist. Later we heard from other prisoners that he had done paintings for the Shah, some princes, and SAVAK agents. He shared his room with Hassan Saharkhiz, whose name translates as "wakes up at dawn" or "early riser." Said and I decided to live in the first room with the Liberation Organization members.

Mohsen and Mahmoud went to the second room, joining the artist and Hassan Saharkhiz.

No regulations were imposed by the prison authorities, nor were there any preexisting commune or collective rules. Left to our own devices, we decided to use the ward's third room as a dining area. The Liberation Organization members got up every morning at five and proceeded to the courtyard, where they put in an hour of hard exercise. After showering, they returned to the room, where each man consumed a bowl of vegetables for breakfast. Still asleep, Said and I woke up to the sound of their chewing. I remember Said remarking, "I feel like I'm in a barn listening to the cows chewing their cud." Gradually we got used to their ways, which were so much different from how we had lived in Qasr.

In Evin we prepared our own breakfast, tea, and snacks; lunch and dinner were prepared for us. Dishes, sheets, and books were not provided; we had to ask our families for money to buy these items, once the news of our transfer filtered out to them. Among the surprises we witnessed in Evin was the periodic arrival of a soldier who would collect a list of things desired by the Iran Liberation Organization, which he bought for them outside of the prison. It seemed that these prisoners were *Nour-e Cheshmi*—literally "the light of the eyes"—that is, favored children. We were told that we could take advantage of this service, but we did not.

Soon other prisoners were sent into the ward. Among them were Shokrolah Paknejad, Fereidoun Shayan, Asgar Oladi, and Aslan Aslanian, who was arrested with us because he used to come to our theater group and participated in the play *The Visions of Simone Marchard*. He had been sentenced to three years.

Intermittently during the first few weeks, we were summoned to Manouchehri's office. He continued to press us to repay SAVAK for our current favored treatment by refraining from mentioning torture to the Amnesty lawyer. After each visit we would discuss this critical issue, trying to reach a reasonable consensus about how we would deal with SAVAK. At one point, Manouchehri told us, "It is better for us and for you that you choose one person to be your liaison to us." I was chosen to perform this function and reluctantly agreed. After two more visits to Manouchehri's office, I realized that I was in a very difficult position. Each time I came back to the ward after my visits with him, the others offered suggestions about our options, some of which conflicted with our previously decided course of action. Exasperated, I finally announced, "I don't want to be put in this position. I don't want to accept the responsibility for all of you. I'm going to tell them that I speak for myself only."

After that decision we had two or three more group meetings with SAVAK. On one occasion, Tehrani, a SAVAK agent who was executed after the revolution, came to the ward to persuade us against talking about torture with the lawyer. He asserted, "I'm not in favor of torture."

We acknowledged his position, but one by one we emphasized that we had been tortured without reason. He kept dodging all our attempts to talk about our specific cases: "That was in the past! We are talking about now! We don't torture anymore! You can help us to push this process forward!"

At one point I said to him very softly, "Mr. Tehrani, please listen to me. Suppose we agree with you. Suppose we deny having been tortured. Suppose we don't bring up this subject when we talk to the Amnesty lawyer. Have you thought of this: if the lawyer asks me, for example, to take off my socks or my clothes and he sees the scars and the marks of torture, what do you suppose he will be thinking? Don't you realize he will believe that you are still torturing and that we are denying it now only because we fear future torture?"

Tehrani paused for a moment, then in a different tone of voice said, "I told those motherfuckers a hundred times: don't hit them so hard!" He stood up and we could see he was completely disarmed. He said, "I don't know, I don't know what you're going to say! I won't give you any more advice! I'll just report your position to my colleagues." And with that he left the room.

We had another meeting, this time with Hossein Zadeh, a high-ranking SAVAK official, whose real name was Reza Attarpour. He came to our ward with Manouchehri and Tehrani. We met in the same room where we had met with Tehrani, but this time all of us stood around the room listening to Hossein Zadeh, who did most of the talking for thirty minutes. He talked about the same issues that Manouchehri had discussed, but with more *chashni*, that is, bits of spice. He seasoned his remarks with lots of little examples as proofs of his positions, points, and arguments. "You know," he said, "you were not criticizing the government. We are not against criticism; we criticize ourselves all the time. You, through your work and your words, were encouraging young, naive persons to take up arms and kill innocent people."

Hossein Zadeh told us that he had been summoned by His Majesty the Shah the week before. "Last week some of my colleagues and I were summoned to the Royal Palace to show a documentary that we had produced. It's about the rug-weaver children of Kerman. We showed it to His Majesty and explained the miserable condition of those children. We made a positive impact on the Shah, and His Majesty decided to change the situation. This is the kind of constructive criticism that is useful. We all recognize that we have a few problems in this country, but with a sensible approach we can correct them. But nothing can be accomplished through your hotheaded, unreasoning attacks."

We stood there mute. We had no idea how to respond to such utter nonsense. At one point I told him, "The way SAVAK confronted us, the way you have dealt with us, it is as if we were guerrillas. It is as if we had taken up arms to commit subversive acts. The night we were arrested, for instance, we were besieged by your agents armed with Uzis, surrounding an entire block simply to arrest a few peaceful actors and actresses."

Hossein Zadeh replied, "We had a report that Mostafa Shoaiyan was coming to your place, so we thought there could be an armed clash there."

We knew he was lying, because it was the first time we had heard this line in the last two years and seven months while undergoing interrogations and torture. It was obvious that he was fabricating an explanation on the fly. His unconvincing tale was proof of both his duplicity and his stupidity.

At the end of the meeting he tried once more to persuade us not to talk about torture. He suggested that we had lots of other things we could talk about: the problems we had with staging our plays, censorship, whatever. Then he added, "In this situation, our country needs you out of prison, carrying on your artistic work. You should know that we don't have any objection to your continuing in the theater."

All of us understood what was at stake the country was restive here and there, intellectuals were distributing letters of protest, expressing their discontent about the climate of fear and repression in Iran. There were reports of scattered protests by workers and the beginnings of pressure exerted by human rights groups, as well as large demonstrations by Iranian students abroad, especially in Europe and most notably in Amsterdam, where they were organized by the Iranian Students' Federation. The latter gathering captured widespread attention from the European media. An anxious SAVAK counterattacked with an unsigned negative report of the gathering, written in exceptionally insulting language and published in the daily

Iranian newspaper *Keyhan*. We understood that it was actually written by SAVAK agents, but the general public did not realize that newspaper editors had no choice but to publish SAVAK's disinformation.

■ ■ ■

One day, Manouchehri came into the ward and told us, "They are going to transfer some *aghayan* [clergy] to this ward. I am sure you all are aware of their sensitivities about issues of *pak* and *najess*." These terms refer to certain religious principles of "cleanliness" and "filthiness." In Shi'ism, for instance, those who are considered as infidels or do not believe in God are najess— filthy, unclean, unholy. In the view of the mullahs, to be forced to live in the same ward with Marxists automatically causes najess; they would risk constant abhorrent contact just by walking on surfaces touched by the najess communists. To combat such najess, Islamists would have to thrust their arms into running water three times. This religious cleansing ritual, called paki, has no relationship to the scientific concept of infectious microbes. Manouchehri continued, "Try to make a comfortable environment for them. Stay separate as much as you can. Stick to your own private spaces."

We tried to reassure Manouchehri that we would treat the aghayan with respect. We told him, "We will use the entry corridor of the ward and let the aghayan have the second corridor, with three living spaces and three bathrooms completely separate from ours. We can make out a schedule to use the showers at different times."

A few days later the aghayan moved into our ward. All of them would become part of the government of the future Islamic Republic of Iran. None of us, including the SAVAKis, could have guessed that soon these aghayan would confiscate the power and wealth of our entire country and become a new ruling class. The mullahs who became our neighbors were Mahmoud Taleghani, Hossein Ali Montazeri, Hoshemi Rafsahnjani, Lahouti, Mahdavikani, Mehdi Karroubi, Anvari, Moadikhanh and a few other members of the future regime.

In 1975, the majority of Mojahedin exchanged their Islamic ideology for Marxism and lost the support of the mullahs. The clergy discussed the new dynamic among themselves and determined that they must clarify and refine its position in regard to Mojahedin and Marxists, both those who were imprisoned and those on the outside. They agreed on a set of principles—somewhere between twelve and nineteen, to the best of my recollection—to guide their relations with the Marxists. For example, only Muslims could become martyrs; no Marxist could aspire to that status. The mullahs' relationship with each group was sharply delineated while the Shah still held power. After the mullahs themselves came to power, they agreed among themselves that unity with the Marxists was not an option; indeed, this attitude extended to the process of overthrowing the Shah, although it was not announced outright. When the despot was overthrown, the mullahs saw their religious duty to be the extermination of any surviving revolutionaries in the ranks of the Marxists and the Nationalists.

SAVAK, through its informers, knew about these discussions and approached the mullahs to suggest that SAVAK could facilitate the fulfillment of any desire on their part to win over other prisoners by sending the aghayan into the wards of whatever prisons they wanted. SAVAK saw this strategy to help the clergy spread anti-Marxist propaganda as potentially very useful for its own purposes. The mullahs decided against splitting themselves among different prisons, preferring to stay together, especially the most influential among them. They sug-gested that SAVAK send specific prisoners to them for informational sessions. They gave SAVAK the names of the people they wanted. We witnessed these prisoners, representing different religious and political organizations, appearing in our ward for one to three weeks and conferring with the aghayan before SAVAK transferred them back to their own wards and prisons to spread the word.

Sometimes there were points of disagreement between some of the visitors and the mullahs. One long-time member of the Mojahedin, Ali Mohammad Tashayod, who had not become Marxist, told me some of what was going on. He stayed with the mullahs for a single week before leaving the ward in anger. Abbas Modaressifar, a member of another religious-political organization, the Islamic Nations, did not like what the mullahs had to say either. A third man, Ezat Shahi, a former member of the Mojahedin, accepted the mullahs' message. Like these three, many revolutionaries in Iran before, during, and after the revolution adhered to different principles, strategies, and beliefs, often modifying their positions several times to meet changing circumstances. Those who fight for a change of society do not necessarily agree on how it should be accomplished.

The first thing the mullahs did after moving in was to wash the floor in their area in order to have a *pak* corridor, that is, a religiously clean living space. Fortunately we did not have much of a problem with them, even though they were imprisoned side by side with us, because both of our groups did our utmost to avoid casual contact. Once in a while we would incidentally encounter each other in the corridor or in the courtyard. The only regularly shared common ground was the television room located on our side of the ward. It was used strictly for eating and watching television. Every night at eight o'clock we would watch the news together—the mullahs and their future victims. Some of the mullahs liked an animal program called *The Mystery of Survival*, for which they claimed a scientific interest when in fact they found the animals' strange behaviors amusing. The aghayan who was most interested in this show was Hossein Ali Montazeri. The program started at four o'clock in the afternoon, once a week, on Wednesday. Montazeri's habit was to venture to our side of the ward just before four o'clock and peer through the door to see if the program had started. Occasionally he would poke his head in a few minutes early and ask, with his distinctive Isfahani accent, "The critter program—is it on yet?" In Farsi, there are several generic words used to refer to animals. The word he chose—*jounevara*, the nearest English equivalent of which is "critters"—was childish and funny in a vulgar way. We would invite him in but he would invariably answer, "When the program starts, I will come." No need to expose himself to najess any longer than necessary, we assumed amusedly.

Montazeri was one of the nine prisoners scheduled to be interviewed by the Amnesty International lawyer. To prepare, he memorized what he thought was an appropriate English sentence from a textbook called *Direct Method*. When the lawyer interviewing him asked about torture, Montazeri replied, "Please don't ask about the past tense." We always wondered what Amnesty International made of that unwittingly cryptic comment.

■ ■ ■

Finally, the day came. A guard came into the ward to inform us that it was time for our interviews with the Amnesty lawyer. He distributed four sets of new prison clothes, pants with jackets, for the auspicious occasion. This was the first time since the interrogations that I had prison clothes. Political prisoners usually wore their own clothes; only criminal prisoners wore prison suits. I hesitated to put on the suit but the guard told me it was required.

He guided me to another building, which housed the prison barber shop. All of us had our hair trimmed and then donned our new suits. We joked and laughed at our changed appearance, but at the same time we worried about the interviews and their possible aftermath.

I recall being the first one called. A guard blindfolded me and led me out of the ward, into another building, and up a flight of stairs to the second floor. We then passed through two corridors before he stopped and removed my blindfold. I found myself in front of a closed door. The guard knocked. After a few seconds the door opened and Hossein Zahdeh came out, dressed in a black business suit and a black tie. There was a bitter expression on his face; in fact, he looked slightly ill. I wondered about his distressed appearance and later I heard that his mother had just died. He stood in the threshold looking at me for a few moments. Then, in a cold voice, he said, "I think we've talked to you enough and you know what you're going to say. I don't have anything else to tell you." Gesturing to the guard, he ordered, "Take him in."

The guard said, "Let's go," and we walked to a second door. When I stepped through the doorway, the guard left. I was in a conference room with a big oval table in the middle that was surrounded by ten or twelve chairs. In the room already were Manouchehri, who sat to my right, close to the door, and two other men seated next to him. A big Grundig reel-to-reel tape recorder had been placed at the head of the table.

As I entered, Manouchehri rose from his chair and approached me. I said hello and he shook my hand. He ushered me to a chair on the left side of the table, next to the tape recorder. "Please," he said, "you sit here."

I shook hands with the unknown men across the table before sitting down. I observed that I would not be alone with the Amnesty lawyer, contrary to what we had been told. Manouchehri said, "The lawyer will be right in. He went to the bathroom."

After a moment, someone else came in. He behaved as if he had already been in the room, nodding to the others rather than shaking hands. I was sure that he was not the lawyer. He was an Iranian, probably one of the SAVAK agents, but I had never seen him before.

I sat there confused and uneasy, not knowing what to say or do. In a few moments, a tall European-looking man entered the room and went straight to the chair at the head of the table, behind the tape recorder. After he sat down he looked at me, then turned to the other people, wordlessly asking them, "Who is this?"

One of the two men across the table from me, an older gentleman whose hair was completely white, introduced me to the lawyer in French, a language I had not yet learned. The lawyer stretched out his hand and introduced himself to me as Yvon Toussaint.

Almost simultaneously, somebody else rushed in and stood at the chair at the foot of the table, across from the lawyer. Before seating himself, this man stretched out his arm to shake my hand, even making a motion as if to hug me. He exclaimed, "Mr. Rahmaninejad! I am so glad to meet you!"

I was taken aback, completely baffled. Who the hell is this man, I wondered, greeting me like a son returned after twenty years in exile? Later I discovered that this person was none other than the political vice president of SAVAK, a general named Motazed.

Apparently this latest arrival completed the cast, because confidence in the meeting's efficacy radiated from all those assembled. This was as it should be, since the whole set was staged. Motazed was there, and Manoucheri was present, along with a mystery guest. Two SAVAK translators, one for English and one for French, sat poised to perform. Most notably, the lawyer and the victim had been introduced, so the curtain could go up and the farce commence.

First, Toussaint asked me to introduce myself for the tape recorder.

I started slowly, in an altogether comfortable tone of voice—name, profession—speaking in short phrases, and not so fast that the translator might miss something. My introduction was brief; I talked about the difficulties we had had in professional theater. I explained the system of censorship as harassment and discussed the play we had been rehearsing and how we were arrested before our work could be staged. I explained that the play would have already been censored when it was translated and published. I tried hard to describe in detail the structure and composition of the censorship committees, both the committee that oversaw publishing and the one for the theater. I noted that there were five members on the theater committee—a SAVAK agent, an agent of the Ministry of Information, a Police Intelligence agent, the director of the Theater Programs Administration, and a rotating member who was a stage director in the employ of the Theater Programs Administration.

At one point, the general, who was in plain clothes, jumped up from his chair, turned to Manouchehri, and said, "What did you tell me? You told me they were prepared!" Red-faced and shaking, he sank back into his chair.

For a moment everyone was silent. Then I turned toward the recorder and continued. When I paused, the lawyer asked me the taboo question: "During the investigation, how would you describe the conditions?"

Before answering, I turned to the French translator and said, "Please, tell him exactly what I am going to tell you." Then I said to the lawyer: "As you see, I am not prepared to describe the situation. We were told that we would be allowed to talk to you alone, person to person."

I don't know what the translator actually told the lawyer, but the lawyer looked at me and said, "Thank you very much." Then he turned off the tape recorder. Toussaint asked if he could take a picture of me, then had Manouchehri take a picture of the two of us together.

Later, back in the ward, everyone said that this fellow, Yvon Toussaint, got "pregnant by SAVAK." Yet Amnesty International and some academic institutions chose him for this highly sensitive mission.

■ ■ ■

The International Red Cross and Amnesty International had been pushing for unfettered access to Iranian prisons because of the multitude of rumors and charges of widespread use of torture. The support of Western governments for the Shah proved inadequate in checking public pressure from human rights groups demanding access to the prisons and their political inmates.

SAVAK initially thought that after they were forced to allow Amnesty International and Red Cross to make prison visits, they could just make some cosmetic improvements to gloss over glaring deficiencies in the penal system. Their efforts were markedly unsuccessful. One ploy was to gather some well-known, ostensibly influential prisoners for a meeting in Evin Prison to solicit their opinions about prison reforms. When I walked into that meeting, there were present a number of men I had known years before. Seeing them proved the only positive result of the proceedings, a febrile show scripted and directed by SAVAK. As usual, Manouchehri was the director, and he made a show of soliciting our opinions, directly asking each person to comment on every point. All of my comments were brief, because I felt distinctly uneasy about engaging in an obvious charade. Unfortunately, a few of my comrades believed it was a serious exercise, a genuine achievement or victory for our struggle. They thought that SAVAK had been greatly weakened and stood ready to grant us important concessions.

Among the issues brought up at the meeting was the lack of any kind of facilities for cooking or at least warming up our food. Everybody seemed to have an opinion about how we could address this problem. When it was my turn, Manouchehri asked me, "What is your opinion, Nasser?" Now we're all friends, I thought wryly, being addressed by our first names. But I am not buying this sales pitch.

"Mr. Manouchehri," I said, "you know better than any of us that this prison, especially *this* prison, was designed so that there is no possibility of cooking. There are no electrical outlets, and nowhere to put frying pans to warm up food. What do you want me to suggest, given this situation?"

This meeting, which was the first and last of its kind, accomplished nothing. SAVAK just went ahead and made the cosmetic changes they had already planned. In Evin, SAVAK brought in a few ping-pong balls and paddles; we already had the tables. Later on, one of the so-called revolutionary reforms was the quasi-installation of a basketball hoop on the courtyard wall. Drills and bolts were not used to install it, just nails, so as soon as they put it up it fell down. We all enjoyed a hearty laugh at this pathetic failure.

Gradually these "revolutionary changes" became a way to measure how close the nearest human rights organization was at a given moment. When the ping-pong balls and paddles were delivered, we joked, "Ah, this time it's the Red Cross delegation; they're just leaving the Hilton Hotel!" The Hilton was conveniently located about five minutes from Evin Prison. As we watched the guards rush to finish installing the basketball hoop, we laughed, "This time there are Amnesty delegates coming; they're just outside the prison gate!"

When a human rights delegation did visit Evin, chaos ensued. Although there were not a lot of us in our ward, there was much coming and going from room to room as we grouped ourselves in twos, threes, and fours to meet the human rights delegates. We used this opportunity to share what little news had been carried in by our families or other visitors. Because some families had two or three members in different prisons, information was easily passed from prison to prison. The regime's control over us was beginning to slip away.

The SAVAK agents were also visibly anxious, rushing in and out of the ward, showing themselves in an effort to intimidate us and to remind everyone of their continuing presence. They utilized different tactics with various groups, trying to shape the nature of the coming visit. The mullahs, for example, were invited to meet with SAVAK in what became a very long meeting. They had lunch together at noon, and the meeting was still going on at six o'clock in the evening. Manouchehri, Azodi, Tehrani, and General Motazed were among the officials present at the meeting. The next day, despite our best efforts, we failed to ferret out any details of the group's discussion.

During this time we perceived the development of two factions among the SAVAK agents. There was no longer good cop/bad cop fakery but an actual hawk/dove division. Azodi and Hossein Zahdeh were the hawks, and apparently Manouchehri and Tehrani were the doves. In his memoir, Ayatollah Montazeri mentions that Azodi "sometimes" came to the prison and met with the mullahs to discuss the differences between Mojahedin and Communists, especially after the majority of Mojahedin had declared themselves Marxist. Montazeri describes how Azodi suggested that the mullahs should explain their position to the other prisoners. He says that Azodi told them the prison authorities could set up a *manbar*, a high pulpit with steps leading up to it, to facilitate the mullahs' preachments to the prisoners about religion and politics. He states, "We understood that they wanted to take advantage of the divisions among the prisoners."

Montazeri's statement is so vague that the average reader would not be able to ascertain exactly where or when SAVAK made these suggestions. He writes simply that "a few times Azodi came to the prison and one time he even had lunch with us." Despite this deliberate vagueness in his writings, the truth is that after the Mojahedin converted to Marxism, the mullahs and their followers withdrew support from them and tried to turn the other prisoners, especially the religious prisoners, against the entire organization. They condemned the Mojahedin as "eclectic." The mullahs preached their views about clean and unclean, and about the impossibility of Marxists becoming martyrs, thus actively sowing discord among the prisoners. In any case, SAVAK and the mullahs, each with their own agenda, worked together to divide and conquer the prisoners.

After SAVAK proposed different options to the mullahs, such as sending them to different prisons to preach their anti-leftist position, the mullahs convinced SAVAK to send them all to Evin—seven initially, later more. Although the lower floor was vacant, SAVAK deliberately housed them on the upper floor with us. Montazeri omits several important facts in this part of his memoir, and there are many other omissions elsewhere in his account. In some ways I respect Montazeri, at least in comparison to most of the other mullahs, but his memoir is unreliable when the standard of measurement is the whole truth and nothing but the truth.

First the pending visits of the human rights groups and later their actual meetings with prisoners severely altered the dynamic in Evin Prison. One especially telling instance of restraint on the part of SAVAK is the following: Manouchehri and Tehrani were in the ward when Manoucheri stopped Said and complained about his behavior. Said defended himself and Manoucheri fell silent and left the ward. No repercussions followed.

On another occasion, small groups of prisoners were talking to various human rights delegations in different rooms. At one point I saw Hadi Jafroudi, the leader of one of the pro-China groups, coming out of one of the rooms, and I asked him, "How was your meeting with the Amnesty people?" We walked together to the first room in the ward and sat down against the wall to talk. Suddenly Azodi appeared in the doorway and looked down at us. "What are you talking about?" he asked, stretching out both arms until his palms touched the doorframe.

I answered, "Hot weather. We're talking about the hot weather."

Azodi paused for a moment, then looked at each of us in turn. "Don't imagine that the situation will stay the same. We can change it at any moment." Then he walked off.

I myself participated in three interviews with Red Cross people. One interview dealt specifically with conditions in the prison, the other two addressed my health. The Red Cross had received reports about my heart problems. I do not know in detail what background they had been given about me, but I learned part of the story from them. They indicated that they had already tried to get me out of prison to undergo heart surgery somewhere in Europe, but SAVAK had told them that if their concern was my heart condition, it could be dealt with in Iran. "We have the best operating rooms, the best hospital, and the best surgeon right here in Tehran. You can inspect the hospital that we will send him to. You can go there, examine the equipment, talk to the surgeon, and judge for yourself. If you determine that everything is in order, we will send him to the hospital under your supervision and he can have his surgery."

My personal doctor had told me that there was a congenital connection between my heart's two chambers, so that oxygenated and deoxygenated blood were intermixing. Later, when I escaped to Europe, a new diagnosis revealed a constriction of the pulmonary valve in addition to the congenital fault already diagnosed. Eventually, when exploratory surgery was done, the only problem the doctors discovered was constriction of the crucial valve.

Two Red Cross doctors visited my ward one day and talked to me about my health needs. They believed I could have the surgery in Iran. They assured me that they had checked the equipment and had talked to the surgeon, who had studied in the United States. He had a good reputation. "We recommend that you accept the surgery."

I was not readily convinced. Obviously I found it difficult to trust SAVAK. I tried to explain my justifiable distrust. I did not believe that SAVAK would actually take the risk of letting me have open heart surgery, because if I accidentally died, nobody would believe that their agents had not murdered me. A few days later the Red Cross doctors visited again and said, "We talked to the government people"—they would not name SAVAK specifically. "We suggest that you come with us to the hospital and see the surgeon, talk to him yourself. If you feel comfortable with the situation, we will proceed from there."

I agreed to do it because I thought I had nothing to lose by merely meeting with the surgeon.

As they left me, one said, "We will let you know what day you are going to the hospital."

A few days later a guard appeared and told me to dress in my civilian clothes. He blindfolded me and guided me to the prison administration building, where Manouchehri's office was located. I was put in a military van with two guards armed with rifles. We drove off in a caravan—one car full of SAVAK agents preceded our van, and two Red Cross doctors followed us in a Mercedes. Behind the doctors there was another car full of armed SAVAK agents.

The hospital was on Takht-e Jamshid Avenue, close to the U.S. embassy. We drove through a private gate into an empty courtyard. It was afternoon on a hot summer day and I was sweating profusely. One of the doctors got out of the Mercedes and instructed me, "Stay here in the van. We will let the surgeon know we have arrived, then we will come back to escort you inside."

The doctors entered the building while I sat in the van, closely watched by the guards. About fifteen minutes passed before one of the doctors came out of the building and stood outside the van, and knocked on the window. One of the guards slid open the door and the doctor announced, "The surgeon is not here yet; we'll have to wait awhile." He did not sound at all hopeful. He went back into the building.

Half an hour later, both Red Cross doctors came back out of the building. They approached the van and one of them explained, "I think there is a misunderstanding. They told us the doctor is not here today, so we have to leave and see if we can arrange another appointment for later."

I could barely understand them as they were speaking in English, but I got the gist of their words and replied, "I told you before, I am not optimistic. I don't think they will actually give me heart surgery here." I never saw the Red Cross doctors again, and the SAVAKis never mentioned the issue again.

Ahmad, one of my original co-defendants, was active in translating the complaints of the prisoners from Farsi into English in the meetings with the Red Cross and Amnesty people. He translated all statements about torture passionately and with impressive conviction. He undertook this risky business although he had never been directly involved in any political activities. He had only done theater with us. I suspect he had been sentenced to four years just for helping our theater group financially. Ahmad was under constant pressure while in prison to write a letter asking for pardon. He was repeatedly told that if he did that he would be released immediately, but his strong sense of morality and convictions precluded this easy avenue to freedom. He remained with us until the prison doors were opened by the people's movement in 1979.

■ ■ ■

After the Amnesty and Red Cross people finished their interviews, everything gradually lapsed into the old routine, with the major exception that SAVAK did not submit us to the harsh torture they had put us through before—mostly, I believe, because outside the prison walls the anti-Shah movement was gaining strength and they feared future reprisals. Our theater group had been arrested in 1974 and all of us had been tortured and beaten. Even those prisoners who received shorter sentences were not released after serving their time, because SAVAK did not want them returning to a society where they would undoubtedly support the movement against the Shah. Actually, just before Amnesty intervened, torture had already become less frequent. Previously they had beaten everyone who was arrested, even for having a pamphlet, a book, or a petition, or for suspicious behavior—all these actions were classified as involvement in an armed insurgency; basically everyone was beaten. However, a few months before the human rights delegates appeared in 1977, SAVAK had cleaned up its act significantly. After everyone's bruises had faded and the ping-pong balls were provided, they allowed Amnesty and Red Cross into the prisons.

By 1977, the issue of political prisoners was becoming an Achilles' heel for the regime as the people's movement was publicizing our situation both within and outside the country. As the movement grew stronger, families of prisoners spoke more openly during visiting hours. They would shout, "Don't worry! You're coming out soon! Everything is finished!" Prison authorities exerted less stringent control, concentrating on the basics—keeping the doors locked and feeding us on schedule—in a pretense of normality.

Outside of prison, however, the government maintained a harsh front as both secular protesters and Islamist groups increased their activities. For instance, in September 1978, after they had transferred me back to Qasr prison, the Shah's military forces, on what came to be called Black Friday, enforced martial law and killed many people primarily from the middle and lower middle classes, both secular and religious, who had assembled peaceably in Jaleh Square in southeastern Tehran. Wild rumors circulated about what had happened, such as "Israeli soldiers shot people in the square." They originated among the Islamists, who hoped to strengthen the movement by fomenting their own anti-Israeli sentiment, an effort that incidentally provided some cover for the crimes committed by the Shah's regime.

Over time, the Islamists aggressively stepped up their confrontation with the government, sometimes openly, sometimes in ways that were morally questionable or downright treacherous. In August 1978, Islamists burned down a movie theater, the Cinema Rex, in the city of Abadan in the south of Iran, killing about 400 people and blaming the government, hoping to intensify the people's hatred of the Shah's regime. During an investigation after the revolution, the Islamists attempted to conceal their arson by scapegoating an innocent man.

These outside events made my situation in Evin more and more uncomfortable, because I felt increasingly isolated and immobilized. Evin housed fewer political prisoners than Qasr, where we had shared what our visitors told us about political activities. At Evin, our ward held at least a hundred political prisoners downstairs, transferred there after our arrival. The few of us housed upstairs were separated from this group, though the doors of upstairs and downstairs were open and prisoners could communicate to each other. We had no opportunities to organize and discuss things over shared meals, no chances to debate issues or to bond politically and socially into a group with solidarity. We did occasionally encounter downstairs prisoners in the courtyard, where we could talk to them a little, but we were not living among them, and they viewed us as "special prisoners" endowed with privileges—more living space and greater access to books, newspapers, and the like. It was not that we were under suspicion—they knew us—but still, we were not seen as being one of them, as had been the case at Qasr. As a result, I started planning to get myself transferred back to Qasr.

My first step was to write a letter to the prison authorities explaining that since I had originally been transferred to Evin expressly to see the Amnesty lawyer, now that the interviews were completed there was no reason to keep me in Evin. I received no reply, and after nearly a month had passed I wrote a second letter, insisting that my request should be addressed and mentioning that if I did not get an answer within two weeks I would refuse to come to the visitors' rooms to see my family. Two weeks passed and there was still no answer. When they called me to the next family visit, I told the guard, "Tell your boss that I have already written to inform them that I will not visit my family until I am returned to Qasr prison."

About half an hour later the guard came back and said, "They say they are going to return you to Qasr soon, but please come and visit your mother. Your mother is worried about you."

I replied, "Tell them I will visit my mother in Qasr. Until I am transferred there, I am not going to visit my family."

Thirty minutes went by and one of the old prison guards, Anousheh, came and implored me, "Young man! Go and visit your mother! She is very worried! I promise you, next week you will be in Qasr."

I replied, "Please let me keep my principles! I am not going to visit my mother. You can do me a favor if you will explain to her that I am fine but that I will not visit her until they transfer me to Qasr. But please do tell her I am fine."

Anousheh left and the next week I was sent back to Qasr. One can readily perceive how frightened and weakened the regime was by this time. A year earlier I would have been placed in solitary, beaten, tortured, and likely exiled in some backwater of a prison, far from my family.

When I returned to Qasr Prison it was like passing through a storm. The prison atmosphere was noticeably calmer, because all of the Red Cross and Amnesty International delegations had departed after completing their missions. Some prisoners had been transferred to other penal institutions in the provinces as punishment for revealing too much to the human rights delegates, but those prisoners who remained were fervently discussing the current political events so crucial to Iran's future.

All of the news reports reflected the spread of criticism of the government to every stratum of society. Here and there, workers put forth demands, staging short demonstrations at their factories. Students and intellectuals were demonstrating and signing petitions to confront the government directly. The Iranian Writers Association insisted on an end to censorship, calling for complete freedom of expression. We were especially heartened by the demands for the release of political prisoners put forth by most of the progressive organizations. The lawyers of the Iranian Bar Association were demanding the revision of parliamentary bills passed over the course of twenty-five years of the Shah's regime that had abrogated legal rights. For the first time, a Bar Association petition specifically mentioned the abolition of torture as a needed reform.

The government counterattacked. When speaking to the press, the Shah, the prime minister, and Farrah, the Shah's wife, would use the opportunity to make statements calling for reason, such as, "We respect the rights of the people. Iranian people have the freedom to criticize the government. This is the way it should be." They would go on to say, "Good criticism, logical criticism, constructive criticism we accept. We are not against criticism, but make it constructive!"

In one of his speeches, the prime minister talked about freedom of expression for writers. He knew very well that there was no such freedom, but he wanted to send a message to the Iranian Writers Association: "You have freedom, but this is not the time to criticize the government." Of course the Writers Association knew his treacherous ways well, because he had tried to buy them off or neutralize them with veiled threats before. Once he offered to send a very influential writer to attend literary events outside the country, all expenses paid. The writer declined the offer, refusing to be bought. Another time the prime minister offered some writers embassy positions in Third World countries such as India or Pakistan, but no one fell for this transparent ruse. Also, as a sign of the government's "liberalism," one of the leaders of the Shah's single legally-allowed political party, Rastakhiz, made an announcement to the effect that whoever chose not to be a member of the party would receive a passport and could leave the country.

The opposition groups viewed all these moves with the disdain they deserved. It could be argued that the regime's belated and clumsy attempts to pose as an enlightened government served only to anger the opposition, which felt insulted and, sensing weakness, redoubled their efforts to overthrow the Shah. One of the early high points of the anti-Shah movement was ten nights of poetry organized by the Iranian Writers Association at the Goethe Institute in Tehran. For the first time ever, thousands of people gathered every night to hear Iranian poets recite their work. The event was held outside during the summer of 1977, and people stood in the garden and all around the building listening. I had just been moved to Qasr when my sister and mother told me about this event.

SAVAK was openly monitoring such events. After the poetry readings, SAVAK agents showed up at a writers' gathering at the Aryamehr University of Technology. *Aryamehr* translates as "Aryan love" and was one of the Shah's honorifics. This man whose commands had led to obscene tortures applied without compunction or mercy wanted to be commemorated as Aryan Love. Unfortunately, Iranian history includes many such examples of megalomania. SAVAK raided the poetry readings at the Aryarmehr University, indiscriminately beating writers and members of the audience alike, wholly unaware of the irony in this demonstration of Aryan love.

Despite these acts of suppression, the opposition's progress moved inexorably forward. Each event triggered another as the cruel countermeasures by the government only elicited fiercer outrage. The Shah had no coherent policy for addressing the problems of Iranian society. The nature of the system did not allow for the formulation of logical policies to make the necessary changes. The tools the regime knew best were force and violence. The mass killings on Black Friday are a case in point. The Shah's policy of force, intended to break the revolutionary thrust for reform, instead led to a nationwide explosion of defiance.

Even in retrospect, it is not clear to me why the government picked the Jaleh Square protest to stage an especially brutal attack. It was probably the only protest ever to take place in that square, which was located in a neighborhood of middle- and lower-middle-class people with a strong religious bent. The protest may have been organized by the Islamists, but that certainly was not clear at the time. Most people in Iran were not yet dividing themselves into religious and secular factions. The people filling the square comprised a cross section of society, indistinguishable from other neighborhoods, villages, and cities. Later, one could identify separate slogans advanced in demonstrations and women showing up in hijab, whereas at the time of Black Friday, this did not yet happen.

The leftist forces in Iran were still in a nascent stage at that time, and if they had seen the different elements in Iranian society objectively, as well as the diversity that characterized the movement, they might have perceived where the movement was heading. I am not sure if a more organized leftist group could have guided the general populace in a truly radical direction. At most they might have shaped a moderate nationalist course, or at least a secular one. A fully realized leftist organization possibly could have bolstered the government of Shapour Bakhtiar, the placeholding interim prime minister, before the followers of Khomeini successfully consolidated their hegemony in the revolutionary movement. The religious leaders saw that if they pushed ahead aggressively, they could realize their dream of an Islamic government. Perhaps they had contact with Western governmental delegations. They definitely knew that Western support against the left was available for the asking, while the naive leftists and Mojahedin were in the streets protesting Bakhtiar, an action that served only the group with the most sophisticated organization, the Islamists.

Meanwhile, in Qasr prison the emphasis of political discussion was on trying to forge agreements between groups that would overcome their ideological differences. At one point we decided to send out a solidarity petition condemning the cruelties that our government was perpetuating against Iranian citizens. Writing it required several days of discussion, as did deciding which institutions and organizations could best channel our manifesto to the general public.

All efforts to achieve common goals and strategy ultimately proved futile. The most extreme among the religious prisoners were the first to separate themselves from the others. Gradually this mood of separatism spread to the other groups, as events in the movement on the outside transpired. The Islamists could sense their version of victory becoming dominant. For years the religious prisoners had attracted little notice; now they became vitally active, well organized, and aggressively outspoken. They would tell the others, "We're going to do things our way, and if you want to be with us, you should follow us." They wanted to start the petition with the names of Allah and Khomeini, and they wanted to distribute it through existing religious organizations. They thought the petition should be seen as coming from them. Even after Black Friday—17 Shahrivar, or September 8, as we called the killings in Jaleh Square—when we wanted to stage a hunger strike to show our support for the victims and our opposition to the government, the religious prisoners refused to participate alongside the leftists, insisting on holding a separate protest at a different time.

12

POLITICS AND THEATER
DURING THE TIME OF
REVOLUTION

Despite continued acts of repression, it was clear that the government no longer wielded complete control of the people. Even the application of martial law failed to prevent the opposition from employing various subterfuges to break curfew. The most common method involved simply going to their rooftops at night and shouting *Allah-o Akbar!* (God is great!) very loudly. After a few nights, people all over Tehran were shouting from their rooftops and were not fazed even by soldiers shooting at them from the streets. People were possibly copying the Algerians, who had used the same tactic against the French during their anti-colonial struggle.

Attempts to placate the populace instead of using violence proved no more effective. The government put some corrupt high officials in prison. The Shah even removed Prime Minister Amirabbas Hoveyda from office. He had been in power for thirteen years, so his removal was a significant concession, but the revolutionary forces were not satisfied, correctly labeling it as a token gesture. Although the issue of releasing political prisoners was raised time and again, the Shah refused, because he believed that all political prisoners were criminals and traitors. However, pressure continued to mount, and finally the Shah felt compelled to bend, grudgingly agreeing to release all political prisoners.

First the government tried to deceive the people by releasing two or three groups of a few hundred each. This move obviously did not fool any of us who were still incarcerated. We knew that those who had been freed initially posed no threat to the status quo. They accepted the traditional SAVAK conditions for releasing selected prisoners—signed confessions, sworn commitments to avoid further political activities, and promises to report anyone from the movement who tried to contact them. They were also required to write a letter addressed to the Shah, "the Father of the Nation," asking for pardon. Activists protesting the regime met these half measures with demands for a blanket release of all political prisoners.

Late one night toward the end of 1978, I was released from Qasr Prison. All during the day, announcements had been made that prisoners from different groups were to be released. Our routine of prison life had crumbled and our mood was complicated and confused. Although we knew the government had no choice but to free us, when the names were being called over the loudspeakers, we did not know whether they would release all of us or just a few. But as the list lengthened, a growing wave of excitement moved throughout the prison, and the regulations that had governed us for so long faded away, replaced by the intoxicating reality of getting out.

One of the clearest images remaining in my mind from that day was the preparation of Safar Khan for release. Safar Khan was one of the longest-serving prisoners in the country; he had spent 29 or 30 years in prison. When a voice announced from the speakers, "The prisoners whose names we are calling—get ready to leave," and the first and second groups were called, we all wondered, "Who's next?" And almost all of us were confident that Safar Khan's name would be called.

Safar Khan was trying to be calm, but you could see that he was really anxious. I was with him on the balcony of ward six as the second group left. He said, "They are not going to call me. I know that."

I could understand his pessimism, because different prison officials had asked on several occasions that his case be sent to the parole committee, but the committee had always refused to release him. When his name finally came over the loudspeaker, the whole prison burst into cheers. Many of us were close to Safar Khan. From all parts of the prison, inmates rushed to find him, to help him prepare for his release. While he strove for calmness, fellow prisoners pushed him toward his room, where everyone seemed to be shouting, "Where is your suit? Where are your shoes? Where is your bag?" I stood and watched the scene, silently rejoicing for Safar Khan, a man I respected with heart and mind.

Salamat Ranjbar was among those helping Safar Khan get dressed. Very excited himself, he was teasing him, joking to keep him calm. It was like ritually dressing a saint for a special religious procession. Once he was suitably attired, Safar Khan walked out into the corridor and made his farewells to all the prisoners, one by one, throughout our three connected wards. The prison authorities agreed to let him go to the other five wards as well to say his goodbyes there.

I was part of the next group to depart after him. I had nothing to take except the clothes I was wearing, but that in no way diminished my elation as I left Qasr behind.

When the paperwork for our group of about forty prisoners was completed, it was about midnight. A large bus carried us to Fozieh Square, one of the principal squares in Tehran and located on the east side. Nasser Kakhsaz and I disembarked together. I knew he needed help getting home because prolonged torture eight years earlier had left him with a damaged brain. I assured him, "I'll come with you; I will deliver you into your wife's hands. Then I'll go home from there."

We hailed a taxi and Nasser gave the driver his address. His wife did not expect him at that time of night, so when she opened the door she cried out in shock. She did not know me, so I simply said, "Here is your Nasser. I'll see you later."

Leaving the reunited couple, I walked down the street until I came to a main thoroughfare and headed toward home, looking for a passing taxi. Eventually I got one, and five minutes later I was standing in front of my family's house.

My mother was the one, as always, who opened the door. It was as if she had been waiting for me behind that door for years and years. Her face beamed with happiness as she hugged me and I embraced her. The lights in the other rooms came on as everyone awakened, gathered in one room, and questioned me about how it had come about that I had been released—and at such a peculiar hour.

I explained that the government had carefully planned to release prisoners in such a way that people would not have the chance to welcome them publicly, because that would have handed the movement a visible victory. Nonetheless, the day after I was released, the rest of the prisoners from Qasr, as well as those from Evin, did have the chance to be welcomed and hugged by their families and friends openly in broad daylight. As the news of our release circulated, the families of unreleased prisoners joined members of the movement in flocking toward the prisons. I would have loved to be with them; however, beginning on my first morning at home, people from the neighborhood, businesses, and shops, as well as friends and family members, formed a steady stream of well-wishers. I enjoyed the welcome home, but I could not go anywhere. In the entire city—indeed, over the whole country—celebrating citizens filled the streets. Still, I got most of the current news from my visitors. We discussed events and speculated among ourselves that the old regime was collapsing; nothing, we thought, could save the old order.

This is not to suggest a unanimity of thinking. Voices grew loud and discussions were heated. Many people were firm believers in Islam and accepted the leadership and authority of Khomeini in the revolutionary struggle, while intellectuals, mostly friends of mine who were leftists, naturally did not want an Islamic government. Yet despite strongly felt convictions, discussion was always friendly and respectful. I recall one discussion about Khomeini and his vision of an Islamic government. The owner of one of the small shops—a repair shop for oil heaters, small oil stoves, lamps, and the like—was a moderate Muslim, not a religious fanatic, but his wife was a strict Muslim. He and I had a lengthy discussion about Khomeini's personality and beliefs, freely expressing our opinions to each other without rancor.

■ ■ ■

The power and magnetism of events in the streets would not tolerate indifference. Some things were also happening behind the scenes; for instance, the mullahs and other religious figures were plotting with some foreign characters, such as General Huyser from the United States, who were there trying to broker a deal between some of the new forces and elements of the old government. The idea was that if the United States could not maintain the Shah, which they knew they could not, they definitely preferred Khomeini over the left.

After a week, I felt an overpowering urge to make physical contact with the activity in the streets. The heart of the movement, not the heart of the plot, against the Shah's regime was in and around the University of Tehran. People from a variety of leftist political organizations and from Islamic groups and mosques mixed with individuals and groups who had come from other cities. All around the university, as well as on the campus itself, small groups of people gathered, sometimes shouting and interrupting one another in their eagerness to express their ideas. A few people, especially devout Muslims, tried to steer the discussions toward the issues they felt were most urgent. They might say, "OK, let's discuss that issue after the Shah has fallen," or "Let's discuss this issue after Bakhtiar is out," or "Let's discuss this issue after the Imam comes." (Khomeini was in France and did not return for another few weeks.)

Among the throngs of people were many ordinary citizens who, for the first time in Iranian history, crossed the barrier between themselves and the university, an institution previously foreign to them. Most could not have imagined that one day they would pass through the gates of the university, express their opinions, and mingle with faculty and students. During previous periods of social unrest, guards had always been posted at the gates of the campus, barring anyone not connected to the university from entering.

Across the street from the university was a row of bookstores, on the sidewalk in front of which various political groups set up tables stacked with political tracts. Revolutionary music filled the air. One could listen to the songs of the murdered Chilean leftist Victor Jara and the American singer Joan Baez, but the unmistakable strains of the revolutionary anthem "The Internationale" dominated. Books with white covers—banned Marxist books with no publisher's name and no cover design—were much in evidence. Books of poetry, novels, anything previously banned was now available—and cheap!

At all the universities in Tehran it was the same: people were discussing or lecturing about the imminent revolution. Former political prisoners, including me, were invited to speak by committees of academicians who shared our fervor for regime change. My future wife, Havva, who was teaching at Iran National University, played a role in these activities and would be kicked off the campus the following year for her involvement.

■ ■ ■

Here I want to flash back to tell an intimate and personal story. As I said before, in the summer of 1974 my theater group had rented a four-story building and had started rehearsals of Maxim Gorkiy's *The Petty Bourgeois,* intending to put it on stage in Tehran after a five-night run in Rasht in northern Iran. Some of the cast members had left and some other friends were replacing them. Mohsen Yalfani was one of those friends. He had decided to come back and work with us after having left the group about two years before when he and Said had had a fight over Brecht's play *The Visions of Simone Machard.* That had been one of the group's rare conflicts, created by Said, because he had not wanted Mohsen to take over as director of the play while he himself was detained by SAVAK. Mohsen had continued rehearsals because nobody knew if Said was going to be released soon, and the group needed to have the play ready for the stage on time. Ahmad Houshmand was another friend who had worked on

The Visions of Simone Machard, and I invited him to come back too and work with us. There were others as well who completed the cast.

We had all agreed to commit ourselves to giving whatever amount of money we could for our monthly rent and expenses. At the same time, we had extended the group's activities and organized a summer acting class in order to train our own ensemble as well as others who were interested in joining the group.

One of the students in our first acting class was Ahmad's sister, Havva. She did not want to join the group; she was only interested in acquiring some skill and knowledge about theater, acting, and play reading to use in the classes she taught at the National University of Iran. She also wanted to participate in rehearsals.

One day a few months into the class, after our rehearsal, Ahmad asked if he could talk to me for a minute. He told me that his sister was interested in seeing me more, that she wanted to know me better. That was a very clear message. He clearly was shy about telling me this, but at the same time he smiled and continued, "I don't know what that means but you will find it out yourself."

About two months earlier I had been asked by Havva, through Ahmad, to help her edit a Farsi text that she was translating from English. The text was her own writing for a speech at the university. It must be said that because Havva had studied in the United States and the Netherlands, she was not confident enough of her Farsi, so she felt she needed a little help. She invited me to her home and we worked together for three to four hours on the text. She was living with her three-year-old son, Nicholas, or Nicky, a very sweet and handsome boy with whom I enjoyed playing a lot. Havva's husband was a skillful British painter and graphic designer who was working for a multinational advertising company in Iran; at the time they were separated.

A week after Ahmad told me about Havva's interest in knowing me better, Ahmad, Havva, and I and two other friends went to a restaurant for dinner after rehearsal. When we left the restaurant, Havva and I walked behind the others and talked about the theater, the Gorky play I was working on, and so on. That first intimate encounter left a very good feeling about Havva in me. I found her to be an intelligent and kind woman. That night I went to bed in a beautiful, warm, colorful mood, with the pleasant voice of Havva murmuring in my ears. After that night, my feelings about Havva were changed. Whenever I would see her, or be reminded of her, a wave of warmth rushed through my whole body and made me happy, and at the same time anxious about something unknown. In the acting class I could not work with her comfortably, and when I would touch her, especially when I wanted to check her breathing, although I was trained well to manage myself and not to be base, that warmth rushed through my body. The most important and trustworthy element in my feelings was innocence. That was something I could lean on and be sure that it did not betray me.

Soon we planned to go hiking together on weekends. The first time we went was early on a Friday morning, when it was still dark. After thirty or forty-five minutes, we stopped for a short break, and in such a natural way we were both drawn to each other, first holding hands and then hugging. I don't know how long we stayed motionless, but it seemed that for the first time I could feel the scent and the taste of love in my life. I should admit that I had never ever had the pure enjoyment of love in my life before Havva. Let me say this now, while I am open, without calculating anything: I should confess that until then, at the age of thirty-six, I did not know how to make love, and it was Havva who taught me this natural but delicate and complicated intimacy.

But the days of my happiness were soon cut short. After a few short months of being together, and before having had the chance of living together, I was arrested with all the members of our theater group and some friends and members of our families.

I would wait for four years, until the revolution, until after the political prisoners were released, to come back and connect my last precious moments with Havva to the rest of my life. Soon after I returned we decided to move in together and live with each other.

Havva's home was now one station north of Gholhak, an old suburb in the north of Tehran, behind the fifty-acre British summer residence on Old Shemiran Road. She was still working at the National University of Iran but in a completely different situation, and her son, Nicky, now four years older, was going to the British School, just a few minutes away from their home. In the new Iran, everything was changing rapidly, and a mood of hostility and aggressiveness could be felt. There was a woman who worked for Havva two to three days a week, one of the millions of ordinary traditional Muslim Iranian women who deeply believed in Islam and in Khomeini. Two of her sons were among the youth who were attracted to mosques and the new Komiteh (the same word used for the infamous interrogation center, but now meaning newly set-up neighborhood committees that enforced Islamic law) and other Islamist paramilitary governmental organizations. There they felt, perhaps for the first time in a patriarchal society, that they were somebody, carrying guns and having the power to stop people, and to question, push, shout at, attack, arrest, and even kill them, and nobody would dare say a word.

The woman gradually became curious about me, because I was new to her. She probably saw me as an intruder, or as somebody coming into the space where she had been working for two or three years with no man around. Now, suddenly, there was a man in the house who seemed prepared to drop anchor there forever. Nobody knows who he is, where he comes from, what exactly his place is in this house, and what his relationship is with her lady, Havva. The man simply comes into the house one day and lives with the other members of the family, exactly like them, and it seems he is too close to her lady, with no clear explanation.

She probably guessed that I might be one of the convicts who had gotten out of prison in the middle of the chaotic revolution, and most probably I was a communist, because there was no sign of Islamic beliefs in me, or in the house. So everything confirmed her suspicion about the situation. Finally, the poor woman unskillfully asked Havva a few questions about me, and the answers revealed her worries about how Havva and I were living together—an un-Islamic way of living together: unlawful, unmarried.

At the time, there were signs and events everywhere in Iran that openly showed the lack of tolerance among ordinary people for any so-called un-Islamic behavior. The questions the woman asked, her relations with the neighborhood mosque, and the role of her two sons in the Komiteh were all signs of concern to Havva and me. After we talked about the matter, we decided to go to the office of the notary public and get married.

On the afternoon of April 14, 1979, Havva and I walked to the notary public office, just a few minutes from our home, carrying our birth certificates, to officially marry, despite our misgivings. When we had entered the office and explained our request, the clerk offered us seats and said that Mr. Such-and-Such would help us after finishing with other work. The man to whom the clerk referred was the head of the office. He was sitting behind a very large table in the middle of the main hall with a very large notary ledger in front of him, the kind that is specifically used in those offices, and he was writing something in the book that I thought would be difficult to read later because of the style of his handwriting.

As we sat there waiting, suddenly a man entered the office whom I realized I knew. He was Bahman Rezakhani, one of the political prisoners with whom I had shared the same ward for a while under the Shah's regime. He was a very funny and sincere man, a religious nationalist (a term that was not used at the time) from a group called JAMA, who had a very mature and friendly relationship with the Marxist prisoners. In discussing any issue with him, even sensitive issues like Islam, one would not have to worry. When our gazes met, his eyes shone, a big smile crossed his face, and he enthusiastically made a commotion and came toward me. We hugged and kissed each other, and after a few words about our new lives, I asked him what he was doing there. He said, "I have a very complicated task. I am trying to find all the notary public offices that have registered court properties and estate transactions. This office is one of them, and I come here every afternoon to document the transactions." He asked me why I was there. I told him the reason, and he began to call people over to congratulate me, because he felt that I was a celebrity and the fact that I had come to register my marriage was an honor for the office. In a few seconds, everything in the office changed. Bahman went to the big desk and jokingly closed the big notary book, lifted it up, and in a friendly way took the arm of the man, pulled him up, and said, "You can do that later, but this job is very important now. Let us celebrate the marriage of our very important artist, who deserves some joy after those years in the prison. Get up, please. Let us celebrate!"

It was like a play by Chekhov to me. All the clerks of the office left their work unfinished and cleaned off the desk that was in the middle of the hall. Everybody was getting ready for something, but I couldn't figure out what. Bahman suddenly disappeared without me noticing where he went. People in the office asked me questions about my profession, why I had been imprisoned, what I had done, if I had been tortured, and so on. They brought tea for us, and the notary office turned into a friendly gathering. They covered the big desk with a tablecloth, and I could see that a serious event was about to happen there. After a few minutes, Bahman came back with two big boxes of pastries and put them on the big desk, which was now set with small plates and cups. He opened the boxes and told the head of the office, "You can start now." The head asked one of the clerks to bring the marriage contract book, then he sat at the top of the desk, as he was sitting before, and asked us to give him our birth certificates. All the while Bahman was making little jokes and laughing and generally trying to make the situation more relaxed, because when the book was placed in front of the head of the office, everybody fell silent and the mood seemed tense.

When all the usual phrases and formal terms of the contract had been entered into the book, the head got to the point where he needed to ask us about some of the traditional elements in the marriage contract. When he asked about the dowry, I said an eight-volume set of the *Shahnameh*. Bahman suddenly jumped and said, "No, no, no. This is not agreeable. Haj Agha"—the head of the office—"don't accept it. With this, officially your marriage is not legitimate." I tried to convince Bahman that this was a deal between Havva and I and that we had already agreed on it. But Bahman jumped up and down and said, "No, no, no! Your marriage is not legitimate and your wedlock is *haram* [forbidden]." He then turned to Haj Agha and said, "Haj Agha, please write down a volume of *Quran-e Kareem.*"

Havva was standing there next to me with a big smile, though perplexed by the whole scene. I tried again to get Bahman to listen to me: "Bahman, listen. Listen, please—" But he interrupted me and said, "Swear to God, Nasser, if I let it happen." All of this was done in such a friendly and funny way that you could not take him seriously—but it was very serious. Finally, Havva told me, "Nasser, let it be. It's fine with me, if you agree." I looked at her for a few seconds, then said, "OK, that's fine. This is just because of you." Bahman was waiting to hear what I would say, and when I spoke as I did he suddenly shouted, "Congratulations! Haj Agha, write it down. It's done. It's finished. Congratulations, Havva Khanom! Congratulations, Nasser! I hope you grow old together."

We had not given any thought to the witnesses. We needed two to be present and to sign the register. The problem was solved very easily. Bahman and one of the clerks signed the book as our witnesses. After everything was done, tea was brought and we had a very good time with all the people of the office, and especially with Bahman. The last thing Bahman did was pay the fee for the marriage. When I asked the head of the office about it, Bahman came to me and said, "This is not your business. You just go. Haj Agha did this as an honor, and we all are happy that we could participate in your marriage." I was going to say something but Bahman did not let me get a word out and said, "The only thing you can do now is hold your wife's hand and go home. And invite us if you have a celebration."

"I am sorry," I said, "I don't think we're going to have a celebration, but a small dinner party with some friends, perhaps."

The head of the office extended his hand, and while he was holding and shaking mine he said, "I am so happy to know you, and I wish you both good luck." He did the same with Havva, and they escorted us to the door. We left the office with our identity paper, within which our marriage was registered.

The street and shop lights outside were already on, and everything was shining.

Havva means Eve in Farsi. I sometimes would jokingly say to friends that I became *Adam,* which means "human" in Farsi. For me this saying was a hint of my great appreciation to be living with Havva.

■ ■ ■

One of the issues under discussion at the time was the fear of a military coup backed by the United States. The mullahs, especially Khomeini, used this fear to unite people behind his movement. He was still in Paris, but from there he issued warnings: "Be careful! They are going to betray you!" He also warned the military authorities, "Don't do anything against Islam! The Shah's regime is not a legitimate regime. Join the revolutionary people and help them finish the job!"

During a presentation I was invited to give at the Aryamehr University of Technology, soon to be renamed the Sharif University of Technology, I warned the audiences, "When a situation is very sensitive, shaky, we all have to be alert." I was primarily worried about a military coup, because I was unaware of the dangerous extent of the mullahs' power. I was not alone in my ignorance or underestimation of Islamic fervor and dedication to power.

In Molavi Hall at the University of Tehran—Molavi is another name of the Sufi poet Rumi—I gave a talk for theater students about the historical background of culture and art during the Shah's regime, its cultural policies, and their purpose. I talked about what kind of cultural policies we needed for the future, and I warned the audiences about the shaky future of cultural and artistic freedom in light of what Khomeini was saying about women and his ordering them to adhere to the rules of Islamic dress, or *hijab*. The lecture was published in an Iranian newspaper, *Sedaye Moasser*—The Contemporary Voice.

For Iran, possible futures proliferated. There was still an official government with a prime minister who considered himself the legitimate leader with a constitutional mandate to run the country. He desperately tried to convince people that he respected the constitution, that he respected the people, and that he would do everything in his power to satisfy everyone. On the other hand, there was Khomeini, supported by a number of mullahs as well as a number of *Kolahi*—lay followers. Finally, there were the mobs in the streets who considered themselves the de facto government for the immediate future.

There were, in effect, two governments at this time—the official one, which was unable to accomplish anything substantive; and the unofficial government composed of Islamists who were actively consolidating power. At night the mullahs met in the mosques and at other designated gathering places and spread the word about what they were doing and their plans for the next day. The people in the streets knew their roles, as well as the people working in various branches of government and workers in factories or on strike. Possessing a ready-made communication system—the mosques were ubiquitous throughout the country— was the key to the mullahs' eventual victory. The Shah himself had given them all the tools, money, and freedom of action they needed, especially after the 1953 coup. Because most citizens had lost all faith in the Shah's government long ago, the majority cared little about the precise nature of possible successors to the dictator's regime, as long as the latter was deposed.

The day the Shah and his wife fled the country marked the end of his dictatorship. On January 16, 1979, the front pages of the afternoon newspapers came out with two huge words: *SHAH RAFT*—"THE SHAH HAS LEFT." People rushed into the streets with copies of the newspaper clutched in their hands, jumping up and down, shouting, crying, dancing, and loudly reciting the headline over and over: *SHAH RAFT! SHAH RAFT! SHAH RAFT!*

I was walking up Old Shemiran Road to Gholhak when the news broke. Standing in the middle of the street, part of the crowd, I thought, "I am one of the lucky people. It is so rare that anybody sees a day like this in the history of his country."

A special demonstration was organized in the form of a march, called *Rahpeimai* in Farsi. Havva and I attended the march, which was announced by religious authorities. At first we stood on the sidelines, reading what the banners proclaimed and seeing who was marching. Thousands of people were there, headscarves and chadors covering nearly every woman, including the wife of one of my friends who was marching in the first row. This friend was a famous leftist poet and I was shocked to see his wife conforming to the strict Islamist dress requirements.

The day before the march, Mahmoud Taleghani, one of the highest religious authorities, had made a statement in the media to the effect that all those with different views and beliefs were destined to become the embodiment of one single movement and to follow one line. Many citizens obviously got the message, but certainly not all of us. He could not have been more clear. At the official starting point for the march, Shemiran Three-Way-Junction, both religious and nonreligious people gathered, but all the women's heads were covered. I said to Havva, "Let's go to the

University of Tehran. We can start from there." I knew that the faculty would have their own banners, with slogans that would more closely reflect our own views.

When we arrived at the gates of the university, there were only a few banners. Near one that stated "Faculty of the University of Tehran" I found my friend, the poet whose wife we had seen at Shemiran Three-Way-Junction. When the marchers came into view, we recognized the various groups by the slogans on their banners. We joined the column and marched through Enghelab Square, Revolution Square. Formerly 24 Esfand Square, it had been renamed. The old signs had been painted over just recently, but everyone was already using the new name. Many streets and squares had been renamed in this fashion.

As we passed through the square, I glanced back and spied a van in the middle of the crowd. A mullah and two or three other men were standing on top of the van observing the crowd. We marched on for a few blocks, chanting our own slogans, which were not strictly Marxist but widely known and recognized as nonreligious and leftist.

Suddenly a group of six or seven young men blocked our way and shouted, "Party—Only the Party of Allah! Leader—Only Ruhollah," a reference to Khomeini's first name, which means "spirit of Allah."

I was in the first row of our group, with five or six others next to me. We drew close to the young men, chest to chest, with our fists in the air. Angry and aggressive, they shouted their slogans in our faces and refused to budge. Moments later a hand grabbed my arm and pulled me backward. Turning, I discovered the hand belonged to my leftist poet friend. He asked, "What are you doing, Nasser? Don't you know who they are?"

"Yes," I replied. "I know them. They want to make us change our slogans."

He said, "Today is not the time to put out our own slogans." Torn emotionally, I quit the march with Havva. We stood on the sidewalk, hurt, angry, and bewildered. I could not really fathom our situation. As we stood watching the marchers pass by, I located the van with the mullah and his companions on top. They were busily directing their followers on the sidewalk, pointing out where they should go next to try to change the slogans by threats and physical intimidation. I said to Havva, "Look what they're doing! Let's leave! I can't be a part of this sham."

What had started so jubilantly had turned sour. I was deeply hurt, even coming to tears. I feared for the future of my country given the ominous portents we were witnessing that day.

Walking home, I felt as if we were navigating an unknown city. Havva shared my disillusionment, but we encountered no others whose manner or expression mirrored our own somber mood.

The rough face of the thug, sweat pouring down his tight, angry jaw, yelling in my face, remained embedded in my memory. In the days to come, his ilk brandished knives in the streets and stabbed people at the university, then dragged their bleeding bodies through the streets. Iranian intellectuals commonly adopted the Marxist term *Lumpen* to describe these miscreants. I could find nothing wrong with their characterization.

The continued participation of the mullahs' minions had the effect of making me stay away from some of the subsequent scenes of the revolution. When, for example, the U.S. embassy was occupied, many went to observe, but I stayed home.

■ ■ ■

Prison and revolution notwithstanding, the theater never left my mind. I could not do theater, at least not the way I wanted to, but I decided it was time to see how I might reorganize the Iran

Theater Association. Some students and political sympathizers were doing short sociopolitical pieces in the parks and streets, but I was not interested in that kind of theater. The form was not the issue, but shallow content and abysmal theatrical skills severely limited the appeal of these productions.

I contacted some of my former colleagues who had worked with my theater group. We discussed the possibility of a new beginning. I found that there were plenty of theater students who wanted to work with me. I just needed a place to rehearse a good play. After reading extensively and weighing my options, I chose *Round Heads and Pointed Heads* by Bertolt Brecht.

There were several plays, including others by Brecht, whose content was politically appropriate to our time and place, that could show the citizens how they were being sold out—how a government not remotely radical or even liberal could successfully pose as revolutionary. This play had a lot of elements that connected to our Iranian situation. It served our goals especially well because it was not specific to a particular time and place. Audiences would be able to identify the play's characters and plot with the Iranian present. Brecht's *Days of the Commune* also dealt with a revolution, one crushed from the outside; by contrast, in *Round Heads and Pointed Heads,* the revolution's fall comes from within.

The play is a parable about an imaginary country called Yahoo. The country is in crisis; its army is called Hua. The country has no king, but it has a ruler, a viceroy. In the south of the country the peasants are arming themselves, starting a rebellion, marching north to the capital city carrying red flags emblazoned with a sickle. The landlords and the aristocracy are withdrawing their support from the viceroy because they do not think that he can control the situation. At the same time, there is a character who has meetings with the landlords and masters and tries to convince them that he is the one who can control the situation and suppress the peasant rebellion. The viceroy consults his counselor and asks him, What can we do now, in this situation? The viceroy and his counselor have a long discussion one night and at the end of the discussion they determine that the situation is grave. The counselor suggests that first the rebellion must be crushed and "the farmers' rising can be curbed only by a man of quite different views." Furthermore, the counselor says that he knows a man who, by the way, has already met with the landlords. He could be appointed by the viceroy to deal with the situation in the viceroy's absence. He describes the man: "He's of the middle class by birth, / Not landlord, not farmer; not rich, not poor. / The unending quarrel of the rich and poor / Enrages him, for it rocks the land and shakes / His class that holds itself the core of all. / Both rich and poor alike he does condemn / As money grubbers; for him the state's decline / Is spiritual and reflects corrupted souls." The viceroy likes the idea that the crisis is spiritual, and the counselor explains more about the man, whose name is Iberin, "He chiefly has the middle class behind him, / Tradesmen, artisans and clerks, / The poorer, 'better educated' kind, / The small depositor, in short the ruined burgher type. / These he has gathered in his Iberin League, / Which, I may add, is very nicely armed, / If anyone can crush the Sickle men, it's he." The counselor tells the viceroy that after everything is calm and the rebellion is suppressed, he can come back and rule as he used to.

The viceroy decides that this is a very good idea. He leaves the country and the new man takes power, pretending that he has forced the viceroy to leave. The Iberin soldiers, Huas, suddenly occupy the city and force people to hang flags and celebrate Iberin's inauguration. Iberin presents himself as revolutionary and tells the people that he has brought them freedom. He declares that anybody who has been victimized or abused by any master can come to the revolutionary courts and obtain justice and compensation. He divides the populace into round heads and pointed heads.

We loved the play because what Khomeini had done was separate people into Muslims and non-Muslims. We expected that the audience would understand the references, because they had experienced it all in their own lives. They would see that the viceroy in the play represented the Shah, and that the new guy, Iberin, was Khomeini, and that the Huas were the Pasdaran—the Revolutionary Guards. The round heads were the Muslims and the pointed heads were the non-Muslims. The peasant rebels represented the leftists. It was as if the play had been written for us, for our situation and the revolution that was betrayed. Nobody could believe that this play was written by Brecht and was first performed in Copenhagen in 1935. Some audiences suspected that we had changed the play.

So the play could perfectly demonstrate our analysis of the political situation. We believed that the new government was reactionary, religiously fanatical, and backward. It did not tolerate any other group, and we could see that the situation was moving very fast toward, as we called it at the time, religious fascism. We realized that they had already started attacking the political and nonpolitical organizations and were arresting people according to a calculated, organized plan. At this time, however, the mobs attacking non-Muslim individuals and gatherings were still more or less spontaneous and unorganized. But the first anniversary of the revolution had not yet been celebrated.

■ ■ ■

I had not had the opportunity to work for years, and now I had a play on my hands that was very complicated, requiring a large cast and with a script much longer than that of most theatrical productions. Additionally, although the new regime was not yet fully established and there were no official censors, opposition groups were being dealt with severely. Our group was a bit apprehensive about how these new government authorities would react to our staging of this critical play.

I did feel a measure of confidence, surrounded as I was with thirty or more young, energetic men and women whose determination and enthusiasm were infectious. We all shared the hope that the new regime had not yet established itself to the point of close state control of artistic endeavors.

The first hurdle was finding a rehearsal space. I knew of several possibilities; however, we had no funds to procure a lease. I was acquainted with the head of the Roudaki Opera House, Zangeneh, the man who had assisted us at considerable personal risk when we produced shows in northern Iran. He had lied to the SAVAK censors in Rasht, telling them that we were a government theater group and that we already had permission to stage *Dr. Stockmann*, the name we had given to *An Enemy of the People*, so they really need not bother reading it. I went to his office and explained our situation, asking whether he could help us once more by locating a rehearsal space and a theater in which to stage our play. He scheduled our production for a two-month run at the Opera House on the spot and provided a small auditorium for our afternoon rehearsals for five to six months, all gratis. We were elated at his generosity, but we still faced the problem of raising the money for production expenses, which would be considerable. I was not at all sure we could manage the way we had before the revolution, tapping actors and friends for money.

The new director of the government's Theater Programs Administration, Jamshid Mashayekhi, had been elected by the actors and actresses in the department. He was one of Iran's finest actors. He called to tell me, "We can finance your production and help you in whatever way you require. If there is one group in the entire country most deserving of financial help it is yours. Why don't you come here to my office? The Theater Programs Administration now is much different than it was under the Shah. You can accept funding without fear of attached obligations. Persons new to the theater have received money. Apply now as we are ready to help immediately."

I prepared a production budget totaling seventy thousand tomans and submitted it with our application. I met with Mashayekhi to arrange a formal contract, that included a statement that the Theater Programs Administration was sponsoring our production. In our request I asked for space for our show in the administration's own theater. The director scheduled a one-month run at the Sangelaj Theater, previously the Twenty-Fifth Shahrivar Theater. Our plan was to rehearse in our originally arranged space for six months, then open in the Sangelaj for a month's run, then move to the Roudaki Opera House for the following two months. With these arrangements completed we could concentrate solely on our preparatory work.

Our excitement grew as we approached the date of our first performance. Music had proved to be a major difficulty. We tried to find the original music composed by Hans Eisler for the play, but were able to uncover only two or three pieces from the whole, despite the help we received from friends in our search. They contacted several foreign countries, including Denmark, where the play had first been staged in Copenhagen in 1936, but they were unsuccessful. For me the music was one of the intrinsic aspects of the play that I did not want to treat lightly, as was often the case in Iranian theater productions. I did not know any Iranian composers familiar with Brecht's work who also had experience writing music for the theater. Fortunately, a friend located one of the few foreign composers who remained in Iran after the revolution. He had been working with the Symphony Orchestra of Tehran under the Shah. A Bulgarian, he had an Iranian wife, which was why he stayed and worked with the orchestra, whose members had mostly fled the country. The composer's name was Vanko Naidenov.

Vanko was very enthusiastic when we approached him and agreed unconditionally to work with us. He obtained a copy of the play for himself, and a German copy as well, because his wife spoke German. He studied it carefully and, after extensively discussing each musical piece and reaching agreement with us about what we needed, he was handed the Farsi version of the song lyrics. Here we had some difficulties, because his Farsi was heavily accented. As a result, he often heard more or less in the Farsi words than was correct, which rendered the matching of notes exceptionally difficult. A second problem emerged: this foreign composer inevitably composed according to the dynamics of Western music, which are totally different than those found in Iranian music. If he were to satisfy Iranian audiences, he would have to achieve the impossible—blend the musical expectations of two cultures in a single piece of music. His task was further burdened by the knowledge that those in the audience—from traditional Muslims to Western-educated modernists—would have wide-ranging levels of education and cultural understanding.

Music rehearsals required that each song be addressed with the actors during hours-long sessions held in my home. The composer sat at the piano playing and rehearsing with the actors. Although we retranslated the lyrics and rearranged them to fit the music, the actors still struggled to stretch out individual syllables that in Farsi would always be brief. Their difficulty lay in their attempts to instill meanings and emotions while conforming to the strictures of the biculturally infused lyrics in such a manner that our audiences could both comprehend and enjoy them.

Opening night finally arrived and we were gratified that during the first month audiences filled the house nightly. Unfortunately, at the end of the month I had to leave for France, where I finally underwent heart surgery. I chose an assistant to oversee the production for the rest of the run. We had a council of five people who had been elected by the actors and other members to manage the theater group financially and administratively. While I was in France, the news from the group was not encouraging; they had problems moving the production to the Opera House because the provisional government had changed the management of the Opera House and the new administrator was a religious nationalist, a Muslim who immediately set about trying to shut down this popular play. His justification: "The people have made a revolution based on their faith and they don't want to see a play that is not Islamic. We don't want to upset people of faith. We want to avoid any possible internal clashes."

At the time, the Falange groups—the terminology we used to identify and characterize the thugs who were organized by the government—were actively and aggressively attacking secular gatherings, especially those of a leftist persuasion. Aware of the growing Islamist threat, our theater council wrote a strong letter to the new head of the Opera House protesting his oppressive censorship. They argued that our month-long run at the Sangelaj Theater had been well-attended and well-received. No trouble had ensued among those attending, thus he had no legitimate grounds for hindering our scheduled run. The council also contacted Jamshid Mashayekhi to ask for his help. He called the new manager and explained that we were a theater group that had been suppressed under the Shah and that some of us had spent years in prison, where we were subjected to torture. He concluded, "As a duty, we in the new government need to support them."

The new head tried to argue with Mashayekhi about who we were, warning him that it was not wise to get further involved in this matter. The manager had been told that we were a leftist group and that the play was leftist in content. He cited a scene in which a red flag is waved from the stage, an affront to all faithful Muslim people.

Our group contacted the new manager again: "We will be at the Opera House on the date that the show is scheduled to open, we will ask people beforehand to attend, and we will explain to those who come that you are not letting us have the show, and that you are the new censors."

Mashayakhi again tried to convince him, "Let them have their show."

The manager replied, "If the actors come to the Opera House, the Revolutionary Guards will be there to protect it, and I'm afraid there will be a violent clash and I don't want anything like that to happen." The conversation grew more heated, and the manager added, "They have a red flag and you know this is a Communist symbol. The Revolutionary Guards cannot tolerate that."

Mashayekhi ended the conversation with "I am coming with the actors to the Opera House. If the Pasdaran want to shoot, let me be the first one to be killed by this new government. Let that red flag be my shroud."

Alarmed, the manager tried to placate Mashayekhi. "We can arrange a few nights for the performance, but we cannot give them the Opera House for two months."

The door was ajar, and some members of the council sat down with the manager and reached an agreement to schedule

sixteen performances scattered over a two-month period, a mod-
ification that made him feel that his compromise was not a total
capitulation.

The council insisted on a single price for all of the seats
whereas the manager argued that higher prices should be charged
for preferred seating. On opening night, Opera House employees attempted to control ticket sales, interfering with our group's
plans. Many people ended up rushing into the theater without
tickets. The Opera House contained around nine hundred seats,
and many theater people and intellectuals knew about the dis-
agreements surrounding the performance, so there was an impressive crowd.

After the sixteen-night run, the council asked for the money
from the ticket sales, but the theater staff claimed that they knew
nothing of the matter. When the council complained to the theater management, they were told, "Nobody told us you were
an independent group. We thought you were with the Theater
Programs Administration, so we deposited all the money in the
account of the Ministry of Culture and Art."

The accountant from the ministry said, "Sorry, we cannot
do anything. We can't withdraw any money for any reason until
the next annual budget comes out. And even then we won't be
able to pay you."

Our council representative protested, "You know, we worked
all this time; aren't you going to pay us?"

The infuriating reply: "We don't have any agreement with
you; we don't know who you are. Go and talk to the Theater
Programs Administration."

Unfortunately, when I returned from France four months
later, the council had still not obtained any payment. I called
a meeting of the group and we brainstormed for hours before

reaching an agreement about our next step. We decided to fix the value of each person's work for six months of rehearsal and preparation, plus two months of performances, and come up with a figure for individual compensation. Ticket sales amounted to more than 130,000 tomans, so we reasoned that the total wages should equal that amount. We penned a letter to the Minister of Culture and Art, Hassan Habibi, explaining all the problems we had experienced trying to get our money and asking him to resolve this problem within a reasonable time. We warned him, "If our problem is not resolved, all the people who participated in the production will come to the ministry and hold a sit-in protest."

The appointed time arrived and we had received no answer. The next day the entire production crew descended on the ministry and sought out the minister's office. Our request to speak with him was refused. We said, "OK, we will wait here until he receives us."

Time passed and no one summoned us. Finally, I asked the man guarding the inner offices, "Please let him know we are still here."

He replied stiffly, "He can't receive you today. He is busy with people in his office. You can come back tomorrow."

"No, we are sitting right here waiting for him," I replied defiantly.

Another two hours passed and we agreed among ourselves to wait and confront him when he emerged to go home.

As the day wore on, the mood in the office and corridor grew quite tense as employees went to and from the minister's inner office. At about two o'clock, one of them came out and asked us to leave, "because it's the end of the workday. The minister promises he will resolve your problem if you come back tomorrow. Tomorrow you will have your money."

I replied, "We have heard a lot of promises before. None of them were realized. So we are going to stay here until the minister speaks to us."

Two hours later a different employee came to ask us "Please leave the ministry. Everyone is gone." Two p.m. was the normal time for offices to close, we were told. "You can't stay in the building after closing time."

"Who says we can't stay?" I asked. "We can stay, and we're going to stay."

We had, in effect, made the minister a prisoner in his own office. He could not escape without talking to us. Finally, the head accountant of the ministry called to me and said, "I'm going to talk to him. I think he'll agree that we can pay you your money."

He went into the minister's office and ten minutes later came out and said, "We can't give the whole amount to one person. We need to give each person his or her wages."

Because they refused the right of our theater council delegate to receive the money and distribute it among us, we went home and returned the next day with a list of what each person was owed. One by one the accountant called us in and we signed for our cash payments. Because I had been away for the last two months of the run, I received a lesser sum. It was a very egalitarian distribution! I was actually happy with this outcome, because it amounted to equal wages for everyone.

We had our victory of principle. None of us were really depending on the payments to live. I, for instance, was teaching in the Faculty of Dramatic Arts, affiliated with the Ministry of Culture and Art. However, it was important not to allow this new government to cheat us—and worse, to use the money to support their Islamist policies.

At the beginning of the reorganization of the theater group after the revolution, I had prepared articles of association for the group. They were intended to help focus our work by defining our goals and principles precisely, and they were to help the members of the group understand why we were there. Newcomers could read this document and clearly understand the goals of the group before deciding whether to join or not. Other independent theater groups had no such structure; a few friends gathered because they liked to do theater without any hard and fast commitment or goals. I wanted people who would be responsible to each other, to the group, and to a social-artistic theater.

The first article emphasized the artistic nature of the theater group. The second emphasized its independence in terms of policy and ideology; we would be independent of any other cultural, artistic, political, or religious groups. At the time, almost all other cultural and artistic groups were closely tied to particular political or religious organizations.

These two principles were very important at the time. In my experience, if a group did not have carefully defined principles, there could be no independent analysis of Iranian society and government. Because I was known as a political artist, and because our pre-revolution theater group was considered, even by the government, to be a political group, sympathizers and members from different political organizations were anxious to commandeer our group and make it over into a mouthpiece for their respective organizations. Many of them approached us to try to influence the nature of our productions to fit their own dogma. Often they knew little or nothing about art. Members of the Tudeh Party, for example, were second only to the government in damaging independent theater groups.

One other item differentiated our theater group from other groups: we published a monthly theater magazine. We were trying, probably not very subtly, to educate our potential audiences, first about our theater group and our productions, but also about contemporary theater around the world.

■ ■ ■

After the revolution, it seemed that our whole society was so strongly politicized that groups of people everywhere were trying to organize themselves to do things that had been forbidden for years and years. During the run of *Round Heads and Pointed Heads,* a number of Fadaiyan who saw the play approached me to discuss it both as art and as an influence on thinking during those heady days of possible change. Although they knew I was not interested in putting our theater group in the service of any particular organization, they persistently tried to persuade me to join them, or at least make common cause with them.

At one point immediately after the revolution, the Fadaiyan occupied a large building on Meikadeh Avenue that had previously belonged to SAVAK. They utilized it as their command headquarters. A. K., a friend of mine who was a Fadaiyan spokesman, sent a message through a mutual friend that he wanted to see me. I went to the occupied SAVAK building, which the Fadaiyan called Setad, to meet him. He described the status of the *sazeman,* the organization, and its need for people "like you, who believe in revolution and the organization." He asked me to organize the theater section of their art workshop, *Kargah-e honar.*

Although I believed in the history and tradition of that organization, I did not wholly subscribe to its current political stance, and this was before it splintered into Tudeh supporters, who constituted the majority, and the non-Tudeh minority. In addition to our political differences, I had some other problems with some of the people who were working with the organization, and I could not bring myself to compromise with them. I was committed to living my life as an artist, not as a mouthpiece for any political organization.

I had a second meeting with A. K. in order to explain thoroughly and frankly my reasons for rejecting his proposal. I continued to run into various Fadaiyan members and sympathizers, some I knew from prison, others on the outside. All of them seemed intent on recruiting me when we met on the street to discuss current events, a national addiction in post-revolution Iran.

Oddly, despite my earlier rebuff of the Fadaiyan outreach, I still ended up working with them. I was approached by an old friend, Massoud. Initially I begged him off, citing my busy schedule with my theater group and teaching at the Faculty of Dramatic Arts. Massoud explained the urgency of the organization's needs: in these revolutionary times the Fadaiyan needed to develop their theater quickly. In a second meeting, I told Massoud that I would accept the offer on one nonnegotiable condition: it must be made clear that I was cooperating as an individual, not as the founder and director of the Iran Theater Association. My theater group's principles of nonaffiliation allowed individual members to belong to different organizations, and many of them did, but always strictly on an individual basis. The Fadaiyan must not assume that my cooperation signaled that the ITA would do likewise. Massoud had no objection to this prerequisite. He told me that the Fadaiyan would rent a place especially for theater people and I would have the key and carte blanche to conduct any other business at this secret address with whomever I wanted.

Two weeks later, Massoud gave me a key and an address and said, "By the way, there are two comrades, theater people you probably know. They are sympathizers of our organization and they also have keys and know about the place. Don't worry; they're trustworthy comrades."

That was the first hint I had that everything would not go as promised. Keeping my misgivings to myself, I replied, "Just make an appointment for me with them at the building." I wanted to ascertain exactly what their status was and if they were to watchdog my movements.

The office was located at the north end of the city in a very crowded commercial neighborhood filled with boutiques and movie theaters. On the appointed day I opened the door to the office to discover the two men were already there. I knew them both as mediocre actors. One of them had worked in a play in my theater group before the revolution; the other, a younger man, I had seen in a street play a few months before. We sat down and I asked them some questions: "What have you done up to now? What do you have in mind to do? What plans do you have?"

They did not have much specific to say; they just wanted to do political theater as sympathizers of the organization.

I asked them, "Do you know any other actors who are members or sympathizers of the organization?"

None that they were aware of, they replied. I did not stay long in the office, which consisted of a small lobby and two office rooms. One of the rooms had a small desk and a few chairs. The space was too small for any kind of theater work. Even a cursory investigation would raise suspicions because no one had bothered to create a believable cover—a dangerous situation given the politics of the time. I resolved to avoid the office altogether.

Nevertheless, I did have a plan for organizing theater groups on a national scale for the Fadaiyan, using their organization to reach out to other parts of Iran. I thought that by creating a Fadaiyan theater group in Tehran we could execute a model that other cities might emulate. I needed to learn the number of actors and actresses in Tehran who were members of or sympathizers with the Fadaiyan. Because of security, this would be difficult, and I was unsure if the Fadaiyan leaders would even have such information. I asked Massoud if he could compile a list as his first contribution to the theater project.

I spent four months trying to organize a theater section for the Fadaiyan. I found ten people working in various theater groups, four in mine, who were sympathizers. Unfortunately I found that the Fadaiyan leaders I was dealing with were not being wholly honest with me. The majority of the organization was moving ever closer to the Tudeh Party.

Despite my having made clear my desire for independence, they expected me to participate in study groups and cell meetings. Massoud was one level below the Central Committee in the hierarchy of the organization and was connected to someone on the Central Committee. He was responsible for supervising some of the cells he kept pressing me to join.

During those four months I became convinced that the organization was poorly led. People were regularly appointed to positions for which they lacked the knowledge or talent necessary for their responsibilities. As often as not they were taken from fields where they did possess some skills, or at least a degree of useful influence. One particularly egregious example was the assignment of a young, educated, beautiful actress who had worked with the ITA to abandon theater and work in a factory, supposedly to organize the female workers. She was one of the Fadaiyan activists whom I attempted to have reassigned to the Fadaiyan's theater section, and she was not the only actor to receive a similarly incongruous position.

Eventually I discovered, through members of my own theater group, that the Fadaiyan organization was trying to enforce its own political line within our Association. At that point I decided to distance myself from the Fadaiyan altogether. I told them I would give them a theater plan that their own people could utilize for whatever would serve their purposes best.

After this misguided foray, I could see more clearly the pressure that the Fadaiyan and Tudeh sympathizers were exerting within the ITA. They were continually trying to get the group to take an official position toward the revolution by endorsing the Khomeini regime. During one meeting of the ITA when this agenda was under discussion, I explained the role of art, especially the theater, in society, and how a group like ours needed to remain aloof from taking political positions. One of the more senior Fadaiyan supporters scorned my argument: "I don't accept your explanation. I believe you have political problems and you are actually assuming a political stance by refusing to take a political stand in favor of the revolution."

Up to this point I had thought this man to be among the honest people in the group and I had trusted him. He had acted as the editor of our theater magazine. I had not tracked his writing because of this trust, which he betrayed by publishing editorials that placed our group squarely in the middle of current political debate. When friends and colleagues read them, my position was compromised and I was left with a lot of embarrassing explanations to make.

■ ■ ■

Our theater group was involved in establishing a syndicate of theater workers. The history of the theater syndicate in Iran, like the history of any other professional syndicate or union in our country, was tragic. The only time theater people had been able to organize themselves as a formal syndicate was during the short period following the Second World War when the Shah's father was sent into exile by the British government. Iran was occupied by the Red Army of the Soviet Union in the north and by the British Army in the south. When the young Shah replaced his father, there was a period of relative freedom, a fragile democracy made possible by the lack of a strong central government. Until 1948, the Tudeh Party as well as the nationalist and right wing parties were free to organize. However, as the young Shah consolidated power, receiving training from the British and later the Americans, he gradually suppressed those organizations. After the U.S.- and British-backed coup against Mossadegh in 1953, nearly every aspect of independent political activity was suppressed, including the theater syndicate.

In 1968 and 1969 there was a second attempt to form a theater syndicate by combining three disparate elements: employees of the commercial theaters of Lalehzar Street, a few television actors, and other popular entertainers, including Mostafa Oskoui from Anahita.

We soon discovered that although there was a syndicate, the majority of theater people were not members, including all the people who were working for the Theater Programs Administration, all the independent or semidependent groups, all students of theater who were working in theater, and almost all the actors in television productions and some of the actors in the theaters on Lalehzar. None of us were aware that the syndicate existed, because Oskoui and others had not publicly announced in the newspapers that they were organizing, meeting, or holding elections. The few people involved just declared the establishment of the theater syndicate and elected themselves as officials. The bulk of theater people were entirely ignorant of its existence or purpose, and when we did learn about it we suspected that the syndicate members would later turn out to be associated with the government and attempt to control the rest of us under the guise of representing us.

Said Soltanpour, Sadegh Hatefi, and I tried to organize all theater people to prevent Oskoui and his friends from obtaining exclusive rights to represent us. We petitioned the Minister of Labor not to recognize the other organization. We gathered more than a hundred signatures from actors who had not been allowed to vote in the so-called election of syndicate officials. We asked the Judicial Department of the Ministry of Labor to investigate the matter. Following the investigation, the authorities invited both sides to a hearing, and after hearing all the claims, they issued a decision dissolving the spurious syndicate. They said, "You can start anew, following the legal procedures—announcing meetings in the newspaper, and so on." But after that, nobody really tried to organize a syndicate until after the revolution.

■ ■ ■

Now, with the Shah's government deposed, theater people, like other professional and industrial groups, tried again to form a union and establish their social identity in the form of a syndicate. We wanted an organization to defend our rights—economic, political, artistic, and social. Despite the general enthusiasm for organizing, there was no consensus about what a theater syndicate should be. Some favored a radical policy that would punish those actors and directors who had collaborated with the previous regime. I recall one young actor who averred, "Those theater people who have collaborated with the Shah's regime should be hanged on the same stage where they played."

More experienced people came forward and suggested that establishing unity among ourselves as theater people should take precedence over seeking revenge on those who had ties to the previous regime. They argued that the government officials responsible for repressive policies had already fled the country, and those actors and directors who were government employees now were more likely victims than villains.

After a few meetings, the majority of actors, directors, and other theater workers were ready to draft our articles of agreement or a constitution. We elected a committee of twelve to write the document. I was included in this group, which would submit its work to the membership.

In due course the new constitution was approved and we finally had a syndicate whose governing board was free from outside political or bureaucratic control, or we thought it would be. The new syndicate was nothing if not inclusive, including theater students, members of independent groups, government employees, and commercial Lalehzari actors.

The syndicate was established as we were rehearsing *Round Heads and Pointed Heads*.

At the same time as we were waging this struggle within our own group, we were preparing for our second show, Dario Fo's *Can't Pay? Won't Pay!* We had chosen this play because of our concern for the plight of the working class. The Islamic government was busily organizing all governmental and nongovernmental institutions, from businesses to higher education. Each had its Islamic association supported by the government, which utilized the associations to control all political activity within the institution or business.

The Islamic associations supervised the activities of non-Muslim workers in the factories, halting any activities that challenged the policies of either factory management or the government, once distinct entities whose boundaries were blurring to the point of being erased. The Islamic government eventually confiscated most of the factories altogether and effectively managed the remaining ones. The official line was direct: "Your property is safe, but the government will manage it for you for ten years." Most factory owners left the country, leaving behind intensifying struggles between Muslim and non-Muslim workers.

Can't Pay? Won't Pay! is the story of two working families who are members or affiliates of rival political organizations, the Communist Party of Italy and the Social Democrats. Although the families work together, they quarrel over their differing political views. We tinkered with the plot to more closely mirror the Iranian working class struggle. Our version featured the Tudeh Party and the Islamic Republic Party; however, for obvious reasons, we employed fictitious names. Of course people could identify them; when the workers ridiculed the Pope, the audience would understand that the Roman pontiff was really Khomeini.

The women in the play are upset about the high price of food and they protest in the supermarkets. The play begins with two housewives who have been involved in looting a supermarket during a protest because they can't afford to buy enough to feed their families. Fearfully they enter their apartments with bags of stolen food, knowing that they have to hide their actions from their husbands as well as the authorities. By the end of the play, after facing various struggles, the families realize that fighting each other is absurd and is not in their best interests as part of the working class. They finally reach a solution: form their own organization to represent their common interests. The play ends literally on a high note, with a song of unity as the workers prepare a feast to celebrate their solidarity.

Serendipitously, the newly formed theater syndicate decided to hold an anti-imperialist theater festival in the Lalehzar district to celebrate the first anniversary of the revolution. Our theater group was given two nights in one of the oldest and largest theaters in Lalehzar, the Nasr Theater. We staged Dario Fo's play before a mass audience. Opening night was made especially memorable when one of the characters ridiculed the pope and two members of the audience loudly took issue, banging their seats as they left the theater. We were confused. We thought they might be typical Lalehzari theatergoers who simply did not like the play because they expected the usual light commercial fare. But the next night, before the performance, we were warned that some Hezbollahi were coming to the theater specifically to disrupt the play.

I sought out the director of the theater and explained our problem. I also called the theater syndicate and asked that some protection be sent to the theater. I did not want them to fight the Hezbollahi, just to sit in the audience and try to contain any disruption by persuading any troublemakers to leave. However, only two or three people from the syndicate showed up—a token gesture.

Luckily, help arrived from an unexpected source: the commercial actors from the Nasr Theater. These were actors usually condemned by the intellectuals as mere commercial players appearing in short skits between belly dance acts. They displayed real fortitude in a situation where nothing was expected of them. They approached me with a shrewd plan to calm us: "Don't worry; just perform your play. We will take care of the troublemakers."

Nasr Theater possessed a beautiful lobby boasting fine plaster moldings and chandeliers, with two doors along the main wing to the auditorium and another door at the top of the steps that led backstage. The Lalehzari actors moved heavy black leather couches, each about four meters long, to form a barricade blocking the backstage door. The audience could exit the play through only two auditorium doors, one leading to the main lobby and the other to the entrance lobby. A group of eight or nine actors would stand in front of the leather couches to bolster the barricade at the stage door, preventing anyone from intruding. They assured us, "After the play is finished, when the audience applauds, don't come out for the curtain call. Run out through the door backstage into the passage that leads to Lalehzar Street." We arranged for cars to speed us away after we fled the stage. I asked one of my friends who was not a member of the group to remain and identify those who wanted to disrupt the play. He would call me after I got home.

That evening, we scrambled off the stage and made our getaway. A half hour after I got home my friend called. He said, "There were about sixty to seventy Hezbollahi, with knives and chains, ready for you to come out of the theater." They were not part of the audience. They were waiting in the street, well aware of the custom in Lalehzar Street theaters that actors leave after the audience has filed out. Some of the theater patrons would wait in front of the theater to watch the actors depart. My friend told me that the Hezbollahi had waited almost an hour. They looked extremely disappointed when the custodians closed the doors and turned out the lights. The gang leader finally shouted, "Motherfucker! We're going to get you! I know you!"

The previous night, when we had left the theater in the normal fashion, I was the last to leave, accompanied by my wife and some other actors. Someone in the crowd who was standing near the entrance of the theater called to me in an uncertain voice, "Nasser!" It was obvious that he did not know me, because he called my name before I stepped near him and again as I passed him. I continued walking, looking straight ahead. Whoever he was, I believed he wanted to identify me as a future target or possibly attack me then and there.

■ ■ ■

One of the many changes brought about by the revolution had to do with the nation's universities. For a short time, before the Islamic government consolidated power, the students at the Faculty of Dramatic Arts and the Faculty of Fine Arts tried to winnow out the reactionary professors and replace them with progressives, especially in the Faculty of Dramatic Arts, where I was hired. Students of both faculties wanted me to teach, but my theater group and other social activities took up much of my time, so I accepted the invitation from the Faculty of Dramatic Arts only. I had no experience teaching, at least not in a classroom, but seeing those enthusiastic students was highly motivating. They were open to new ideas, to innovative ways of analyzing plays, stories, and characters on the basis of the social and political backgrounds of whatever subject was at hand, during a period of revolutionary change.

Unfortunately, I could not teach more than a year, because at the time my first priority was the theater group, and my personal priority was performance and direction. I fervently believed that the sociopolitical situation demanded an immediate artistic response. That is why in 1980 I accepted an offer from a professional theater to direct Nikolai Gogol's *General Inspector*, a nineteenth-century play.

I directed this theatrical piece using actors from the Pars Theater in Lalehzar. This was a wholly new experience for me as I was used to working with student and intellectual actors. The Lalehzari actors were not used to performing in plays with strong social, political, and literary themes, or to engaging in probing analytical explanations of the text. They were accustomed simply to memorize their lines and immediately perform onstage. The traditional role of the director in Lalehzar was limited to offering mechanical advice. For example, you might instruct the actor,

"When you say this line or sentence, remain in the chair. When you get to this word, you can move from here to there." It was an old-fashioned kind of direction, which the actors also completely ignored during actual performances after the first week's staging.

I did not want to do Gogol's play this way. I held a few readings with the actors in order to give them some ideas, discussing the play's text and context as a means of defining our goal in staging the production. Although most of them possessed no higher education, they were talented actors, and I consciously avoided intellectual language to further our mutual understanding.

I allowed them free rein with the stage action during rehearsals, not stopping them, just suggesting changes when I thought their notions were wholly unworkable. In this way I hoped to stimulate their creative spirits without resorting to subverting the play's thrust by ad-libbing, inserting vulgar words, and making inappropriate gestures to invoke the audience's laughter. They were used to simple farces, not Gogol. I told the actors, "Bring any new ideas that will further the goals of the play, but please don't bring your Lalehzari tricks that will sidetrack the drama for the sake of comic relief."

During the first week of the run I went to the theater every night to watch and show the actors I was serious about faithfully delivering Gogol's message. It turned out to be a very good learning experience for us all, and they seemed pleased to be dealt with in a serious fashion. One of the popular comedians appearing in the play, Ardeshir Sohrabi, began discussing politics with me and asking me for political petitions and books. He was a very talented, energetic, and inquiring actor and we built a good friendship.

The Lalehzar audiences, in fact, responded very positively to the play. I had changed the plot slightly, taking two characters who were in the action of the play and putting them in front of the curtain before each act to clue the audience in about the forthcoming action. Bobtchinski and Dobtchinski were two noisy fellows who hung around the town and always knew what was going on, beginning with the arrival of the inspector general. I thought this device would make the play more accessible to audiences unfamiliar with more serious theatrical fare.

Almost a year later I was invited to be the managing director of the Alborz Theater, another Lalehzar company. A significant condition was attached to the offer: theirs was one of the confiscated movie theaters and they wanted me to be a hidden collaborator, a literal behind-the-scenes director. They were trying to avoid trouble with the Bonyad-e Mostazafan, the foundation that had confiscated the wealthy Pahlavi Foundation previously controlled by the Shah's family. The Mostazafan Foundation ("Foundation for the Poor") had also taken over several factories and companies in their insatiable quest for profits. It was one of the richest financial institutions associated with the Islamic government, wealthy enough to compete with the government itself. For years the head of this foundation, Mohsen Rafighdoust, was one of the *obash*, the thugs who illegally siphoned off vast sums from the foundation's earnings. This scam operated with the full knowledge of the government. I had known this cutthroat while I was imprisoned, and I remembered that he was always indignantly complaining that SAVAK had confiscated one of the banana boats he had used to smuggle fruits and other commodities into Iran. He was obsessed with his lost banana boat to the point of tedium, but he had certainly overcome this earlier setback to accumulate a pile of cash.

I agreed to work secretly with the Alborz Theater to produce a number of plays, none of which carried my name as director. I was able to bring some intellectual actors to mix in with the Lalehzari actors, an experiment that proved fruitful for all the participants. Unfortunately we could not continue long, because the political situation deteriorated as the new regime consolidated power, using its secret police and the Pasdaran to involve themselves in all aspects of Islamic life. Theatrical revenues suffered, and within a few short months all of the professional theaters were abruptly closed by the government.

Another highly negative development occurred with the second syndicate election, which proved to be unpleasantly different from the inaugural poll. The Tudeh Party had prepared for the election by manipulating people and events behind the scenes, which was standard behavior for the party as its agents colluded secretly with the management of the commercial theaters to control the elections.

The elections were to be held in the Pars Theater in Lalehzar, where I had directed *The Inspector General*. I knew the management and the actors of this theater. Although it was late, I talked to them and let them know our theater group's concerns about the election and the issues we thought were important.

A few days before the election, I heard from several sources that the actors associated with the Tudeh Party were campaigning hard for Tudeh candidates. I called a meeting of the actors and actresses in my theater group for early afternoon on election day, shortly before we were to leave for the Pars Theater to cast our votes. In the meeting I tried to explain what issues I thought were important and what kind of candidates I thought the syndicate needed. I did not have any specific candidate in mind. I wanted to know what the other actors had to say about the candidates and hoped we could collectively back the most promising from our perspective. We settled on four candidates to support.

When we arrived at the Pars Theater, however, I was blindsided. Expecting that we would sit together as a group, I was taken aback when the Tudeh and Fadaiyan sympathizers of our group chose to sit in the combined Tudeh-Fadaiyan block. At first I just stood there with the few of us remaining, watching the others in disbelief. Nothing was left for us to do but sit down and wait for the voting.

Different groups and individuals went up to a big board and nominated their candidates by giving the names to those appointed to write them down. The Tudeh and Fadaiyan followers from our own group were among those offering names, none of which were the ones they had agreed to support at our meeting—a shocking betrayal, in my view. These tactics succeeded and the syndicate was theirs—another victory for the "socialist camp."

In our theater group we had people with different political viewpoints, ranging from Tudeh Party members to Fadaiyan to Maoists to people who were not very political. Because society was extremely politicized at that point, almost nobody could be neutral. When we had discussion in our meetings, one could see that everyone was in some sense political, because everyone was taking stands and expressing certain points of view. You could hear it in the language; it was as if language itself had totally changed. Everybody felt that he or she had a duty to take a specific political position toward events. Gradually some of the members of the group started to suggest that the group as a whole should take a position toward the situation, the revolution, and the government. They came forward step by step over a long series of meetings and finally posed this question to the group in clear language: "What is the position of our theater group toward the revolution?" By "the revolution" they meant "the Islamic Revolution," as both the Islamists and the Tudeh Party claimed it.

My answer, as always, was, "First of all, we are an artistic group. Our starting point is always art. We start from the field of art. We have to start always from the artistic point of view, not from the political point of view. As a theater group, we are first of all artists, and then activists. So we have to follow our own rules, the rules of art, but the kind of art that is always concerned with the political situation."

Sometimes we used terms that were prevalent among leftists, such as *engagement* or *commitment* or *committed artist*. The artist must be committed "to the society" or "to the struggle." But everybody had his or her own interpretation of these terms, usually according to the views of whatever organization he or she belonged to. Underlying this discussion was the push from certain members of the theater group who were trying to align us with the Tudeh party. At this point, even the majority of the Fadaiyan were aligned with the Tudeh Party. (The Fadaiyan, by this time, had officially split into "The Majority," which was aligned with Tudeh, and "The Minority," which was not.) A few opportunists were trying to push this discussion as well.

Of course this push was not limited to our theater group. After the revolution, the Tudeh Party was sneaking into all political, cultural, professional, governmental, and women's organizations, as well as into labor unions and local paramilitary committees belonging to neighborhoods or mosques. It was trying to insert its members and sympathizers into every organization. The big problem with all of this was that the general policy of the Tudeh Party was to support the Khomeini government. In the service of their cause, they were collecting information about all the groups they had joined—names, political positions, activities, everything—and turning it over to the government run by the Islamists. They were, in fact, informers. Their goal, the goal of their party, was to either co-opt each group or destroy it. Those they could not co-opt they attacked each day in their newspaper. As it turned out, the only group they were unable to either co-opt or destroy was the Iranian Writers Association, which expelled its Tudeh members and forced the party to form its own writers association.

■ ■ ■

One of the problems I had with friends who were pushing me to take a stand in support of the Islamic government had to do with the issue of street theater. At the beginning of the revolution, street theater was a hot "new" thing to present to the people; it had more to do with furthering political aims than with theatrical craft. There were not many street theater performances, nor did they draw large audiences. When plays were given in Laleh Park, north of the Tehran University campus, there just were not enough people in the park to form a decent audience. When the street theater groups went to the poor neighborhoods on the south side of the city, Khomeini supporters in the neighborhood would forcefully interrupt the plays, and the subsequent violence often resulted in the arrest of the actors as instigators of the disturbances.

The primary problem, however, was the poor quality of street performance in terms of both the acting and the plays. Usually the actors were amateurs whose only motivation was expressing their politics. Their texts were mostly chosen from the editorials of their political organizations' official newspapers. Little was done to develop the texts; they just lifted sentences from their newspapers, pasted them together, and labeled the result a play. One or two rehearsals was deemed sufficient to memorize the lines before going into a park or the streets.

I personally knew Augusto Boal, the Brazilian director who created the "Theater of the Oppressed" and the Invisible Theater. We had met in Paris when I was there for my heart surgery. His work was well suited to revolutionary times. I still hesitated to do street theater because I was not sure it would be effective and

I did not have any good texts for street theater in Farsi. I was constantly arguing about these points with friends in my theater group who were trying to push me to do street theater. Finally, one of them, Arman, who was a playwright, handed me a text and asked, "If you like it, will you produce it?" We held a meeting to read and discuss the play. I told Arman that if he would remove the overly obvious propagandistic parts of the play, I would produce it. We were mutually enthusiastic about the piece because the form and subject were innovative.

The Biggest Boxing Match in the World was set in a boxing ring. One of the boxers was Iran and her opponents were various people from different periods in Iran's past, from the 1953 coup to the revolution. The referee was the United Nations, which invariably sided with Iran's opponents, who were capitalists or surrogates pushed into the ring by capitalists. The opponent's coach was always the United States while Iran had no coach. The only problem was the staged spectators who shouted current propaganda slogans all too easily identifiable as those of the Fadaiyan majority, Arman's political affiliation. For me the slogans resembled a political patch unskillfully sewed onto a historical play. I wanted to see how street audiences would react to the play without the artificial prompting of a fake audience. I believed that the patched parts would make a mockery of the play's most attractive feature, its Brechtian quality of forcing audiences to interact with the characters and think for themselves.

The fake audience was eliminated before the play had its first public exposure in front of the Union of Needleworkers, whose members were exclusively male. Our venue was the roof of their union hall in Lalehzar.

Our second showing was in Darvazeh Ghar, the Cave Gate, one of the poorest districts in the southern part of Tehran. This performance was interrupted by two young Muslims from the neighborhood who objected to some of the lines in the play. They shouted their protests and, playing the narrator, I tried to calm them down and continue the play. They subsided briefly but started shouting again. I tried to persuade them, saying, "Please, let us finish the play. Afterward we can discuss it together."

At that juncture I spied Revolutionary Guards arriving. One of them, who I later discovered was head of the neighborhood's Revolutionary Committee, shouted, "Please stop the show and leave this place. People here have faith and they don't like your show. You should not force it on them." Despite my efforts to engage him in discussion, we were forced to close the performance.

The third and last time the play was staged, we once again found ourselves in south Tehran, in a very busy bus terminal called Khazaneh. We drew a big audience, mostly because one of the actors marched around the terminal beating a military drum, followed by a second actor shouting, "We are putting on a really great show, *The Biggest Boxing Match in the World.* It's great and it's free!"

When enough people, about three hundred, had gathered, we began. Halfway through, in the middle of a scene that took place after the Revolution during the reign of the provisional government, Revolutionary Guards appeared and surrounded the cast and physically restrained the actors one by one. As narrator, I was standing off-stage when the raid began. When I saw the Guards actually arrest six of the actors and haul them off, I thought I had better accompany them. I located the commander of the Guards and told him, "The people you have arrested are not the ones responsible for the play. I am the director. Please let them go. I will come with you."

He said, "OK, you come with me, but I am not letting them go."

I knew that, in this kind of situation, if the authorities wanted to make a case, they would come after me anyway. I wanted to make a statement to the effect that it was our right to present a play to the people, and that we were not attacking the Islamic faith in any way.

We were interrogated briefly at the Komiteh in the Khazaneh bus terminal. It took about two hours to prepare files on the seven of us. They then transferred us to another Komiteh, which was named after the neighborhood, *Ghassab-Khaneh*, the Slaughterhouse Committee. From its inception, this revolutionary committee had tortured and beat people as its preferred method of interrogation. We were taken one by one into separate rooms and held there until eight o'clock that night. From there we were transferred to the Komiteh Markaz, the committee of the central district, which had taken over the entire parliament building in the center of Tehran. The basement was used as a prison and the rest of the building was given over to offices and interrogation rooms. We were put in the building's lobby, which allowed us some time to consult one another and devise a clear, coordinated plan for how we should deal with incarceration if that proved to be our fate.

A half hour passed and I was sitting on one of the old black leather sofas that had belonged to the parliament when I saw a door opening at the other end of the lobby. A man stepped through and walked toward us. He had almost reached the middle of the lobby when I realized that I knew him from prison. I hesitated, weighing my options, then I got up and went to him, even though I was not entirely sure this was a good idea. When I approached, he smiled and said hello, and I replied hello. He immediately added, "I asked the brothers, and they said they behaved respectfully toward you. Now I want the brothers to give you a respectful ride home."

I was vastly relieved, but at the same time I was still indignant. I protested, "We didn't struggle and have a revolution so that we would come back to the bad old days. It isn't right that just for staging a play in the street they arrest us and throw us into prison."

He said, "Let me tell you, it is not a good time now. We are in a very touchy and sensitive situation. Please go home now and come back later. We will have this discussion then. But right now, go home, please!"

He wanted to call the guards and the drivers, but I told him, "No, we can go by ourselves. I appreciate your help."

He gave me his phone number and said, "Call me and come whenever you like and we can talk."

I said, "Tomorrow or the day after, I will again be in the street, putting on our play. I don't want anyone interrupting the show or arresting us."

He said, "Please, don't do that! Please, come here and talk to me before making that decision."

We were allowed to leave. The guards opened the gates and we simply walked out.

The man who let us go was Ezat Shahi, a former member of the Mojahedin-e Khalq, the "Iranian People's Mojahedin." He had been arrested in 1973 in a street clash with SAVAK, had become famous for his resistance under interrogation and torture, and was much celebrated by the Mojahedin. He was one of their heroes. But in prison, after the 1975 Mojahedin split, when most of his fellows declared themselves Marxist, Ezat left the Mojahedin and developed a close relationship with the mullahs.

When I was transferred from Qasr Prison to Evin, he was one of those selected by the mullahs to talk to prisoners from different political groups in different prisons.

I had met him when he was brought into our ward to talk to the mullahs, and we had talked with each other there a few times. He was one of the very few Muslim prisoners who still possessed a sense of common humanity; he talked to me as one human to another. He did not let Islamic politics cut him off from others. He tried to relate to the old prisoners and leftist inmates of all kinds. After he was released, he was appointed head interrogator of the Komiteh Markaz. A week after our recent encounter, I went to see Ezat again. I was not feeling optimistic about obtaining any substantive help, but I was curious to learn what was happening inside the government. I also had another very practical reason for the visit: I wanted to show the Islamists that I had nothing to hide, that I was merely doing theater openly and with no hidden agenda.

Once I was there he tried to convince me that "the situation is dangerous and for a period of time we have to be careful and cautious and ready for compromise. The most dangerous elements now are the Mojahedin. They are trying to force us to pick up our guns first, but we don't want to do that. We want them to make the first aggressive move. For example, last week Maleki [one of the members of Mojahedin] came here and stole a car, hoping to provoke us into a rash action. Another example is the theft of parts from Bell Helicopters at an airbase. We asked for their return but they denied any responsibility for their raid. These are stupid things that the Mojahedin are doing to provoke us. What do they want with those parts? They can't use them!"

He tried to convince me that he was an honest man and faithful to the revolution. He insisted, "After the revolution, everybody asked for their share from the revolution, but I did not ask for anything. I am doing what I am able to do in my position. If I didn't care, I could already have had a higher position. I know there are some wrongdoings that have occurred, but this is normal for a new government with less than two years' experience in wielding power. I know we have only fourteen saints; we don't have a fifteenth one."

This was an obvious but unspoken reference to Khomeini. Islamists believe that there are only fourteen saints, twelve Imams and two others, and that the rest of humanity sins.

Ezat spoke at length and I just listened. When I was ready to leave he said, "Wait a minute. I want to introduce you to a man who can help you with your theater group, help you show your plays in different places." He picked up the telephone and dialed, then said, "I am sending someone to you who is one of those brothers who have suffered under the Shah's regime. I want you to help him in whatever way you can."

I knew right away that I would not go anywhere near a person recommended by this Islamist, however friendly he acted toward me.

Ezat wrote a letter of introduction for me to present to the man he had called. "I am sure he is going to help you."

I thanked him and left the Komiteh. I read the address on his letter: the Sepah-e Passdaran, the Revolutionary Guard Corps. That address alone was sufficient to convince me to forego Ezat's proffered assistance. I realized at that moment that there was no viable future in street theater.

■ ■ ■

Foremost among my ambitions for our theater group was that we would all understand the social aspect of art. This goal became even more significant after the revolution. Toward that end, I suggested we study the original writings of Marx and Engels that dealt with art, because I believed that studying the original texts could build a basic understanding of the nature and function of art in relation to society. After some discussion, the group finally agreed that one afternoon each week we would gather to study Karl Marx and Friedrich Engels. It would require a few sessions of studying their concept of history to understand the dialectical development of phenomena in general. To comprehend this was especially important because there was a paucity of knowledge and understanding about the historical and social implications of recent events in our country.

Behzad, who was working with our group and active in the subgroup devoted to research and education, had a Ph.D. in the sociology of art from the Sorbonne and was particularly helpful in organizing our study. Another friend, Hamed, who had a Ph.D. in history, also from the Sorbonne, agreed to help us with our program.

After two meetings with Hamed that provided a historical context, we began studying specific Marxian concepts about art. We used *Marx and Engels on Literature and Art,* edited by Lee Baxandall and Stefan Morawski. Havva translated the individual sections we needed to study, topics such as "Tendency Literature," where Marx and Engels oppose the idea of a party line in literature, or "Class Value in Literature" and "The Problem of Realism." These were problematic topics, often misinterpreted, especially in those days of revolutionary unrest and confusion, when seemingly everyone felt free to style himself as a theoretician. Most individuals' theories were derived from bulletins and newsletters published by political organizations.

Our study and analysis were severely undermined and foreshortened by the partisan pressures exerted by the Tudeh Party and the Fadaiyan Majority sympathizers in the group. Outside pressures intruded as well. The government, in an aggressive and insidious manner, searched commercial buildings hoping to uncover front companies whose real purpose was conducting underground political activities. The first floor of the building where we met also housed a new English language newspaper called the *Tehran Times*, an unofficial mouthpiece of the government. The editor of the newspaper was Ghotbzadeh, one of three Western-educated men who were close to Khomeini. The two later fell out and the editor was executed on Khomeini's order. The two other Western-educated men were Ebrahim Yazdi, who served a term as secretary of state and worked for the Islamic Republic of Iran until his death in 2017; and Abolhassan Banisadr, the first president of the Islamic Republic, who is currently in exile in Paris.

The newspaper staff was curious about the other offices with which they shared the building. One staffer, adopting a friendly demeanor, repeatedly approached me in the hallways and asked questions about our group's activities. I was suspicious, with good reason, because the newspaper's intent to control the building eventually became obvious. Workers arrived one day and covered all the windows facing the street with perforated steel sheets. Then a very imposing physical specimen was posted at the building's entryway. He did not wear a uniform or other badge of authority, but everyone who entered the newspaper office was questioned about their business and reason for being in the building. When I was asked the first time, my reaction was to check with some acquaintances in other offices about this intrusion. Before we could meet to discuss a formal protest, the new gatekeeper's attitude changed drastically—no more queries, and instead, hostile stares. I never felt completely comfortable after this, because I realized that the newspaper staff had developed an overweening interest in the building's other tenants. Not long after we left the building, a friend on the third floor was arrested for no apparent reason and spent five years in prison, with no specific charges ever filed against him.

■ ■ ■

The Tudeh Party and the Fadaiyan Majority sympathizers ceased contributing to our group's expenses. They began raising issues, noting that the theater group did not have any particular stance or any rigorous analysis of the current political situation, that is, a statement regarding the Islamist government. This claim ignored the fact that the group held a very clear position of opposition to the government. What they really wanted was for us to alter that stand. They claimed that the council that governed our association was inept and ineffective and that early elections should be held to replace the group's leadership. Through a series of secret meetings that I came to know about, they persuaded the majority of the group to hold early elections, in the hope that they could seize control.

We had elections, and the Tudeh and the Fadaiyan Majority sympathizers won four out of the five council seats. Inexplicably, I was reelected to fill the fifth seat, perhaps because I was the founder and the artistic director of the group and they felt my presence was needed to sustain the flow of outside financial contributions. Also, because they had a majority of the council seats, they doubtlessly thought of me as politically neutered.

At the first seating of the new council, everyone waited for me to open the meeting. I knew their intention was to affiliate our group with the Tudeh Party, which considered the Islamic regime to be a legitimate revolutionary government. Finally tired of waiting for me, Hassan A. said, "Mr. Rahmaninejad, please; you start."

I looked at him directly and replied, "Why me? Why don't you open the meeting?"

He turned red and said, "Because you are the head of the group. You know all the issues we need to discuss. It is better if you begin."

I responded, "For the last six to eight months you have labored hard to take control of the council. You should be prepared to run things."

The others entered the conversation, all stating basically the same theme: the association had reached a dead end. No one accused me directly but they said things like, "Because of the group's policies we can't move forward and stage the kind of plays that could be proposed to television and to the Theater Programs Administration."

I replied, "That is not true. We submitted a play to television but it was not approved. I don't want to do plays that follow guidelines laid out by government censors or that are simply propaganda pieces supporting government policies. If you are suggesting that we do those kind of plays, I must tell you that this is not in the tradition of the Iran Theater Association."

Everyone began protesting at once, until I stopped the discussion by telling them, "What you have done is contrary to the principles of the Association and I am going to explain everything you have done during the last six to eight months in writing and distribute it to all members of the Association. It will expose your secret meetings and the generally undemocratic manner in which you have conducted yourselves. I will explain all this and then ask the other members to expel you from the group for violating the Association's principles."

On that jarring note, the meeting was adjourned.

I penned a three-page report outlining the issues and had one of the group's members circulate it to the others and ask those who agreed with me to add their signature to the document.

The majority of our group signed the letter, and I tried to contact the membership about a date for a general meeting. Meanwhile, I discovered that those who did not sign my document, including all four of the council members, had written up their own version of the situation, explaining their intentions and asking all those who agreed with them to sign their letter. I also heard that the Fadaiyan and Tudeh sympathizers had decided not to participate in the general meeting—in effect expelling themselves. About ten of them left our group, a little less than half of our total membership.

A week later, two of the dissenters, representing their faction, asked for half of the Association's costumes, accessories, tools, furniture, and whatever property we had accumulated. "Name a day and time," I told them, "and come and take anything you want, whatever you think is your share based on your contributions. In terms of money, we owe thirty thousand tomans for the last six months' rent. You should bring your share of the rent money also." The two representatives, the youngest of those who had left, were nonplussed, and without a word they turned and left. No one showed up on the appointed day to settle accounts. I was not surprised.

Shortly after my manifesto was distributed, an old friend with whom I had been imprisoned visited my home. We sat across the kitchen table from each other while my wife and one of her university colleagues conversed in the living room. My friend criticized me for what he termed the harsh and condemning tone of my letter. He ended his comments with a threat: "You won't get away with it!"

I understood his meaning. The Tudeh Party and Fadaiyan Majority members had been instructed to denounce to their cell leaders all "counterrevolutionaries" in their neighborhoods and workplaces. Such reports would then be passed on to intelligence-gathering cells in their organizations, who would turn over the damning statements to the Islamist government.

I had personal knowledge of such practices, so when my friend made this threat, I straightened in my chair and told him "Get out of my home!"

He jumped up, as if shocked, and left the kitchen. I heard him call to my wife, "Bye, Havva!" as he left the house.

Havva rushed into the kitchen and asked, "What happened?"

I replied, "I will tell you later, go back to your friend." I sat at the kitchen table trembling with mixed emotions.

■ ■ ■

In order to illustrate our theater group's legitimacy, I submitted a play about war to television. The story centers (rest of the description of the story is in present tense) on an old woman, a mother, in the city of Susangerd in southern Iran, which the Iraqi army had occupied in 1980 at the beginning of the Iran-Iraq war. Iraqi soldiers rape a young girl, the old woman's daughter. Her son-in-law has been killed earlier by an Iraqi bomb. The Iraqi soldiers stay in her home, forcing the old woman to cook for them and to serve them. The old woman decides to poison the food and to kill the soldiers who have raped her daughter and killed her son-in-law.

The soldiers are wily. At each meal, before eating, they insist that the old woman eat first. The woman prepares the poisoned food, calls the soldiers, and as instructed, eats some of her preparation first. The soldiers eat and die, as does the determined woman. This play was a slightly altered retelling of an actual newspaper account.

The play was written by one of the members of our theater group, who was trying to show the attachment of the peasant family to the land, the source of their livelihood. The play included no Islamic clichés such as having the family members be practicing Muslims. They were portrayed as ordinary people who kept their faith a private matter.

The head of the theater section of the television company was a young man who was the younger brother of Prime Minister Mir Hossein Mousavi. In spite of the fact that he had not studied theater and possessed no experience in theater, he would have the final word on our proposal. He called me to discuss the play and tried to convince me that "the way you see the motivations of the old woman does not reflect reality. Our people are not fighting the Iraqis over land; they are fighting as an expression of their faith, just as they did earlier against the Shah. They know that without faith family, land, and a country are meaningless. In this play the old woman should poison the Iraqi soldiers as a matter of faith."

I tried to explain to him that "in reality there is something else. The old woman has her own reasons, among them revenge, in making her decision to sacrifice herself. The Iraqis have killed her son-in-law and raped her daughter, and the family has lost their land, the source of their livelihood. She herself is badly injured and feels she has nothing left to lose. These are readily understandable motivations for her to give her life to kill the enemy."

The young man did not agree. He only repeated the same nonsense about faith as the sole credible motivation. I left his office after telling him that I needed time to think about his suggestions. I did not want to say anything that would lead him to believe that we did not want to work in his medium. In reality, I was resigned to the fact that this was the end of our television ambitions. I desperately wanted the members of our theater group to be safe and not go through the same experience they had under the Shah. I would pretend that we were legitimate—as the government would define it.

Even more disquieting than our truncated television aspirations was another experience our group had with a government agency, the Center for Dramatic Arts. We submitted a play written by one of my friends, a story about the loss of a bullet in a small village. Villages in Iran were policed by local gendarmes, not central government forces. One of the gendarmes loses a bullet and his superior tries to find it, because even one bullet is considered dangerous and must be accounted for. If someone else finds it first, he can threaten the village government or the gendarmerie itself. The gendarmes think the bullet was stolen and that the thief may also have stolen a gun. The head of the gendarmerie interrogates one of the villagers who had been in the village teahouse when the off-duty gendarme who lost the bullet was there. This innocent villager is tortured and the frustrated gendarmes question and torture the entire village, with no result. The head of the gendarmerie decides to burn the whole village, on the theory that the bullet will explode in the fire, thus revealing the identity of the thief.

While the fire is raging, men emerge from each dwelling carrying rifles.

The play was an allegory about the disarmament of Kurdistan; however, we carefully made no overt references to Kurds or Kurdistan in the play.

We were denied a permit to stage the play. I received a letter from the Center for Dramatic Arts inviting me to discuss the play with one of the censors. The center was located on the second floor of the Roudaki Opera House, which had been built as a showplace for the Shah's regime. In terms of architecture and interior design, it was one of the finest, most expensive buildings in Tehran. Only people from the upper classes, the *nouveau riche*, and some foreign residents could frequent the opera.

I went there to talk with the censor, a fanatic with no real knowledge of religious Muslim culture. I entered the building and went upstairs, where the Office for Dramatic Arts was located. Finding no signs on the office doors, I asked for the person responsible for play permits. As I entered the room, I stopped in the doorway in shock. The interior had been completely changed since I had been inside the Opera House two years before. The walls had been stripped of all decorations, and expensive furniture had been pushed against the walls. Brother Hossein Jafari, the official, sat cross-legged on a broad seat cushion placed on the floor, with his back propped against the wall. A young boy squatted on his knees in front of Brother Jafari and bent over some files spread out on the carpet.

I froze, uncertain how to proceed. I took one hesitant step, nearly stupefied, and finally managed a weak hello. I could see my greeting dangling in the air between the floor and the ceiling. I decided to sit on the nearest couch pushed against the wall. Brother Jafari, who was saying something to the young boy, stopped, turned his head toward me, and answered "Hello."

"I am Nasser Rahmaninejad. I've received your letter, and I am here to discuss the lines and sections of the play that you mentioned should be cut."

Brother Jafari quickly moved from the cushion and told the youngster to leave the room. After he was gone, Brother Jafari spoke again. "Hello. How are you?"

I said, "I got your letter about the play, *The Bullet*, Mr. Jafari." I called him "Mister" even though revolutionary etiquette required the usage of "Brother," unless one wanted to make a political statement—which I did. "I have come to find out what these 'problems' are, what the sections you mentioned are that need to be cut."

Jafari called one of the brothers from the next room and asked him to bring in the file on the play. In the meantime, he informed me that he was familiar with me and my works during the past regime. He said, "I'm trying not to be harsh. I don't want to comment on your past works, because those are history. But I want you to understand that then and now are two separate times. Today, for example, Miller and Brecht won't work. The issues are different, the people are different; everything is different. The issues of today must be put on the stage today..."

Brother Jafari continued preaching for some minutes about the artistic mission appropriate for the day. Blessedly, the assistant brother came back with a thin file containing two or three sheets and said that he could not find the play itself. Brother Jafari protested that it had been placed next to the file. The other brother said that he had looked everywhere but could not find it. Brother Jafari said, "Oh, well, I will find it myself later. Thank you anyway." And the assistant brother left.

I worried that, without the text as reference, my arguments might not be as effective as they might otherwise have been.

Brother Jafari said, "I have marked those sentences and phrases that should be cut, but the most important thing is the opening scene, where the barber is talking to his customer."

"What do you mean?" I asked him.

He said, "I mean those explanations about the ceremony for cutting hair and trimming beard—the barber's shaving rules."

Luckily he had begun with a point I could challenge easily.

I explained, "The barber is speaking from his own experience, from his professional knowledge."

"These explanations don't do anything! The barber should get to the main subject right away!"

I replied, "Well, that is a technical matter, a matter of the style of storytelling and establishing a scene. It is better left to the playwright and the director."

Brother Jafari argued passionately, "What I am saying is that those speeches are superfluous! They don't advance the play!"

"Well," I said, "that is a technical matter, a matter of style. Do you have a problem with the content of the barber's speech?"

Almost shouting, he retorted, "Whatever the barber is saying is just nonsense."

I repressed an impulse to jump up and walk out, but controlled myself and asked, as calmly as possible, "Mr. Jafari, are you suggesting that everything the barber says is nonsense?"

"Yes, yes! It's all nonsense!"

"Do you know whose words they are?"

"I don't care whose words they are. They're nonsense! They must be excised from the text and thrown away!"

Calmly, with great confidence, I told him, "Mr. Jafari, all the barber's words are from the *Hilyat al-Muttaqin*."

Hilyat al-Muttaqin is one of the authoritative texts of Shiism. It contains rules and regulations for everything a Muslim Shia should know and follow in life, from details about how to walk into a restroom to how to complete a pilgrimage, and including how to make love with one's wife and how to clean oneself after defecating, what colors to wear when one wants to seduce his wife, and virtually everything else.

It was like extinguishing fire with water. Brother Jafari kept staring at me for some moments, sunk a little more deeply into his cushion, then said, "I have to see it myself."

I assured him, "All the barber's words were quoted from one of the old lithographic prints, not from one of these new editions."

Mr. Jafari said, "I believe, however, that those words must be omitted. They are misplaced."

I replied, "Find the play first. I'll come back later with the copy of *Hilyat al-Muttaqin*. Then we can talk more precisely."

As I was telling him this, I was certain that I would not be coming back. Going home, I marveled, could this fellow, a censor, be unaware that the barber's words were taken directly from a famous text? Or was he pretending, perhaps trying to convince me that he was not a religious fanatic? At any rate, opening with the barber's speech would immediately set the play in the current period. The barber's discussion of the rules of the shave and haircut would communicate to the audience that the play dealt with Iran under the Islamic government. If we were to cut the speech, the audience could very well read the play as being set in the previous regime, an unacceptable interpretation.

■ ■ ■

In 1982 we were on the brink of closing down our theater group because all our efforts had been thwarted by politics and censorship. About two years earlier, the Islamic Revolutionary Court of Tehran had issued a decree to all print shops that they could accept orders only from those customers who had received permission from the Ministry of Islamic Guidance. This edict included any printed matter.

All independent newspapers and magazines were attacked and shut down. Some bookstores were burned. All newsstands in front of the University of Tehran and other areas had been shut down even before the printing decree was issued. Many people who had operated those newsstands had been personally attacked, stabbed with knives. The barricades that had been set up throughout the city during the revolution were converted into checkpoints. Many additional checkpoints were added to all parts of the city. Motorists and pedestrians were constantly stopped and questioned, especially at night. All political organizations, conventional professional gatherings, and union meetings were banned.

The police state grew more restrictive each day. Fear showed in people's faces. The very fabric of society changed. Many people grew beards and adopted traditional Islamic garb; the former rich diversity of colors and clothing styles vanished, leaving only darker hues. Previously well-maintained streets now bore a permanent patina of filth. People cautiously minded their behavior when outside their homes. The subjects they spoke about and even their manner of speech were guarded. Normal daily activities such as garbage collection ceased.

In the area where Havva and I lived at this time, a relatively upper middle class section north of Tehran known as Darband, the streets had always been notably clean. Now, less than four years after the revolution, only a few houses south of our house a huge and growing pile of garbage blocked the middle of the street. Restriction and suppression reigned. People were careful about what they said, even at home, especially if they had children going to school, where the new teachers hired by the government to apply Islamic principles questioned them about their parents and what transpired in their homes. Fear of denunciation was so prevalent that people turned music up to high decibels lest their neighbors hear and report seditious conversations.

Before the revolution, many people from all walks of life had their own private faith whose tenets did not include spying on their neighbors. After the revolution, that kind of private faith was gradually replaced with a religious mandate that required public actions as a duty and pious acts to protect the sanctity of Islam. We had experienced this personally, in the suspicion and scrutiny from Havva's cleaning lady.

When on June 20, 1981—the 30th of Khordad of 1360—the Mojahedin tried to draw people out into the streets to confront the regime's heavy-handedness, they made a serious political miscalculation. The Islamic government used these protests as an excuse to further clamp down on those in opposition. Many people, mostly young, were killed by government forces, especially the Pasdaran whose orders specified to take no prisoners and to shoot demonstrators after lining them up against the nearest wall. A chain of executions began the next day. The Mojahedin had given the government a perfect excuse to get rid of those who were guilty only of criticizing the regime. One of the victims was my old friend Said Soltanpour. The poet, actor, director, and political activist had been arrested a few months before, in his own home, at his marriage ceremony. Beginning on the thirty-first of Khordad, the media daily announced a new round of executions, in a conscious effort by the government to foster an atmosphere of fear. The strategy worked. People began destroying any political literature that might be construed as leftist, as well as most printed material of a nonreligious nature. One could smell the smoke of burning paper in the air, while piles and bags of books and papers overwhelmed the city dumps and clogged gutters and flooded channels. Many people were arrested at checkpoints set up by the government, just because they had books in their cars. Ironically, in many cases, those arrested were not political; they were simply carting their relatives' books away. I knew of one case in which a mother and sister were stopped with a load of a son's books in their car. They were put in prison, where the mother was soon freed, but the daughter was sentenced to five years. This was the famous Iranian novelist, Shahrnush Parsipur, the author of *Touba and the Meaning of Night*. (This novel was years later translated in America into English by my wife Havva Houshmand.)

No one, including me, felt safe. It was hard to sleep, to rest fully, when one might be arrested for as little as being acquainted with someone who was under suspicion.

Working in theater was out of the question at this point. There were many nights for over a year that I would lie next to my wife pretending to be asleep, my senses hyperalert, listening to outside noises—sounds that had once been nonthreatening, like cars, footsteps, and wind in the trees. After a while I discovered that my wife was doing the same thing. Late one night, after hours of wakefulness, I opened my eyes and silently turned my head to see if she was sleeping, only to behold her watching me. We tried to comfort each other by saying, "There is nothing to be afraid of. Don't worry."

From that night on we tried to spend more nights at my mother's house, to be with the family.

Within months, all those who had been in prison under the Shah, or anyone who was under suspicion of being a leftist, was also arrested. I could no longer stay at home after a very close friend was arrested, and I was warned not to be seen outside. I had already started working with a friend in his office at a construction company so that I would not be sighted on the streets. Only Havva, who was working for another friend as a lifeguard at a day-care swimming pool, knew my actual whereabouts. She was not "in hiding" herself, because if both of us were perceived to be absent, that in itself could pose an additional danger.

There were threats all around us, visible and invisible. I felt the situation was deteriorating. I did not feel secure—on the contrary, I felt that I was being followed by shadows, about to be ambushed in a dark, dead-end alley. Given the circumstances I felt I could stay with Havva more, that we could spend more time together, and concentrate on the baby she had been carrying inside her womb for more than eight months now. Our baby would soon be in our arms—a shining sun in that politically dark, socially cold winter. The closer we got to the baby's due date, the more our excitement grew.

Our son Nicky was even more excited than his mother and I. About two years before, he had told his mother that he felt so lonely, and he had asked her to bring him a brother or a sister, or at least give him a dog. When the British School he attended had been closed down and we had to enroll him in an Iranian school, he had had a very difficult time adapting himself to a new system of education, a new language of instruction, a whole new environment and culture with new schoolmates. Having spent years in Britain, he had little knowledge of the idiosyncrasies of Iranian culture and had difficulty engaging with his classmates inside or outside the school. His closest playmates were my nieces and nephews. He played with them when we went to their homes or they came to ours.

The day finally came. All the arrangements had been made at Tehran Clinic. We rushed there, and they took Havva straight to the delivery room. Doctor Houtan Adib, a close friend and medical school associate of Havva's brother Houshang, was assigned to take care of everything.

After the revolution many things had changed, and a husband's presence in his wife's delivery room was no longer permitted, so I had to wait outside in the hallway, impatiently counting the seconds. It was the first time in my life I found myself waiting for such a moment, waiting for the arrival of so precious a being. I didn't know how I would feel when I would see her, touch her, and hold her in my arms.

I could not turn my eyes away from the delivery room door. Finally it opened and Houtan called my name. I rushed in and went straight to Havva. She was pale and held the baby to her chest. For a few moments I did not know what to say or what to do. Then I carefully took Havva's hand in my hands and kissed her. With a faint smile she turned her eyes toward the baby, inviting me to do the same. I looked at the baby, and I could not believe how such a little creature could defend itself in this cruel world.

They transferred Havva to a private room where she would stay for the next few days. We knew that Nicky was anxious to see his sister, so I stayed with Havva for a few hours and then went to pick him up from school and bring him to the hospital. Nicky was so excited that he finally had his sister in reach. We took a picture of all of us together, and Nicky got as close as he could to the baby, practically grabbing her in his arms, his eyes wide open, shining.

We named her Khorshid, for warmth, light, and life—and what a glorious shining gift she was. I would be attached to her to such a degree, to such an extent, that I could never even have begun to imagine it.

13

FLIGHT TO TURKEY

After much discussion, Havva and I agreed to leave Iran. We decided it would be better for me to leave first and Havva to leave later. Eventually a friend of mine found a Kurdish man from Turkey named Salaheddin to get me out of the country.

I would travel through Kurdistan with a group of Turkish Kurds under the leadership of Salaheddin. He agreed to renew the expiration date on my passport and take me from Tehran to Istanbul, although nobody could guarantee my safety. According to Salaheddin's instructions, I could take nothing with me. A week before I left I stopped shaving and trimmed my mustache like Muslims. I thought I could disguise myself as an ordinary, uneducated person for the Revolutionary Guards who would question us at the checkpoints.

I would wear a pair of secondhand pants and an unironed shirt of rough material, and I would carry my birth certificate. If a guard outside of Tehran asked me where I was going, I would tell him that I was heading to the military base in Salmas, an Iranian city at the edge of Kurdistan, to inquire about my nephew who was fighting against the Kurds.

The morning I left Tehran we met at the bus terminal. I found out later there were other people, fleeing like me, traveling on the same bus. Salaheddin had arranged for us to depart in the early morning. While we were traveling, there would be as little contact with him as possible. We were to converse only when absolutely necessary.

Salaheddin was pacing back and forth just a few yards from me while smoking. I spied one of the Lalehzar actors whom I knew very well. He was one of the opponents of the Islamic regime who was radicalized when they closed all the Lalehzar theaters. All the actors and actresses, musicians and dancers, singers, magicians, acrobats, and the other workers in these theaters, including the office workers, had lost their jobs. Most of them possessed no skills that would afford them a chance at a new career.

He came straight up to me and hugged me as we kissed each other. He was the one who forged the validation on my passport, so he already knew I was leaving the country. He told me, "When I got your passport from Salaheddin, I got so angry at this fucking regime, and at the same time I was happy that you were leaving. I wish I could leave this damned country like you, but I can't because of my family. I have to stay here and take care of my wife and kids."

He told me his story since the closing of the theaters in Lalehzar. "For a year I was making sandwiches and selling them on the sidewalks in Lalehzar, right in front of the Nasr Theater, where I played for years. Many people knew me and I purposely explained to them who I am and why I was now doing this job."

We did not talk long because of the danger. Then he surreptitiously handed my passport to Salaheddin, who would give it back to me along with some money he was holding for me when we reached Kurdistan.

On the bus, a middle-aged Turkish man sat next to me on the window side. He did not speak Farsi, only Turkish. I could understand a few words but I tried to talk to him anyway, with limited success, because he was not at all talkative.

As Salaheddin explained to me before boarding, there were other people in the bus who had political problems like me. He told me not to try to communicate with them. He suggested that I pretend that I was traveling by myself. He also explained his plan that in Khoy, when the bus stopped for tea, we would leave the bus. After the bus departed I was to follow him on the opposite side of the street. Eventually he would cross the street and climb into a Jeep, and I was to join him as quickly as I was able. Others would follow my lead, and the Jeep would speed away.

Just before Khoy there was a checkpoint where all the busses and other vehicles were inspected by the Pasdaran. They would board the busses and question the individual passengers about where they were going, what business they had there, and so on. As Salaheddin explained, this checkpoint would be a critical juncture, after which we should experience no problems.

At the checkpoint, two Pasdars (guards) boarded and stood by the first row of seats. Turning left and right, they looked straight into the eyes of the occupants. I was sitting on the aisle toward the back of the bus. I had bought a small package of sunflower seeds at the teahouse during the previous stop and was sharing them with my seatmate, the Turk. I started to speak, pretending we were acquaintances from the same village. I asked him to talk with me while at the same time, out of the corner of my eye, I tracked the Pasdars' progress. When they reached our row, I glanced at the guard casually, as if by accident. The guard who was the active questioner looked into my eyes for three to four seconds. I fixed my eyes on him, then very naturally turned to my seatmate, and the guard passed on.

The guards finally got off the bus and waved the driver to continue on. In an hour or so we were at the teahouse, our last stop. The bus left the teahouse, with Salaheddin still inside and I waited outside. I watched him come out and start walking up the street. As instructed, I followed a few paces behind on the other side of the road. About 200 meters later, Salaheddin crossed the street and entered the waiting Jeep. I quickened my pace and climbed into the Jeep too, closely followed by five other people, one an aged woman with a preteen girl and teenage boy. A young woman with an eight-month-old baby entered last.

The Jeep pulled away, turned to the right, and drove out of the city. In half an hour we came to a rough road leading up hill, which soon disappeared altogether. I noticed that the Jeep was laboring hard to climb the hill, which was scattered with trees. At a predesignated spot, Salaheddin stepped out and told us to jump out quickly. He told the driver goodbye, then told us, "We are climbing up the hill. At the top there are horses."

It was late afternoon and I had an adventurous feeling about this part of the trip. While we were climbing, I was wondering what our next step would be. Ten minutes into the climb, the old woman, whom I later knew as Haj Khanom, started breathing heavily. Salaheddin said, "The horses are just ahead; we don't have far to go."

Minutes later we saw the horses and their riders, all of them Turkish Kurds. Salaheddin's father and two brothers were among them; the rest were from their village. After Salaheddin told us who would ride which horse, I found that we didn't have enough horses for all of us to ride solo, so each of us had to sit behind a horseman with our arms around his waist. It proved to be an uncomfortable ride, because we were perched on the raised back edges of the saddles, which were rough and pointed.

At first it was exhilarating, because I was able to compensate for the jostling of the horse's steps by rising out of the saddle or swaying right and left. However, after an hour I realized that it was impossible to keep up this motion as my muscles tightened painfully. I had ridden donkeys and camels before, but I had never been on a horse.

After two hours of riding I developed a painful injury between my legs, and others in our group had already started to complain. Finally I requested that the horseman let me get down and walk.

That first night we were to cross into what was then called Liberated Kurdistan. The democratic Kurds who controlled this safe area knew that we were fleeing Iran. Salaheddin paid them for a guarantee of safe passage as we crossed their border. We rode most of the night until we reached a safe house in a village, where we rested for two or three hours. Early morning and a quick breakfast saw us on our way. After three hours of alternating riding and walking, we stopped. Salaheddin explained the situation. In front of us was a vast meadow that faded into a sparse forest. To our left was a grassy hill. Salaheddin warned, "Here is the only dangerous place. We have about a twenty-minute gallop across this meadow. Everybody should hold tightly to his or her horseman. If you hear gunshots, don't worry; we will protect you. We have to pass through this area in any case."

Standing there facing the meadow, a vast open landscape with the sun shining on it, I began to sense the reality of freedom, an image I still savor. I saw one of Salaheddin's brothers, Nader, produce and brandish a huge handgun with a long barrel, the kind one would see in the hands of German military officers in World War II movies. With exaggerated movements, while holding the reins of his horse, he was, I thought, somehow relaying the danger of the situation and the importance of his job. He was the youngest brother, still in his twenties, a tall, handsome fellow with very light skin and an irresistibly charming manner.

Salaheddin asked the young woman if he could hold her baby so that she could hold onto him more securely. He held the baby to his chest with his left hand in a very protective way. It was obvious that he could be trusted and that the baby would be safely returned to her mother's arms. For the last time Salaheddin told us, "Get ready. Hold tight to the horsemen. We will be galloping very fast."

When we were all checked and ready, Salaheddin, speaking in Kurdish, commanded everyone to start, and we took off across the field.

For about fifteen minutes we clung to the horses as they ran. I was trying to watch the hills to our left, where Salaheddin had told us the Pasdaran held a position. Because of our speed, coupled with the uneven pace of horses covering rugged terrain, it was impossible for me to do more than cling to my perch. Salaheddin had warned us that the Pasdaran sometimes shot at those who were crossing the field. We had come about halfway through the meadow when I heard shouts from the hilltops. The guards yelled and gestured at us while Salaheddin and the other Kurds shouted among themselves as we sprinted across the field. I could not understand what they were saying, but I presumed they were encouraging the horses and each other.

At one point I thought I would lose my balance as my mental focus and arm strength wavered. I kept exhorting myself, "Hold on! Just twenty minutes. Just half an hour! Hold on! Hold on!" while simultaneously somewhere else in my head I exulted, "I am free! I am free!"

I was expecting gunfire but luckily no shots were fired. We reached the other side of the field and, without slowing, galloped through the trees until our horsemen felt safe. All of us were exhausted and breathing fast, as if we had been galloping ourselves.

Salaheddin told us that after a short distance we would stop and have lunch. "After lunch we will be safe, and the rest of the way is easy. My father and my brothers will take you to Istanbul."

An hour later we arrived at a cool, shady place. We dismounted and the Kurds unsaddled the horses. Nader, the charming gunman, and two other horsemen rode on to the village to pick up the lunch that had been prepared for us.

We were all desperate to find at least a semiprivate place to relieve ourselves while the horsemen fed and watered the horses. Nader and his companions arrived with two big pots of food and fresh-baked peasant bread wrapped in squares of fabric. One pot contained rice and the other held lamb stew. We had a delicious lunch there in the shade. That was the best meal we had on our six days' journey to Istanbul.

After lunch, Salaheddin came and sat next to me. He gave me my passport and showed me the pages where the expiration date had been changed. Right away I saw that the Lalehzar actor had done a sloppy job. The old date had been scratched off so unskillfully that it made a hole in the paper. The new date was typed with an obviously different typeface. No expert would be needed to see that it was a forgery. You could make out a black fingerprint next to the date, and a piece of Scotch tape had been placed over the changed writing. I could have done it much better myself. I had expected a professional job, and I realized immediately that my actor friend was responsible.

I showed it to Salaheddin and said, "This is terrible!"

He assured me, "Don't worry, no one will check it. You don't need a passport in Turkey."

He gave me some Turkish currency, liras, in exchange for the sum I had given him in Tehran. He explained the exchange rate of the lira to the rial. He said, "Don't worry. My friends will take care of everything. You will get to Istanbul safely."

And we did.

I will never forget that broad, grassy plain, and the vista like out of a Hollywood Western, the sun beating down, and the wind blowing. The young smuggler pulling his long-barreled pistol from its holster with a proud flourish. Seven horses with fourteen riders gathering their strength for a quivering, tense moment, then taking off in a great burst and flying across the plain toward a horizon of trees. From the ridge to the left, distant shouts rising from the Revolutionary Guards at their posts on the heights. On the plain a confused flurry of wild hoofbeats, of snorting, panting horses, and the hunched figures of desperate fugitives clinging to the broad backs of the smugglers, all of our minds screaming, "Hold on! Freedom! Don't fall! Freedom! Freedom! Freedom!" Every muscle, every nerve, straining with elation and fright, as if we, not the horses, were galloping across the field, urged on by the shouts of the smugglers in Kurdish and Turkish, foreign-sounding to our Iranian ears.

All my life, in a special part of me, we fly into the distance, little doubled-up, hunched figures on straining, scrambling horses, growing smaller and smaller, with clouds of unintelligible languages roiling like dust in our wake—and then, freedom!

ACKNOWLEDGMENTS

Let me begin by saying that there is always a strong and ceaseless inspiration, a muse, present throughout my creative work: my precious daughter, Khorshid, who generously shines in and on my life. I owe this book, and so much more, to her.

I should add that, had my dear friend Kathleen Au not encouraged me to sit down with her and tell my story, this memoir would not now be in your hands. From the very start she wanted my story to be told, and in those initial interchanges between narrator and writer we began to compose my memoir, to give it form. Kathleen was the engine that set this journey in motion, and she was as important as I in shaping it, giving it direction; I owe her tremendously.

Nor would I ever have been able to share my story if another dear friend, Terry Wilson, a scholar and writer, had not openheartedly offered to edit the manuscript. This he did enthusiastically, patiently, and professionally. I owe him deeply, too.

Cyrus Samii, my dear friend and a writer himself, followed my personal and literary trajectories with concern from beginning to end, and was always ready to help me whenever and with whatever I needed; my special and warm thanks to him.

I would also like to thank two friends, Abbas Sadrai and Kamran Nayeri, who read the manuscript attentively and gave me valuable suggestions for improvements and refinements.

Here, I would like to express my gratitude to an extraordinary woman, Lynne Elizabeth, who saw the value in my story and decided to share with the public my attempts at artistic creation and survival in pre- and post-revolutionary Iran. I am proud be included on the list of New Village Press authors, and I am grateful for Lynne's incredible support throughout the publishing process.

My sincere appreciation goes to my editor Ignacio Choi, for his keen eye, for his attention to context and detail, and for his fine work in making the publication process smooth and enjoyable throughout.

None of this would have been possible without their assistance.

I hope in these following passages I can bring to light at least part of the ordeal that Iranian artists endured during the previous regime and those they are currently enduring under the present regime.

And if the artists have suffered, then clearly, so have the people of Iran.